Literary Drowning

Irish Studies
Kathleen Costello-Sullivan, *Series Editor*

Select Titles in Irish Studies

Fine Meshwork: Philip Roth, Edna O'Brien, and Jewish-Irish Literature
Dan O'Brien

Irish Questions and Jewish Questions: Crossovers in Culture
Aidan Beatty and Dan O'Brien, eds.

J. M. Synge and Travel Writing of the Irish Revival
Giulia Bruna

Kate O'Brien and Spanish Literary Culture
Jane Davison

The Rebels and Other Short Fiction
Richard Power; James MacKillop, ed.

Respectability and Reform: Irish American Women's Activism, 1880–1920
Tara M. McCarthy

Science, Technology, and Irish Modernism
Kathryn Conrad, Cóilín Parsons, and Julie McCormick Weng, eds.

Trauma and Recovery in the Twenty-First-Century Irish Novel
Kathleen Costello-Sullivan

For a full list of titles in this series,
visit https://press.syr.edu/supressbook-series/irish-studies/.

Literary Drowning

Postcolonial Memory in Irish and Caribbean Writing

Stephanie Pocock Boeninger

Syracuse University Press

Some material in chapters 3 and 4 reprinted with permission from "'I Have Become the Sea's Craft': Authorial Subjectivity in Derek Walcott's *Omeros* and David Dabydeen's 'Turner'" in *Contemporary Literature*, vol. 52, no. 3, 2011, pp 242–92.

Reprinted by permission of Farrar, Straus and Giroux (chapters 3 and 4):

Excerpts from "The Sea at Dauphin" and "What the Twilight Says: An Overture," from *Dream on Monkey Mountain* by Derek Walcott. Copyright © 1970 by Derek Walcott. Excerpts from *Omeros* by Derek Walcott. Copyright © 1990 by Derek Walcott. Excerpts from "The Sea Is History" from *Selected Poems* by Derek Walcott, edited by Edward Baugh. Copyright © 2007 by Derek Walcott.

First Edition 2020

20 21 22 23 24 25 6 5 4 3 2 1

∞ The paper used in this publication meets the minimum requirements of the American National Standard for Information Sciences—Permanence of Paper for Printed Library Materials, ANSI Z39.48-1992.

For a listing of books published and distributed by Syracuse University Press, visit https://press.syr.edu.

ISBN: 978-0-8156-3672-4 (hardcover)
978-0-8156-3682-3 (paperback)
978-0-8156-5497-1 (e-book)

Library of Congress Cataloging-in-Publication Data

Names: Boeninger, Stephanie Pocock, author.

Title: Literary drowning : postcolonial memory in Irish and Caribbean writing / Stephanie Pocock Boeninger.

Description: First edition. | Syracuse : Syracuse University Press, 2020. | Series: Irish studies | Includes bibliographical references and index. | Summary: ""Literary Drowning" is the first book-length study of drowning in literature. It examines depictions of the drowned body in Irish and Caribbean postcolonial literature, uncovering a complex transatlantic conversation that re-evaluates memory, forgetfulness, and the role that each plays in the construction of the postcolonial subject and nation"— Provided by publisher.

Identifiers: LCCN 2020004823 (print) | LCCN 2020004824 (ebook) | ISBN 9780815636724 (hardcover) | ISBN 9780815636823 (paperback) | ISBN 9780815654971 (ebook)

Subjects: LCSH: Drowning victims in literature. | English literature—Irish authors—History and criticism. | Sea in literature. | Memory in literature. | Postcolonialism in literature. | English literature—20th century—History and criticism. | Caribbean literature (English)—History and criticism. | English literature—Caribbean authors—History and criticism.

Classification: LCC PR8723.D76 B64 2020 (print) | LCC PR8723.D76 (ebook) | DDC 820.9/9415—dc23

LC record available at https://lccn.loc.gov/2020004823

LC ebook record available at https://lccn.loc.gov/2020004824

Manufactured in the United States of America

Roll on, thou deep and dark blue Ocean—roll!
Ten thousand fleets sweep over thee in vain;
Man marks the earth with ruin—his control
Stops with the shore;—upon the watery plain
The wrecks are all thy deed, nor doth remain
A shadow of man's ravage, save his own,
When for a moment, like a drop of rain,
He sinks into thy depths with bubbling groan,
Without a grave, unknell'd, uncoffin'd and unknown.

—Lord Byron, *Childe Harold's Pilgrimage*

Contents

Acknowledgments

This book has been a long time coming and gratitude is due to more people than I will remember to name here. Susan Cannon Harris has seen this project through from its earliest stages and her wisdom, support, generosity, and good humor have continued unflaggingly in the years since I left her classroom. Special thanks are also due to Richard Rankin Russell, whose love for Irish literature and his students first drew me to the field, and in whose classes I first started to notice the drowned body. Many other mentors have read and given feedback on this book, including Maud Ellmann, Luke Gibbons, Romana Huk, and P. J. Mathews.

I am grateful to Providence College for the sabbatical that allowed me to put the finishing touches on this book. My colleagues at Providence College have created an environment in which it is a pleasure to teach and to work. Special thanks are due to Alex Moffett and Bill Hogan for reading and commenting on portions of this work. Thanks also to Bruce Graver and Peggy Reid for their support and hard work as department chairs. I have loved working alongside Licia Carlson and Margaret Manchester, who have taught me more than I can quantify here. The members of the Best Committee Ever (you know who you are) gave invaluable advice on the book proposal process, while also providing solidarity, laughter, and a sense of community. My students have been and remain a source of inspiration, challenging me to see these texts from new perspectives.

Part of chapters 3 and 4 are adapted from an article that first appeared in *Contemporary Literature* in 2011. My thanks go to the University of Wisconsin Press for their permission to reprint that work.

Thanks also to David Dabydeen for his generous personal response to my request for permission to quote from "Turner." I am grateful to the readers for Syracuse University Press for their encouragement and helpful suggestions. Special thanks to Michael Malouf for his careful reading and trenchant criticism of this book; engaging with his critique made this book much stronger. Most of all, I thank Deborah Manion at Syracuse University Press for her enthusiastic support of my book and her patience with my questions about the publishing process. I'd like also to thank my copyeditor, Jessica LeTourneur Bax, whose attention to detail prevented many errors. Any that remain are my own.

There are people who may never read this book who have nonetheless been vital to its creation. The loving support of my parents and siblings has been a constant source of encouragement. While the birth and infancy of my two sons, Samuel and Micah, delayed the progress of this book considerably, they are the best distraction anyone could hope for and have enhanced my life immeasurably. My deepest gratitude is always due to my husband and best friend, Brian, for the love, laughter, and intellectual honesty that saw me through this decade-long process.

Literary Drowning

Introduction

Burial at Sea

On May 1, 2011, after a ten-year pursuit, US Navy SEALs invaded the Pakistan compound where the Al-Qaeda leader Osama bin Laden, the architect of the September 11, 2001, attacks, was hiding. They shot and killed the terrorist leader and, within hours, before President Barack Obama's late-night announcement to the world, bin Laden's body had been taken aboard the USS *Carl Vinson* and "buried" in the North Arabian Sea. The Obama administration's decision to rapidly bury bin Laden at sea perplexed many and outraged some. Why, many wondered, dispose of the body furtively, before Americans, especially those bereaved on 9/11, had a chance to see images of the body and accept them as proof that the infamously elusive terrorist was, in fact, dead? Why give conspiracy theorists such ample fodder and leave Al-Qaeda loyalists room for hope?

According to news sources, the decision to rapidly bury bin Laden at sea was based on two factors: (1) a desire to respect Islamic burial tradition, which stipulates that a body be buried within twenty-four hours of death; and (2) a belief that no country would accept the body for burial.[1] If, however, respect for Islamic tradition was truly at the top of the Obama administration's priority list, they did a poor job of showing it. Within twelve hours of President Obama's announcement, the Associated Press journalist Hamza Hendawi published an article titled "Islamic Scholars Question bin Laden's Sea Burial." According to the religious scholars interviewed by Hendawi, Islamic tradition allows for sea burials only when the death occurs aboard a ship: "'If a man dies on a ship that is a long distance from land, then the dead man should be buried at the sea,' said the Shiite cleric Ibrahim al-Jabari. 'But if he dies on land, then he should be buried in the ground, not to be thrown into the sea. Otherwise, this would be only inviting fish to a banquet.'"[2] With the claim to be honoring Islamic tradition a problematic one at best, journalists began to speculate about the administration's true motives. The most common theory, stated in the *New York Times*' front page story on the morning after bin Laden's death, was that "by doing it at sea, American authorities presumably were trying to avoid creating a shrine for his followers."[3] A grave could potentially provide a rallying point for Al-Qaeda sympathizers, a pilgrimage site for the radical Islamic fringe among whom bin Laden was a hero. Yet one of the curious factors in the Obama administration's decision is this: had they chosen to bury bin Laden on land they would not have been required by Islamic tradition to mark the grave. Hendawi's religious scholars suggest that an unmarked grave on a remote unpopulated island would have been an easy option, and the one most respectful to Islamic burial tradition.

Bin Laden's burial at sea suggests several intriguing things. First, it highlights an intense contemporary awareness of the power of memorial sites, a power so dangerous that the leaders of the most powerful nation in the world chose to act against their stated desire to honor Islamic tradition, and against the desires of many of their constituents to see the body, because they were afraid of a grave. Even an unmarked grave, they seem to have decided, was too risky; it would contain too much potential to unite and inspire. Second, the decision suggests that there is something unique about burial at sea that resists these potentially dangerous memorial tendencies. The Obama administration appears to have assumed that there cannot be a shrine or a memorial in the sea—being buried at sea is incompatible with being memorialized in certain ways. Although bin Laden's followers could correctly argue that his body has become part of the North Arabian Sea and thus claim that a pilgrimage to the seashore would serve to honor his memory, such an outcome seems unlikely. The sea diffuses and disturbs memory, making it impossible to consecrate a specific gravesite as a rallying point. The US authorities responsible for bin Laden's burial were probably not thinking specifically of the sea's effects on memory. Yet their decision to risk the displeasure of Muslims and the suspicions of conspiracy-mongers by disposing of the terrorist leader's remains in the ocean shows how deeply the notion of a sea burial as a disturber of memory and memorial sites has pervaded contemporary cultural consciousness.

Much like this political episode, literary depictions of drowning or burial at sea provide fascinating glimpses into the often conflicted human relationship with memory. For most cultures and religious traditions, properly remembering the dead involves burial, a funeral or memorial service, and some kind of grave marker.[4] The grave site provides a memorial for the individual, holding at bay the reality of bodily dissolution and providing the illusion that the human body can remain a separate, unique individual even after death. In the modern United States in particular, the popularity of embalming enhances this illusion for mourners who bid farewell to a corpse that looks as lifelike as possible.[5] Burial at sea—in which the body disappears from sight, leaving no trace on the sea surface—troubles these meaning-making processes, rendering memory itself problematic.

Postcolonialism and the Drowned Body

Literary drownings have been accompanied by questions about memory since some of their earliest manifestations, as I demonstrate in chapter 1, "'Full Fathom Five': A Brief History of Literary Drowning." The book's primary focus, however, is on postcolonial texts from Ireland and the Anglophone Caribbean. For many postcolonial writers, the subject of memory is especially fraught. Leela Gandhi writes that "postcoloniality can be described as a condition troubled by the consequences of a self-willed historical amnesia," since postcolonial nations and individuals often repress the painful memories of colonialism.[6] Yet not all of the amnesia attending the postcolonial condition is self-willed. Colonialism as it was practiced by the British Empire involved the deliberate suppression or eradication of native languages, religions, and cultural practices, all essential to the work of preserving memory.

Postcolonial is a fraught and not always helpful term, as scholars like Neil Lazarus have demonstrated. While the term originally indicated only historical information, it has become both universalizing and ideologically laden. In an important passage from *The Postcolonial Unconscious*, Lazarus criticizes postcolonial scholars like Homi K. Bhabha for their tendency to submerge all postcolonial writing under one ideological paradigm: "For most such writers simply do not write from the perspective that Bhabha spells out for us—and that he himself clearly believes is uniquely responsive to the social and historical condition of 'postcoloniality.' Moreover, in the case of a significant number of these writers, at least, they do not fail to write from this perspective by omission or default, but on the basis of the strictest conviction. Put baldly, their assumptions about identity and community and cultural value and politics are quite different from those revealed in the passage by Bhabha."[7] Bhabha and other postcolonial scholars enshrine hybridity, fragmentation, and the resistance to grand narratives as necessary features of postcolonial writing. Yet many postcolonial artists, according to Lazarus, value and even celebrate class or national identity, and emphasize community and togetherness rather than fragmentation. Postcolonial scholars have often, intentionally or not, written in ways that homogenize and flatten the vast and vibrant reality of both the lived experience and the art of former colonies.

Though turning back the clock on postcolonial studies is both impossible and ultimately undesirable, this book attempts to use the term *postcolonial* as much as possible in its historical sense.[8] The writers whose work I examine live and write in former colonies of the British Empire—or, in the case of J. M. Synge, in a colony emerging from colonial rule. They do not share political or ideological commitments beyond a general resistance to colonialism (or at least to its violent effects). All of them face the reality of memories that are no longer accessible, though their attitudes toward those lost memories differ drastically. I do not attempt to flatten those reactions into one experience of postcoloniality; rather, I highlight the clear and profound disagreements between these authors about how to address memory loss on a national and an individual scale. As Jahan Ramazani writes in his introduction to *The Cambridge Companion to Postcolonial Poetry*, when used thoughtfully, "A postcolonial perspective . . . continues to be a powerful tool for revealing linkages across regions emerging from colonial rule, even as it avoids dissolving all writers in an undifferentiated globality, heedless of the differentials of power, history, and language."[9] While these writers all connect the image of the drowned body to the experience of remembering and writing in a postcolonial context, they do so in ways that cannot be reduced to a single ideological stance, and in ways that draw intersectionally on race, class, and gender as well as on cultural or national identity.

Faced with fissures in cultural memory, postcolonial writers often identify their situation—and their nation's—with that of the drowned body. Floating aimlessly without a grave, unmemorialized and perhaps unremembered, the drowned corpse embodies the memory troubles of the postcolonial nation or individual. As the drowned body disintegrates and dissolves, so colonialism erodes the memories of the cultures and individuals it encounters. For writers from island nations where the threat of drowning is a part of everyday life, the image becomes especially important as it carries both local relevance and symbolic strength. This book examines depictions of the drowned body in Irish and Caribbean postcolonial literature, arguing that rather than simply being the marginal detritus of these island literatures, drowned bodies have been central to the project of postcolonial writing in Ireland and the Caribbean, providing a focal point for a transatlantic discussion of memory. I follow a trail of drowned bodies and literary confluence from the Irish playwright J. M. Synge, through the poems and plays of the St. Lucian Nobel laureate Derek Walcott, to the lesser-known work of the Guyanese-British novelist and poet David Dabydeen, and finally back to the contemporary plays of the Irish playwright Marina Carr. Each author, while borrowing from those who came before, reinflects the image of the drowned body in new ways to reflect different facets of the project of remembering postcolonially.

British Imperialism and the Drowned Body

For writers from British colonies or former British colonies, writing about the sea and the drowned body is almost inevitably an act of resistance. While the sea is of universal interest and drownings are by no means exclusive to British literature, the representation of the sea and the drowned body in British literature from the sixteenth century onward is unique in its intense political focus. Starting with the plantation of Ulster, Britain built an empire that, by the eighteenth century, made the small island the world's dominant colonial power. This imperial power was based largely on Britain's possession, beginning with the defeat of the Spanish Armada in 1588, of an unrivalled navy.[10] As Jonathan Raban writes in his introduction to *The Oxford Book of the Sea*, the rhetoric of British imperialism turned the sea itself into a uniquely English place of memory:

> For the English writer . . . the sea was swollen with historical significance. The sea shaped and defined the nation. It was the terrain on which the Englishman's major wars had been fought, his road to the markets of the world, his route to Empire. It was his wilderness and the chief testing-ground of his young manhood. It was impossible for him (or her) to write about the sea without summoning some or all of these clangorous echoes. He could barely look out over the end of a pier without thinking of Drake, Hawkins, Raleigh, Nelson.[11]

National pride over their navy and vast empire led many British writers and thinkers to conceive of the sea itself as an extension of the British Empire. In 1881 Robert Louis Stevenson wrote in his essay "The English Admirals": "We should consider ourselves unworthy of our descent if we did not share the arrogance of our progenitors, and please ourselves with the pretension that the sea is English. Even where it is looked upon by the guns and battlements of another nation we regard it as a kind of English cemetery, where the bones of our seafaring fathers take their rest until the last trumpet; for I suppose no other nation has lost as many ships or sent as many brave fellows to the bottom."[12] In these kinds of passages the imperial urge is so strong that it cannot stand the specter of the unmarked sea, resistant to human ownership. Instead, it transforms the sea into a cemetery, filled with English places of memory.

Stevenson's central conceit of the sea as cemetery is by no means an uncommon one; what may surprise readers is the audacity of his claim that the sea is an English cemetery. No longer confined to moss-covered graves in sleepy churchyards, the English dead have the entire sea for their national resting-place. They have earned this oceanic cemetery, according to Stevenson, not by their naval victories but by their defeats, by the vast numbers of English dead whose bones rest on the sea floor. This strange depiction of the dead body as effective colonist recurs throughout British imperialist rhetoric; perhaps the most obvious example being Rupert Brooke's 1914 poem "The Soldier":

> If I should die, think only this of me:
> That there's some corner of a foreign field
> That is forever England. There shall be
> In that rich earth a richer dust concealed;
> A dust whom England bore, shaped, made aware,
> Gave, once, her flowers to love, her ways to roam,
>
> A body of England's, breathing English air,
> Washed by the rivers, blest by suns of home.[13]

With his imagined dead body, Brooke claims a piece of "foreign" earth for England, much as Stevenson's drowned sailors claim the sea. Thus the dead English body becomes a powerful colonizing force, taking the land and sea for England one grave at a time.

For attentive readers, the glaring irony in Stevenson's essay occurs in his claim that "no other nation has . . . sent as many brave fellows to the bottom." Although Stevenson is writing well after slavery was abolished in England, he is nonetheless writing from a nation that was, for well over a century, one of the largest players in a trade that sent millions of men, women, and children to the bottom of the sea against their will. Although Stevenson's claim that England has sent the greatest number of human bodies to the sea floor may be correct, the fact that his jingoistic words conceal is that many, if not most, of those bodies were African. Estimates of the number of deaths vary, but most historians agree that between one and two million Africans died during the Middle Passage, their bodies unceremoniously thrown into the sea.[14] While not all of these deaths can be blamed on the British slave trade, the vast number that can be attributed to British slavers casts a dark shadow over the imperialist rhetoric of the sea as an English possession, filled with English graves.

In writing about the sea and the bodies in it, the authors considered in this book resist or rework the British claim to ownership of the sea, rediscovering the hidden bodies beneath the ocean's surface. Not all of the bodies they uncover are those of African slaves; some are Irish peasants or Caribbean fishermen. All of them, however, speak to the gaps left in the wake of British colonialism, to the ways it erased and troubled memory. Each drowned corpse also speaks to the difficult process of reconstructing collective memory and national identity postcolonially.

Ireland and the Caribbean

In his groundbreaking 1993 book *The Black Atlantic: Modernity and Double Consciousness*, Paul Gilroy calls for a transatlantic model of cultural studies that resists previous nationally or ethnically focused models. Instead, he writes, "In opposition to . . . nationalist or ethnically absolutist approaches, I want to develop the suggestion that cultural historians could take the Atlantic as one single, complex unit of analysis in their discussions of the modern world and use it to produce an explicitly transnational and intercultural perspective."[15] Gilroy uses the image of a ship, traveling "between Europe, America, Africa, and the Caribbean as a central organizing symbol," noting that transatlantic ships inevitably recall "the middle passage, . . . the various projects for redemptive return to an African homeland, [and] the circulation of ideas and activists as well as the movement of key cultural and political artefacts."[16] Gilroy's focus on "the black Atlantic" has proven fruitful for subsequent scholars seeking to escape the limiting confines of the nation-state and attempting to understand the kinds of cross-cultural influence and intermingling that occur as a result of colonialism and the transatlantic slave trade.[17] This book draws both on Gilroy's example of transatlantic scholarship and on his image of the slave ship, while shifting focus from the ship itself to the trail of bodies left in its wake.

While transatlantic scholars often focus on the exchanges between the colonizing country and the colony, or between Africa and the Americas,[18] recent scholarship has shown that there is much to be learned by comparing the literature, history, and politics of Ireland and the Anglophone Caribbean, former British colonies on opposite sides of the Atlantic. Spurred on by the conference hosted by David Lloyd at the University of Southern California in 2007, "Black and Green Atlantic," and by Lloyd's subsequent publication with Peter O'Neill of *The Black and Green Atlantic: Cross-Currents of the African and Irish Diaspora* in 2009, comparative scholarship has flourished in recent years. Such work has revealed the extent to which postcolonial Caribbean nationalism and self-fashioning was informed and inspired by the example of the Irish. In *Transatlantic Solidarities: Irish Nationalism and Caribbean Poetics* (2009), Michael Malouf shows how the shared history of being colonized by the British and of emigrating in large numbers to New York and London brought Irish and Caribbean peoples into much closer contact than has been previously recognized. The nationalist discourse of Ireland, Malouf argues, together with the nation-building literature of the Irish Literary Revival, had a profound impact on the development of key Caribbean political and artistic figures as they sought to shape the postcolonial identities and art of their own nations.

Maria McGarrity's *Washed by the Gulf Stream: The Historic and Geographic Relation of Irish and Caribbean Literature* (2008), though it traces the Irish presence in the Caribbean as far back as 1612, focuses on the geographical similarities between the two regions. She argues that as small islands—or groups of small islands—both Ireland and the Caribbean have developed a sense of identity shaped by the sea. While for Great Britain—a small island, but one with a powerful navy and unbounded imperial ambition—the sea serves as "a means through which to pursue power and domination";[19] for Ireland and the Caribbean, "The sea functions not simply as a physical restriction but as a new means of potential union."[20] This geographical similarity, McGarrity argues, illuminates correspondences between the cultural output of Ireland and the Caribbean. While her geographical argument tends toward the metaphorical rather than the literal or the historical, it provides a suggestive way of approaching the connections between the two regions. This book combines elements of McGarrity's metaphorical approach with Malouf's historical focus; I explore the drowned body as a metaphor while also looking at specific historical conversations taking place between Ireland and the Caribbean.

More recently, McGarrity's publication of *Caribbean-Irish Connections* (2015), together with Alison Donnell and Evelyn O'Callaghan, provides an interdisciplinary look at the historical, literary, and political networks that have emerged between the regions. In their introduction, the editors remark that "a striking kinship between Irish and Caribbean peoples is a constant, if modest, feature of many Caribbean literary works."[21] Certainly this kinship is evident to a greater or lesser extent in each of the major Caribbean texts I consider in this book. But as Donnell, McGarrity, and O'Callaghan note, the connections between Irish and Caribbean writers go deeper than direct influence or specific allusions: "Even where explicit intertextuality is not apparent, writers across the two postcolonial spaces share mutual concerns: the haunting of history; a deep attachment to land denied them for centuries; the presence of the sea; the importance of orality and storytelling; experiments with non-English linguistic registers; and the need to constantly break and reinvent language and form."[22]

To this helpful list I would add the bodies lost in that sea, which haunt the literatures of Ireland and the Caribbean with obsessive regularity.

My argument adds to this exciting field of transatlantic scholarship by identifying the drowned body as a trope used by Irish and Caribbean writers to examine the memory troubles of the postcolonial nation, and to consider the responsibility of the artist in dealing with those lost or submerged memories. For some, the artist's duty is to mourn and to memorialize, a task rendered more difficult by the missing or disintegrating bodies that mirror the fading memory of the postcolonial nation. For others, the drowned body represents a kind of freedom for the postcolonial artist, who emerges from the painful past into a new creative fluidity and hybridity. In either case, discussions of drowning reveal a transatlantic conversation in which authors build on, challenge, and complicate the ways in which their precursors address the colonial and precolonial past.

By placing Irish and Caribbean texts in conversation I do not intend to equate their experiences of colonialism or of postcolonial independence—quite the contrary. The Irish experience of colonialism, because of race and proximity to the imperial center, was far less extreme and harsh than the Caribbean's. The Irish, as historians such as Liam Kennedy have shown, were privileged colonial subjects, and were at times complicit in British imperialism themselves—serving as civil servants in the Caribbean, for example. Kennedy writes that "Ireland, in effect, was a junior partner in that vast exploitative enterprise known as the British Empire."[23] As Hilary Beckles observes in his foreword to *Caribbean-Irish Connections*, despite the appealing narrative that constructs the Irish as victims of colonialism whose whiteness was in question: "Even when as indentured servants they were described as 'white niggers' and 'white slaves,' the power of the prefix presupposed a privilege that could not be denied."[24] It is crucial not to elide these differences in a desire to render Irish literature fashionably subaltern.

The Caribbean authors considered in this book—Derek Walcott and David Dabydeen—clearly consider the Irish to be allies and important models in their quest to create a Caribbean literary and cultural identity. Both draw on Irish authors as models and include positive Irish characters in their work. Yet while the Irish share the common colonial experience of losing much of their language and many of their cultural traditions to the British colonizer, this loss of memory is minute compared to the one experienced in the Caribbean. The genocide of native populations combined with the displacement of African slaves left irreparable fissures in the memory of the Caribbean. It is partly this difference that makes comparing the literature of the two regions so fascinating. Irish and Caribbean authors deal with memory loss on a different scale, and the scale of that loss shapes the role that each imagines memory playing in the development of the postcolonial nation or individual.

In selecting the Irish and Caribbean authors and texts to focus on in this study, there have been inevitable and regrettable omissions. Drowning is such a ubiquitous trope in both literatures that once I began noticing it, I found myself metaphorically surrounded by dripping corpses. Fred D'Aguiar's *Feeding the Ghosts*, Kate O'Brien's *The Land of Spices*, James Joyce's *Ulysses*, Conor McPherson's *The Weir*, Marie Jones's *Stones in His Pockets*, M. NourbeSe Philip's *Zong!*, and Shani Mootoo's *He Drown She in the Sea* all beckoned, and any of them would be worthy topics for further study.[25] Ultimately I chose to focus on authors whose work contained complex and recurring treatments of drowning—not just single incidents. I also selected authors whose explorations of drowning related clearly to concerns about postcolonial memory and whose work added to, challenged, or altered previous depictions of drowning. Some of the authors discussed in this study are responding specifically to others: Walcott and Carr's work writes back to Synge's, and Dabydeen's answers Walcott's. But even those works that do not directly address one another are clearly responding to the layers of meaning that have accreted around the trope of the drowned body. While each of the drownings examined is a reflection on memory, the authors advance or question one another's portrayals of memory by layering new concerns onto the drowned body. Notably, they differ in their observations regarding the artist's role in relation to memory and in their conclusions about the impact of gender on the work of remembering postcolonially. I doubt, for example, that Marina Carr had Walcott's *Omeros* in mind when penning *The Mai* and *Portia Coughlan*, but her drownings work to reveal the gendered oversimplifications that attend his depictions of drowning and authorship. This book is constructed not as an exhaustive treatment of postcolonial drownings but as a first foray into this important topic. Each artist and each text adds layers to the image of the drowned body, while retaining a central interest in memory and its impact on the postcolonial artist.

Places of Memory

In his monumental collection *Les Lieux de Mémoire* (1992), the French historian Pierre Nora emphasizes the importance of graves, archives, monuments, and other memorial sites to modern consciousness, particularly to any modern sense of collective or national identity.[26] Modernity, Nora argues, has been marked by a move away from memory. Where once memory was preserved in *milieux de mémoire*, or "environments of memory," "settings in which memory is a real part of everyday experience," now it has been replaced by history.[27] History, as opposed to memory, is "willful and deliberate, experienced as a duty rather than as spontaneous; psychological, individual and subjective, rather than social, collective and all-embracing."[28] Yet the desire for memory remains, collecting around certain sites, which Nora calls *lieux de mémoire* ("realms" or "places of memory").[29] These places of memory serve as "the ultimate embodiment of a commemorative consciousness that survives in a history which, having renounced memory, cries out for it,"[30] arising "out of a sense that there is no such thing as spontaneous memory, hence that we must create archives, mark anniversaries, organize celebrations, pronounce eulogies, and authenticate documents because such things no longer happen as a matter of course."[31] The places of memory sacred to a particular group or nation provide important insights into the group's values and anxieties; thus Nora proposes to study the history of France, "not in the traditional thematic or chronological manner," but by "analyzing the places in which the collective heritage of France was crystallized, the principal *lieux*, in all senses of the word, in which collective memory was rooted."[32] The resulting collection spans seven volumes, each chapter examining a different *lieu de mémoire* seen by Nora and his contributors as an important facet of French identity.

While Nora's theory provides a fascinating approach to historical writing, it may raise some questions for a careful reader. The problem that most frequently perplexes English speakers who encounter the notion of places of memory is the fact that many of them are not physical places. Nora uses the term *lieux de mémoire* broadly, including literal places such as palaces or graveyards alongside objects such as textbooks and intangible ideas like literary symbols or "the concept of a historical generation."[33] The confusion on the part of English-language readers is perhaps due to the difficulty of translating the word *lieux*; in any case, it is best when encountering the term to think of Nora's reluctantly given "official definition": "A *lieu de mémoire* is any significant entity, whether material or non-material in nature, which by dint of human will or the work of time has become a symbolic element of the memorial heritage of any community."[34] In this book I often use the term *place of memory* to refer to literal places—graves, memorials, archives, and statues that carry significant memorial weight for a community. In the midst of these physical memorials, however, I place the literary symbol of the drowned body, asking whether or in what ways it serves as a place of memory for the authors studied and the cultures they represent.

Another pressing question for a reader of Nora is how to distinguish a modern *lieu de mémoire* from the kinds of memorials that have existed throughout human history—the Egyptian pyramids, for example, or the stone altars frequently consecrated by the Israelites to memorialize important moments in their collective lives. The difference is difficult to pinpoint precisely; it seems one of scale rather than kind. A powerful nostalgia, even a fetishization, surrounds the modern place of memory, a desire to remember accompanied by a profound lack of living memory. What distinguishes places of memory from "simple memorials," according to Nora, is less their relationship to the past than their role in the present:

> The *lieux* of which I speak are hybrid places, mutants in a sense, compounded of life and death, of the temporal and the eternal . . . For although it is true that the fundamental purpose of a *lieu de mémoire* is to stop time, to inhibit forgetting, to fix a state of things, to immortalize death, and to materialize the immaterial . . . —all in order to capture the maximum possible meaning with the fewest possible signs—it is also clear that *lieux de mémoire* thrive only because of their capacity for change, their ability to resurrect old meanings and generate new ones along with new and unforeseeable connections (that is what makes them exciting).[35]

Places of memory are powerful because they not only tell the story of the past, but they also help onlookers to access collective identity in the present, drawing a memory-less modern people together and providing them with a fleeting sense of unity.

Colonialism, Postcolonialism, and Places of Memory

Nora's work is concerned almost exclusively with France, and yet his concept of *lieux de mémoire* has been adopted by scholars across a variety of disciplines, working in different national contexts. As Homi Bhabha notes, for the postcolonial individual, "Remembering is never a quiet act of introspection or retrospection. It is a painful remembering, a putting together of the dismembered past to make sense of the trauma of the present."[36] The cultural critic and literary scholar Ian Baucom adapts Nora's framework to the British Empire in *Out of Place: Englishness, Empire, and the Locations of Identity* (1999). Baucom fruitfully applies Nora's concept of *places of memory* to the postcolonial context by examining how places of memory encode national identity, turning certain English sites into carriers of "contagious" Englishness.[37] Yet the exchange went both ways; as the colonized adopted elements of English culture they also began to change its sacred places, to alter Englishness from within.[38]

The fraught nature of postcolonial remembering leads to a certain ambivalence about places of memory. For Caribbean writers, there is often a sense that such places simply do not exist. Traditional places of memory, such as gravestones and statues, are largely absent from the Caribbean, partly because British imperialists with their guns and their diseases often wiped out the native agrarian peoples, replacing them with African slaves and East Indian indentured servants who worked the sugarcane fields. There is also a climatological element to this absence—on tropical islands, vegetation is quick to overgrow the traces left by human beings. This combination of factors leads the Caribbean author Derek Walcott to claim, somewhat hyperbolically, that in the Caribbean, "There are no memorials on land"; instead, "In the Caribbean we have something around us that you can't make a mark on—which is the ocean."[39]

In Ireland, by contrast, places of memory abound. The Irish landscape is littered with gravesites, ruined churches, round towers, ancient castles, and memorial statues. Many of these memorials, however, are not nostalgic sites of authentic Irishness but signs signifying the successive waves of domination and violence that have racked the small island throughout its long history. For the Irish poet Eavan Boland the true places of memory in Ireland exist only as fading scars on the landscape, scars such as the famine road in "That the Science of Cartography is Limited." Though such places of memory still exist, overgrown and almost-forgotten traces of unimaginable suffering, Boland notes that the famine road "will not be there" on the official maps—and, by implication, in the official histories—of the island.[40] For Irish writers like J. M. Synge, a turn toward the sea signals a turn away from such incomplete official histories and toward the stories and lives left out or suppressed. As the sea dissolves bodies that ought to be buried and marked by a gravestone, so the British colonization of Ireland diluted the language and cultural traditions that kept memory alive.

Oona Frawley's impressive three-volume collection, *Memory Ireland*, brings the lessons of memory studies to bear on the unique postcolonial situation of Ireland. In her introduction to the collection's first volume, subtitled "History and Modernity," Frawley acknowledges Nora's influence but also the insufficiency of applying his insights to a postcolonial context. She writes: "Irish cultural memory must necessarily be less monumental and more fragmented than other counterparts because of Ireland's colonial and postcolonial experience," and thus she portrays "cultural memory as processual, fluid, and dynamic."[41] The fragmentation of the past in the postcolonial nation highlights the instability of all memory. The interest in drowning among Irish and Caribbean authors speaks to this sense of cultural memory as fluid and ever-changing.

In their representations of drowned bodies, postcolonial Irish and Caribbean writers express their ambivalence toward places of memory. Given the human desire to memorialize the dead, corpses often become places of memory, at least for the families that mourn them. Their immersion in the sea, however, troubles this desire. Traditional rituals of memory are disturbed by the drowned body, which may remain lost at sea, or wash up unrecognized on a distant shore. For the authors discussed in this book, the drowned body captures both the powerful desire to remember and the sense that available ways of remembering may not prove adequate for the unique situation of the postcolonial nation. Statues, gravestones, and memorials are too often tied up with the imperialist desires to possess and lay claim to land, to erect and maintain a dominant narrative of history. While such places of memory may embody collective or national identity for France or England, the situation of the colonized nation is not so straightforward.

In the image of the drowned body, postcolonial authors experiment with a version of memory, and by extension of national identity, that is not fixed but fluid, one that is concrete and yet elusive. In so doing, they create a place of memory that changes the terms of what it means to remember. As Barbara Misztal notes in her contribution to Frawley's collection, decolonization led to "a newly important politics of identity, which proclaims memory as the basis of the collective identity of a community and sees memory as a resource for the construction and defence of cultural identities."[42] Newly formed nations seek to establish their identity by developing a sense of collective memory, and thus "memory is used strategically: not merely to explain the group past but also to transform it into a reliable identity source for the group present."[43] For many—though certainly not all—authors, this co-opting of memory by the nation represents another potential danger. While the erasure of memory under colonialism can lead to a fragmented sense of self or a loss of identity, a monolithic reconstruction of collective memory could be seen to promote nationalist violence. According to Frawley, Irish collective memory can be alternately healing and divisive: "Irish cultural memory can be said to retain names of physical sites long since disappeared, genealogical histories of particular parishes, reverence for land even in the face of overwhelming modernization and urbanity. It can also retain mighty hatreds for individuals or for groups, and it can fortify itself with the illusion of forgetting major traumas such as battle failures, famines, religious violence, bombings."[44] By engaging with the drowned body rather than the gravestone or statue, postcolonial authors recognize the dangerous potential of collective memory. Instead they seek out a sense of memory that is shared and meaningful but also multivocal, uncertain, dynamic, and fluid.

As Frawley's aforementioned quote suggests, postcolonial memory can be viewed as a deliberate negotiation between memory and forgetfulness. In *The Ethics of Memory*, Avishai Margalit considers whether we as human beings have a moral or ethical obligation to remember, and if so, what kinds of things we should remember. For Margalit, this question goes hand in hand with its opposite: "An ethics of memory is as much an ethics of forgetting as it is an ethics of memory. The crucial question, Are there things that we ought to remember? has a parallel, Are there things that we ought to forget? Should we, for example, forget for the sake of 'forgiving'?"[45] Margalit concludes that forgetting in order to forgive is neither truly possible nor desirable, choosing to embrace the biblical metaphor of "crossing out" sins rather than the alternative image of "blotting out."[46] Yet he acknowledges that for newly born democracies, forgetfulness is a crucial piece of moving forward: "Communities must make decisions and establish institutions that foster forgetting as much as remembering."[47] Margalit concludes that victims of trauma do not owe forgiveness to their oppressors but that forgiveness is beneficial to the victim and the community in order to suppress dangerous attitudes such as revenge and recrimination.

For the authors analyzed in this study, the drowned body provides a space to consider the artist's position on this spectrum of postcolonial remembering and forgetting. As Frawley perceptively concludes, postcolonial nations paradoxically suffer from both a deficiency and an excess of memory: "Postcolonial memory might thus be said to embody at its extremes two disparate forms of memory: the inability to forget that has been so often noted by cognitive scientists studying the impact of trauma, and the need to remember and reconstruct a history and a past that might have been forgotten: postcolonial memory would thus seem to involve the too-much-ness of memory that is nostalgia faced with the too-little-memory that is forgetting."[48] Both memory and forgetting may be difficult or impossible for the postcolonial individual. For Synge, the author's responsibility in the face of this dilemma is to remember and to mourn. By contrast, Walcott finds a deliberate, informed amnesia more artistically fruitful. For writers like Dabydeen and Carr, decisions about where to place themselves on this spectrum between remembering and forgetting are inescapably inflected by race and gender. Each author thus uses his or her depictions of the drowned body to stake out a different position on the continuum of memory.

While Synge, Dabydeen, Walcott, and Carr all draw on Irish or Caribbean literary traditions in their representations of drowned bodies, part of the power of their depiction of postcolonial memory comes from the way that they resist or redirect some of the most canonical British images of drowning. Allusions to Ophelia and *The Tempest*, to John Milton's "Lycidas," and to *The Waste Land* abound. Meanwhile, the more subtle influence of serial literary drowners like Charles Dickens and George Eliot can be glimpsed in the background. Thus chapter 1, "Full Fathom Five: A Brief History of Literary Drowning" examines the historical representation of drowned bodies in *The Tempest*, "Lycidas," and *The Waste Land*, demonstrating their concern with issues of memory and memorialization. These texts' use of drowning to express anxiety about memory lays the groundwork for the appropriation of the drowned body by postcolonial authors as a symbol of their far more pervasive memory troubles.

Milton and Shakespeare worry about the human ability to remember particular individuals once they have died, but postcolonial authors deal with memory loss on a larger scale. Chapter 2, "The Lost Body: The Author as Mourner in J. M. Synge's Travel Writings and *Riders to the Sea*," shows how in a postcolonial context, literary depictions of bodies lost at sea often stand in for the losses of cultural memory caused by colonialism. For Synge, the drowned body is the lost body, wandering in the vast ocean space or sunk far from sight in a deep lake or river. Drawing not only on *Riders to the Sea* and *The Aran Islands* but also on his lesser-known *Travels in Wicklow, West Kerry, and Connemara*, chapter 2 argues that for Synge, the drowned body, the center of a deeply personal experience of grief, simultaneously signifies a more general sense of cultural loss. Decaying, free-floating, often unrecognizable even to their own mothers, the "power of young men floating round" in Synge's sea allow the author to interrogate the relationship of the Irish artist to Ireland's multiform histories. In the process, Synge's work becomes a keen for cultures that are passing away. This view of the postcolonial artist as a mourner for the "lost bodies" left in the wake of colonialism and modernity directly influences the work of later Caribbean artists such as Derek Walcott and David Dabydeen, who reject or reinflect the tearful solemnity involved in this form of memory.

Chapter 3, "The Regenerative Body: Creative Amnesia and the New World Author in Derek Walcott's *The Sea at Dauphin* and *Omeros*," focuses on the radical changes made by the St. Lucian poet and playwright Derek Walcott to the image of the drowned body and to the project of postcolonial remembering. His early play, *The Sea at Dauphin*, an adaptation of *Riders to the Sea*, hints at those changes, which are more fully developed in his epic poem *Omeros*. Where

Synge's play focuses on the death of a young man and the waning of a way of life, the drowning of the suicidal widower Hounakin in *The Sea at Dauphin* can be read as a sign of the healing that can be enabled by forgetting the wounds of the past. In *Omeros* Walcott extends this vision of drowning as a regenerative process, as the drowned body hosts the growth of a coral reef, a growth that mirrors the birth of the postcolonial nation. Walcott's work rejoices in the sea as a fertile common space for art because it erases history, enabling the postcolonial artist to rename the world from a space where cultures and traditions converge.

Chapter 4, "The Disintegrating Body: The Unstable Author in David Dabydeen's 'Turner,'" examines the Guyanese poet and novelist David Dabydeen's poem "Turner," which writes back to *Omeros*, warning against its too-easy conflation of forgetting and regeneration. The drowned body that narrates "Turner" is disintegrating, and its memory is gapped and unreliable. Its forgetfulness, however, does not inspire rebirth but instead enables a destructive kind of revisionist memory, a memory that allows the speaker's prejudices to become part of the story of the past. Thus "Turner" highlights the ways in which Walcott's work challenges its own fluidity and heterogeneity in order to foreground the creativity of the individual artist. Unlike *Omeros*, however, "Turner," in its attention to the drowned body's disintegration and decay, offers little hope that the postcolonial nation and individual will able to move beyond the wounds of their past.

Chapter 5, "The Ghostly Body: Gender and Memory in Marina Carr's *The Mai* and *Portia Coughlan*," considers the drowning deaths of the heroines of two of Carr's most successful plays. By making the drowned postcolonial bodies female ones, Carr brings an intersectional focus to her examination of drowning and memory. Her Irish heroines long for a romanticized precolonial past, but as women they find themselves trapped in the limited domestic roles that come with that past. For the Mai and Portia, water represents a chance for freedom and escape, but immediately after they drown themselves, both women's bodies are found and returned home by their husbands. Carr's innovative temporal structure places the suicides in the middle of the plays, going back in time for the final act to examine the period immediately before the death. This technique effectively turns her heroines into ghosts, forced to return to their restrictive and unfulfilling lives even after their deaths. For women, Carr suggests, memory is both alluring and dangerous, imprisoning them in roles and routines that should be buried in the past.

Paraphrasing Bhabha, Leela Gandhi writes: “Memory is the necessary and sometimes hazardous bridge between colonialism and the question of cultural identity.”[49] In moving forward to construct new cultural identities, postcolonial artists and intellectuals must contend with memory. In revealing the role played by the drowned body in Irish and Caribbean literary negotiations with memory, I illuminate a few of the myriad approaches postcolonial authors have taken to crossing this “hazardous bridge.” In the literary drowned body, these authors have created a uniquely postcolonial place of memory—one sensitive to the complex balance of memory and forgetting that attends the development of the postcolonial individual or nation.

1

"Full Fathom Five"

A Brief History of Literary Drowning

"Fear death by water," Madame Sosostris tells the narrator of T. S. Eliot's *The Waste Land*.[1] Yet drowning is popularly imagined as an easy death, as evidenced by the frequent figurative use of the verb to describe states of submersion ranging from the irritating to the blissful. We are drowning in paperwork, so we drown our sorrows in drink. We may drown in erotic or religious ecstasy. Literary depictions of drowning deaths are typically gentle, or at least quick. Much like the common understanding of freezing to death, drowning is pictured as a gentle submission to the elements, even a way of uniting oneself with the natural environment.

Though it is of course impossible to know what death by drowning feels like, it seems likely given the descriptions of near-drowning victims or survivors of waterboarding that it is in fact a traumatic, though reasonably quick, way to die. Drowning deaths occur as a result of suffocation, which happens when the victim passes out from lack of oxygen and inhales water. Drowning victims usually die of brain damage or lung injury within four to six minutes of this final watery breath.

Whatever the victim's experience, the aftermath of a literary drowning death often involves more hand-wringing anxiety than deaths by other means. Confronting a corpse, particularly the body of a loved one, can be a terrifying experience. The absence of a corpse, however, may be more troubling than its presence. Missing bodies disrupt mourning processes, making closure difficult. In many cases, the literary text attempts to fill the place of the missing monument or gravestone, as in the case of *Justa Edouardo King Naufrago*, the 1638 collection of elegies for the drowned Cambridge student Edward King, in which John Milton's "Lycidas" first appeared. Milton's elegy—and those of his classmates—is animated by the absence of King's body, by the desire to poetically "locate" it and fill a threatening emptiness.

Drowning thus serves an ambivalent function in literature, uniting the human desire for a peaceful death with the equally powerful terror of being forgotten. While a broad history of literary drowning, illuminating these competing desires, would be a worthwhile endeavor, this chapter is primarily concerned with setting up the tradition of representing the drowned body within and against which postcolonial Irish and Caribbean writers work. Thus, while literary drowners such as George Eliot, Charles Dickens, Henrik Ibsen, Kate Chopin, Flannery O'Connor, Herman Melville, and many others beckon, here I focus on three British drowning texts that have been particularly influential for the Irish and Caribbean writers who make up the main focus of *Literary Drowning*, as evidenced by frequent allusions and thematic connections. The drowned bodies in William Shakespeare's *The Tempest*, John Milton's "Lycidas," and T. S. Eliot's *The Waste Land* demonstrate the intense anxieties about memorialization that surround drowning in the Western literary tradition. The authors' concern with the dissolving boundaries and disappearing memory of the drowned individual reveals a parallel concern with the boundaries of nation and national identity. Thus the drowned bodies of Alonso, Lycidas, and Phlebas the Phoenician sailor provide fertile ground for later authors interested in exploring the role of memory in a postcolonial, transatlantic context.

The study of literary influence has become suspect in recent decades, largely because it can be used to enforce ethnocentric narratives in which creativity and innovation flow outward from the imperial center to the periphery. As Ankhi Mukherjee writes, "The canon is often represented in postcolonial fiction as portable property, a library of carefully vetted works that carries out its work of global dominance in the farthest outposts of empire. Often in postcolonial representation, the classics distil, usually for the tragically deluded protagonist, the very meaning of civilization and sanity."[2] In beginning this book with Shakespeare, Milton, and Eliot, I am especially aware of the danger of falling in to these kinds of insidious templates. As Jahan Ramazani writes in *The Hybrid Muse*, the "gift" of an English education "may also have been the greatest curse of empire, purveyed by missionaries and by imperial governments as a tool for altering native minds and even turning them against themselves."[3] To oversimplify the nature of British literary influence on writers from former British colonies or to suggest that the influence only goes one way is to risk occluding these important realities.

Yet as Paul Gilroy argues in *The Black Atlantic*, thinking transatlantically often means acknowledging and addressing such influence:

> The intellectual and cultural achievements of the black Atlantic populations exist partly inside and not always against the grand narrative of Enlightenment and its operational principles. Their stems have grown strong, supported by a lattice of western politics and letters. Though African linguistic tropes and political and philosophical themes are still visible for those who wish to see them, they have often been transformed and adapted by their New World locations to a new point where the dangerous issues of purified essences and simple origins lose all meaning. These modern black political formations stand simultaneously both inside and outside the western culture which has been their peculiar step-parent.[4]

By beginning with these three texts, I do not mean to suggest them as some kind of drowning urtext, providing the raw materials from which later texts are assembled. Rather, I highlight these drownings in order to demonstrate the multiple ways in which postcolonial authors have made the drowned body new. For some authors, their ability to move freely in and out of the canon of Western literature is creatively enabling. As Salman Rushdie writes, "It is perhaps one of the more pleasant freedoms of the literary migrant to be able to choose his parents."[5] For others, the relationship is a more antagonistic one. In choosing to frequently reference *The Tempest*, "Lycidas," and *The Waste Land*, the authors discussed in this study emphasize the usefulness of these texts but also their dangerous oversights, the extent to which their depiction of the human desire for memory is blind to the vast erasures of memory occurring as a result of Britain's imperial project.

"Sea Changes": Drowning in Shakespeare

In Shakespeare's plays, the bottom of the sea is a monstrous, magical place, littered with riches and human bones. In a vividly imagined speech from *Richard III*, the guilt-ridden Clarence describes a nightmare in which he falls overboard and visits the sea floor:

> O Lord! methought what pain it was to drown!
> What dreadful noise of waters in mine ears!
> What sights of ugly death within mine eyes!
> Methoughts I saw a thousand fearful wracks;
> A thousand men that fishes gnawed upon;
> Wedges of gold, great anchors, heaps of pearl,
> Inestimable stones, unvalued jewels,
> All scatt'red in the bottom of the sea:
> Some lay in dead men's skulls, and in the holes
> Where eyes did once inhabit, there were crept
> (As 'twere in scorn of eyes) reflecting gems,
> That wooed the slimy bottom of the deep
> And mocked the dead bones that lay scatt'red by.[6]

Clarence's dream is an unusually terrifying depiction of drowning, clearly emphasizing the pain and fear of the drowning person. Yet after the first three exclamations, his terror seems less related to the actual experience of drowning and more to his contemplation of what happens to the bodies of those who drown. They are, he remarks twice, "scatt'red," gnawed on by fishes, mocked by gemstones pretending to be eyes. Shakespeare's foregrounding of the word *scatt'red* hints at the real source of terror underlying Clarence's dream. The ocean does not respect the Christian traditions of funerary rites and memorialization that have as their goal the peaceful rest of the deceased. A scattered body suggests a disturbed and wandering soul, as evidenced by Clarence's continued dream journey from the bottom of the sea across "the melancholy flood / With that sour ferryman which poets write of, / Unto the kingdom of perpetual night."[7] While it is ultimately Clarence's treachery that earns him his vision of hell, the sea's disordering of the bodies in it certainly does not aid the journey to a peaceful afterlife.

The bottom of the ocean is not a fit resting place for "peace-parted souls,"[8] as evidenced in Shakespeare's *Pericles, Prince of Tyre*. When his beloved wife, Thaisa, dies in childbirth aboard a ship in the middle of a storm, Pericles is persuaded by the superstitious sailors to throw her body overboard in order to calm the storm. His speech to her body indicates his anxiety about this unfitting resting place:

> Th' unfriendly elements
> Forgot thee utterly; nor have I time
> To give thee hallowed to thy grave, but straight
> Must cast thee, scarcely coffined, in the ooze;
> Where, for a monument upon thy bones
> And e'er-remaining lamps, the belching whale
> And humming water must o'erwhelm thy corpse,
> Lying with simple shells.[9]

Pericles worries about what the hasty sea burial will do to his wife's memory; just as the "elements / forgot" her, Thaisa's body will lack a "monument," overwhelmed by the ocean's tides and massive denizens. The letter Pericles includes in Thaisa's coffin, directing "who finds her" to "give her burying" further indicates his apprehension about the fate of his wife's body.[10] Shades of Clarence's eerie sea floor, disturber of human memory, remain.

Yet in Pericles's vision of the underwater world, there are no "scatt'red" bones; Thaisa's corpse remains, in her husband's imagination, relatively fixed, "lying" in one place, surrounded by shells. The relatively peaceful depiction of the sea floor hints at the fact that Thaisa will not in fact land there; she has been too hastily pronounced dead and survives the trip ashore in her improbably well "caulked and bitumed" coffin.[11] Shakespeare's unwillingness to consign Thaisa to the bottom of the sea may indicate that his ocean possesses a kind of moralizing duality. For the morally corrupt—or narratively insignificant—the tides and currents of the ocean are disrupting forces, separating their bones and comically intermingling them with the wealth that may have been their downfall. The dissolution of the body cannot be separated from the moral peril of the soul. For the morally upright Thaisa, the same tides and currents wash her safely to shore, eventually to be revived and reunited with her husband and daughter. Her body remains intact, an outward symbol of the purity of her soul.

Shakespeare makes this connection between spiritual straying and bodily dissolution most explicitly in the drowning case that has become his most famous—the drowning of Ophelia in *Hamlet*. Unlike Clarence, Thaisa, or Alonso, Ophelia is immersed in a brook, rather than the ocean. While she does sink, weighed down by "her garments/ heavy with their drink,"[12] Ophelia's death is observed, and her body is immediately retrieved; she does not become one of the scattered skeletons that Clarence imagines. The ambiguous, possibly suicidal nature of Ophelia's death, however, ignites a controversy about burial, and the majority of the next scene is spent discussing bodily decay. The clowns who dig Ophelia's grave converse about their task, suggesting that the gravedigger's role is to preserve deserving bodies from decay for as long as possible. The first clown jokes that the only person who "builds stronger than either the mason, the shipwright, or the carpenter," is "a grave-maker," since "the houses that he makes last till doomsday."[13] Later, when Hamlet appears, he asks the gravedigger how long a body will last in the earth before it rots. The gravedigger replies that a nonsyphilitic corpse "will last you some eight or nine year," and "a tanner will last you nine year."[14] The reason that a tanner will last longer, the gravedigger jokes, is that his hide "will keep out water a great while, and your water is a sore decayer of your whoreson dead body."[15] While this is a humorous scene, it clearly underscores the play's anxiety about bodily dissolution and its connection between a sinful life and a speedily decaying corpse. In addition, it supports the idea from elsewhere in Shakespeare's oeuvre of water as a disturber of human bodies and human legacies.

While all bodies rot, from that of Yorick the court jester to "imperious Caesar, dead and turned to clay," the clowns' discussion suggests that proper burial and memorial rites are designed to temporarily keep decay at bay.[16] They also suggest that Ophelia's body may not deserve such consideration; the scene begins with the clown's question: "Is she to be buried in Christian burial when she willfully seeks her own salvation?"[17] The rites given to Ophelia are, according to Hamlet, "maimèd rites," the word *rites* designating both the truncated funeral service and the hastily prepared body.[18] The doctor, maintaining that "her death was doubtful," remarks that instead of flowers or prayers, "shards, flints, and pebbles should be thrown on her," the sharp-edged objects indicating a desire to speed, rather than arrest, the disintegration of Ophelia's body.[19]

Ophelia's death thus reveals a complex web of connections between drowning, which speeds bodily dissolution, and suicide, which endangers the eternal fate of the soul. Michael MacDonald notes that the reactions of these lower-class characters to Ophelia's death are historically accurate responses to drowning: "Drowning was one of the most frequent causes of accidental death in Tudor and Stuart England, and it was obviously difficult in many cases to be sure that people found drowned in a pond or river had actually committed suicide. Juries nevertheless returned large numbers of drowned bodies as *felones de se*. Throughout the whole early modern period, drowning was the second most common cause of deaths found to be suicides, and it was the most common cause of such deaths of women."[20] This cultural association of drowning and suicide, which almost certainly resulted in some accidental deaths being labeled as suicide, may explain the ambiguous nature of Ophelia's death. Gertrude's detailed account of Ophelia's death clearly describes an accident, in which Ophelia climbs out on a branch overhanging a brook in order to pick some flowers and, as the branch breaks beneath her, falls into the brook. Her wet garments are so heavy that she is unable to climb out again, and she is eventually pulled beneath the surface. Yet the clowns and the doctor, those who are not emotionally invested in the fate of Ophelia's soul, seem certain that Ophelia has chosen to drown herself.

Ophelia is the canonical drowned woman, so famous that she may be the figure most responsible for the ongoing association of drowning and femaleness. As Magda Romanska argues, Ophelia was "the single most often represented female figure" during the nineteenth century; her wet and helpless body, surrounded by the lush natural world of Gertrude's description, became an erotic subject for countless painters.[21] Gertrude's account, in which Ophelia sings "snatches of old lauds, / As one incapable of her own distress," emphasizes Ophelia's passivity.[22] So do paintings like John Everett Millais's *Ophelia*, in which the drowned woman's vacant eyes mirror the resigned gesture of her hands. Here, drowning is submission, giving one's body to the water's deadly embrace.

Ophelia looms large in Western culture's imagination of drowning, but for postcolonial writers, Shakespeare's most significant description of a drowning occurs in *The Tempest*. The play opens on the deck of a ship, a raging storm threatening to drown all aboard. The storm causes the sailors to abandon ship, and although Prospero's magic ensures that no one dies, the ship's occupants are scattered on the island, each group believing the others have drowned. The spirit Ariel taunts Ferdinand, the son of Alonso, the king of Naples, by singing a song describing his father's drowning. The song, "Full Fathom Five," echoes Clarence's description of the sea floor as a mingled heap of bones and jewels:

> Full fathom five thy father lies;
> Of his bones are coral made;
> Those are pearls that were his eyes;
> Nothing of him that doth fade
> But doth suffer a sea-change
> Into something rich and strange.
> Sea nymphs hourly ring his knell:
>   Ding-dong.
> Hark! Now I hear them—Ding-dong bell.[23]

Although Alonso has not actually drowned, Ariel's depiction of his corpse transforming into a coral reef has provided one of the richest intertexts for later literary drownings. The frequent allusion by postcolonial writers to the song demonstrates its complexity, the way in which it brings together individual concerns about memory and forgetfulness with broader political worries about the permanence or permeability of the nation.

Unlike Clarence's terrifying vision of the sea floor in *Richard III*, Ariel's description of Alonso's drowned corpse is an ambivalent one. For Ferdinand, the (supposedly) bereaved son, the transformation of his father's body by the sea is undoubtedly tragic. The father and king that he knows has disappeared, replaced by a "strange" collection of underwater objects. The brief lapse of time between the shipwreck and Ariel's song, between Alonso's supposed death and the complete transformation of his body, calls into question any notion of the king as transcendent or more than mortal. The once-powerful king is quickly overpowered by the denizens of the sea, who have no more respect for his body than any other organic matter. The scene echoes the boatswain's claim that the sea is no respecter of political hierarchy: "What cares these roarers for the name of king?"[24] Ariel's song thus depicts the fragility of human government, its susceptibility to a radical "sea-change."

Yet this benthic scene is noticeably more positive than the one observed by Clarence, who describes the bones as "scatt'red," the sea floor as "slimy," and the gems as having "crept" into "the holes / Where eyes did once inhabit."[25] By contrast, Alonso's coral bones and pearl eyes seem to remember and respect the shape of his former body. This is not, perhaps, an appropriate tomb for a king, but it is a monument nonetheless, one that may remain intact long after gravestones on land have crumbled. In its refrain, "Full Fathom Five" underscores this sense that Alonso will be remembered despite his inaccessibility to traditional mourning rituals; while he does not have a proper funeral service, "sea nymphs hourly ring his knell." In her excellent article tracing a natural history of coral, Shannon Kelley reads Alonso's "coral body" as an image of immortality: "Alonso's corpse offers this stunning alternative to decay: a wondrous constancy whose ontological status is unclear."[26] For early modern thinkers, coral and pearls, unlike the gold and other jewels that are strewn across the sea floor in Clarence's vision, occupy a unique space between living but impermanent plants or animals and dead but enduring stone. Kelley writes of coral: "If it began as a mere underwater plant (herb, shrub, grass, or tree), its mineralized form was curative, perpetual, and exceedingly valuable. Alonso's second, coral body, then, was a significant improvement on his pre-tempest mortality."[27] While the sea is typically portrayed as an eraser and scatterer of human remains, here the frightening process that "changes" Alonso's body serves to make his body more permanent and durable even as it lies inaccessible on the sea floor.

Despite the boatswain's assertion that "roarers" do not care "for the name of king," it seems in Ariel's song that they do. Kelley writes that "Full Fathom Five" literalizes the early modern political theory of the two-bodied king. While Alonso's physical body is threatened by the tempests and plots afoot on Prospero's island, his body simultaneously incarnates the "body politic," which is immortal: "As a half-transcendent being who embodies the mystic body politic, [Alonso] cannot die, he cannot err, and he cannot be subject to Aristotelian accident. Alonso's coral skeleton, an apt metaphor for the body politic, will never fade, diminish, or decay in any context; coral's seemingly infinite capacity for skeletal endurance contrasts with the vulnerability of the human body."[28] The image of Alonso's coral corpse thus foreshadows the resolution of *The Tempest.* The Neapolitan political order, though threatened, will be reformed and resurrected. The sea water that promised destruction instead brings cleansing and restoration.

Shakespeare's placement of the king's body in the sea indicates his interest in the changes to the European nation-state brought on by its imperial exploration and expansion. The "strange" and wondrous new places and people encountered by Europeans on their voyages of exploration and the subsequent efforts by explorers to claim such places threaten to irreversibly alter the nation. As Dan Brayton notes, "Shakespeare's preoccupation with marine phenomena . . . suggests that he was acutely aware of his nation's growing status as a sea power."[29] "Ariel's song," he continues, "enacts a carefully orchestrated *coup d'état* in which nature itself is enlisted for political purposes; it cannot help but evoke historical questions about the European ventures at sea in early modernity."[30] The intense otherness of the sea threatens to unsettle kingly power, much like the unruly otherness of the rebellious Caliban, who is possessed, as Brayton notes, of "an ontological hybridity that encompasses man and fish."[31] *The Tempest* asks whether the European nation can expand to encompass such difference, or whether it will suffer an irreversible "sea-change" as a result of its imperial ambitions. Ultimately, its answer, while complex, seems to find in favor of European expansion. While Prospero, Alonso, and Antonio are undoubtedly changed by their experience in the sea and on the island, they are changed for the better. Alonso emerges unscathed from his imaginary drowning and the body politic is not only reformed and restored but promises to continue through the marriage of Ferdinand and Miranda. While the scattered mix of human bones, jewels, and gold in *Richard III* clearly satirizes the human greed that leads to imperial expansion, the coral and pearls that take the place of Alonso's body in *The Tempest* gesture toward the immortality of the monarchy and the nation.

"The Genius of the Shore": Drowning in Milton

Largely thanks to the much-discussed relationship between Prospero and Caliban, *The Tempest*'s position in postcolonial literature and criticism is indisputable and unsurprising. Ariel's song, combining concerns about individual mortality and memory with political concerns about the boundaries of nation in an age of empire, has understandably become the drowning most frequently referenced by postcolonial writers. What is more surprising is the frequent reference in postcolonial literature to another, much less obviously political, literary drowning.[32] John Milton's poem "Lycidas," written approximately twenty-five years after *The Tempest*, describes the poet's grief over the drowning of a friend, the Cambridge student

Edward King. Written as a highly allusive pastoral poem, "Lycidas" seems unlikely to be of interest to the same authors who are drawn to "Full Fathom Five." Yet the speaker's concern over the whereabouts of his friend's body and about what the sea's battering of that body will do to the processes of memory and grief have proven compelling to later postcolonial writers, who understand such concerns on a larger and even more tragic scale.

The well-known circumstances of Milton's composition of "Lycidas" need not be repeated in detail, but a quick overview illuminates the poem's concern with the way that drowning disturbs memorialization. On August 10, 1637, Edward King, a Cambridge student three years Milton's junior, an amateur poet and aspiring priest, drowned when the ship he was aboard wrecked while crossing the Irish Sea. King had been born in Dublin, where his father was an English civil servant, and he was traveling to Dublin during the school break to visit family and friends. On learning of his death, his school commissioned a collection of elegies by his classmates titled *Justa Edouardo King naufrago, ab Amicis maerentibus* (Rites to Edward King, Drowned by Shipwreck, from His Grieving Friends).[33] Milton's "Lycidas" was the final poem in this volume. The volume's title, with its emphasis on "rites" and its mention of the specific mode of King's death, draws attention to the fact that King's missing body disturbs traditional mourning rituals. Drowning makes certain consolatory rituals—anointing the dead, burying the body, laying flowers on the gravesite—impossible. In the face of these absences, *Justa Edouardo King naufrago* attempts to stand in for more conventional rites.

Critics are quick to clarify that Milton was not particularly close to King, and that he uses the occasion of King's death for his own poetic and political purposes in "Lycidas." Whether or not Milton's grief was deeply personal, however, there is no question that his speaker is profoundly disturbed by the method of King's death and the loss of his body. Milton writes "Lycidas" in the pastoral mode, transforming King into the poet-shepherd Lycidas. Yet Milton does not create a more likely means of death for his shepherd character, choosing not only to maintain King's drowning but to saturate his poem in water imagery. Richard Adams estimates that "no less than fifty lines, out of a total of 193, are concerned with water in one way or another."[34] Lycidas's death is particularly troubling not just because he was young and full of promise but because it is a watery death. Thus the disturbing cry: "For Lycidas is dead, dead ere his prime, / Young Lycidas, and hath not left his peer," is quickly followed by: "He must not float upon his watery bier / Unwept, and welter to the parching wind."[35] Just as Lycidas's youthful death is unnatural, so is the current state of his body. Milton underscores this sense that Lycidas's drowning goes against nature by his rapid juxtaposition of the words *watery*, *welter*, and *parching*. Both *watery* and *welter* are sea words, appropriate to their task of describing the drowned body, rolling and tossing in the ocean waves. But *parching*, which the *Oxford English Dictionary* defines as "drying to excess" or "scorching," is a desert word, jarring in this context.[36] A world in which Lycidas dies young is an unnaturally cruel world, where desert winds blow across the surface of the ocean, where it is possible to be both waterlogged and thirsty.[37]

Milton's speaker is troubled by the mental image of Lycidas's body lost and weltering amid the waves. In one of the poem's most moving cries of grief, the speaker imagines how far the tides might have taken the body:

> Ay me! whilst thee the shores and sounding seas
> Wash far away, where'er thy bones are hurled;
> Whether beyond the stormy Hebrides,
> Where thou perhaps under the whelming tide
> Visit'st the bottom of the monstrous world,
> Or whether thou, to our moist vows denied,
> Sleep'st by the fable of Bellerus old,
> Where the great Vision of the guarded mount
> Looks toward Namancos and Bayona's hold.[38]

The sea has not been gentle with its young charge. Lycidas's "bones" have been "hurled" "far away" from where he first sank; the undersea world he visits is "monstrous." Rosemond Tuve writes: "It is the human pain over the remembered body wandering untended and unstrewn that gives the sense of wild displacement to that image which most mixes grief with pity."[39] Death in the sea is disordered, and it is left to the survivors to find new ways to grieve and to remember the lost individual.

As the sea aimlessly wafts Lycidas's body, disturbing both the grieving processes of his friends and their ability to remember, the poet-speaker of "Lycidas" recognizes his responsibility to create a poetic memorial. Lycidas "must not float upon his watery bier / Unwept . . . / Without the meed of some melodious tear"; it is instead the poet's job to see that Lycidas is remembered and mourned.[40] Milton connects the task of the elegist to the ritual trappings of burial; in imagining his own death he hopes that "some gentle Muse," will "with lucky words favour my destined urn, / And as he passes turn / And bid fair peace be to my sable shroud!"[41] The poet's words must replace the "urn" and "shroud" that Lycidas's body lacks. Eric Brown writes that "Lycidas" attempts to give a kind of poetic stability to the wandering body: "The honorifics of the elegiac seem intended to becalm, finally, the aimless floating, the 'weltering' of the dead."[42] This process of poetically burying the drowned body culminates in the famous passage where the speaker calls on the valleys to bring a wealth of "vernal flowers" in order "to strew the laureate hearse where Lycid lies."[43] Despite Milton's knowledge that Lycidas will not have a "hearse," that there is no place to bring flowers, he cannot imagine Lycidas's death unaccompanied by memorial rituals. As Tuve notes, this is "not a simple grief . . . How can we not come with tributes, though there is no place to lay them?"[44] The human need for memory and ritual cries out, lost without the body and the grave to serve as its focal point.

The fact of Lycidas's drowning and the loss of his body troubles Milton's speaker, rendering sinister most of the water imagery in the poem's first 164 lines. In the poem's final 30 lines, however, Milton reverses this trend, drawing on the positive imagery of water from the Christian tradition to connect Lycidas's drowning with baptism and spiritual rebirth. In a passage directly following the grief-filled search for Lycidas's body, tossed to the furthest reaches of the Irish Sea or resting at "the bottom of the monstrous world,"[45] the speaker consoles the weeping shepherds by asserting that Lycidas is not dead as a result of sinking beneath the waves but is instead spiritually reborn:

> Weep no more, woeful shepherds, weep no more,
> For Lycidas, your sorrow, is not dead,
> Sunk though he be beneath the watery floor.
> So sinks the day-star in the ocean bed,
> And yet anon repairs his drooping head,
> And tricks his beams, and with new-spangled ore
> Flames in the forehead of the morning sky:
> So Lycidas, sunk low but mounted high,
> Through the dear might of Him that walked the waves,
> Where, other groves and other streams along,
> With nectar pure his oozy locks he laves,
> And hears the unexpressive nuptial song
> In the blest kingdoms meek of joy and love.[46]

Just as the sun appears to sink into the ocean at the end of the day but rises again in the morning newly bright, so Lycidas is "sunk low but mounted high." His drowning becomes not a death but a baptism, a washing in "nectar pure" that leads him to "the blest kingdoms of joy and love."

This passage embodies one of the fascinating complexities of writing about drowning within the Judeo-Christian tradition. While a drowned body causes anxiety about funeral rites and the state of the eternal soul, the experience of drowning also mirrors one of the most important rituals of Christianity—baptism. In many Christian traditions, including Milton's Anglican Church, baptism is considered one of only two sacraments instituted by Christ, and it is necessary for salvation. In baptism, being submerged in water—or, in many traditions, having water poured over one's head—signals the spiritual cleansing that attends salvation. It represents both death and rebirth: the death of the old, sinful self and rebirth into a new Christian life. In his letter to the Romans, the apostle Paul outlines the connection between baptism, death, and resurrection:

> Do you not know that all of us who have been baptized into Christ Jesus were baptized into his death? Therefore we have been buried with him by baptism into death, so that, just as Christ was raised from the dead by the glory of the Father, so we too might walk in newness of life. For if we have been united with him in a death like his, we will certainly be united with him in a resurrection like his. We know that our old self was crucified with him so that the body of sin might be destroyed, and we might no longer be enslaved to sin.[47]

In baptism, one self dies and another, eternal self is born. Awareness of the significance of this Christian ritual makes writing about drowning a complex business. Both one of the most troubling forms of death and an echo of the baptism that leads to Christian resurrection, drowning has the potential to be seen as either disturbing or cleansing the eternal soul.

Although Paul does not connect baptism with drowning in his letter to the Romans, the author of I Peter uses the story of the biblical flood, in which nearly all of the human beings on earth are drowned, to explain the significance of baptism. He writes that the flood prefigures the sacrament of baptism:

> For Christ also suffered for sins once for all, the righteous for the unrighteous, in order to bring you to God . . . God waited patiently in the days of Noah, during the building of the ark, in which a few, that is, eight persons, were saved through water. And baptism, which this prefigured, now saves you—not as a removal of dirt from the body, but as an appeal to God for a good conscience, through the resurrection of Jesus Christ, who has gone into heaven and is at the right hand of God.[48]

In the Book of Genesis, God uses the flood to blot out the wickedness of humankind, saving only a righteous remnant in Noah and his family. Thus the floodwaters cleanse the earth of evil, as the sacrament of baptism cleanses the believer. In an interesting twist, the author of I Peter compares the experience of baptism not to the experience of the victims of the flood, who are submerged in water, but to the family of

Noah, who are "saved through water" not by dipping below it, but by floating on top of it in the ark. The image is similar to Milton's claim that the drowned Lycidas is raised to resurrection not, as one might expect, by the Christ who was baptized in the Jordan, but "through the dear might of Him that walked the waves."[49] Christ is seen here as the one whom water cannot defeat, as the one who walks on the water and commands the wind and the waves. Baptism, with its imagery of dipping below the water only to emerge reborn, identifies the Christian with this Christ whom the sea obeys. Thus in baptism, the Christian symbolically overcomes and transcends the terrifying experience of drowning.

Milton, however, is not satisfied with a purely Christian tale of baptism and resurrection. "Lycidas" does not place Lycidas in a Christian heaven and leave him there. Instead, Milton gives the drowned shepherd an important role on earth:

> Now, Lycidas, the shepherds weep no more;
> Henceforth thou art the Genius of the shore,
> In thy large recompense, and shalt be good
> To all that wander in that perilous flood.[50]

This passage not only demonstrates Milton's participation in a pastoral tradition but also subtly gestures toward concerns that are more national and political than religious. In "The Genius of the Shore: Lycidas, Adamastor, and the Poetics of Nationalism," Laurence Lipking argues that "the collaboration between poetry and nationalism . . . supplies a quiet, persistent undertone to forms like the pastoral elegy of 'Lycidas,' which blends personal grief with a sense of how much the country has lost."[51] Lipking notes that King was traveling to Ireland, where his father was a colonial administrator. In the speaker's poetic search for Lycidas's drowned body, he is also scouting out Britain's borders: "The circulation of Lycidas's body most fully reveals what is at stake for Milton. In their imagined journey, the bones obey no ocean current, but rather the extreme margins of the Irish Sea, the limit of Britain."[52] Just as the angel Michael watches over Britain's borders, looking toward Spain, so the drowned Lycidas becomes a kind of border guard; as the genius of the shore he will not only watch over those who "wander in that perilous flood," he will also keep an eye on the threats that come from both outside and inside Britain's borders.

Lipking's reading does much to explain why "Lycidas," a poem that seems both too local and too hidebound to be of use to politically focused postcolonial writers, shows up so frequently in their subsequent stories and poems of drowning. "Lycidas," with its nymphs and shepherds and oaten flutes, can seem both artificial and inaccessible to modern readers. In his introduction to "Lycidas," Edward LeComte wonders whether, without classical training, the modern reader can appreciate the poem, since "there is no major strand in the poem for which a precedent cannot be found."[53] Besides this potentially inaccessible erudition, the personal nature of the poem's inspiration would seem likely to limit its later applicability. Unlike *The Tempest*, where a shipwreck threatens to wipe out Naples's social and political elite, "Lycidas" describes the drowning of a twenty-five-year-old student. Yet as Lipking cogently demonstrates, the poem subtly unites the personal and the political: "Even as Milton was mourning a friend, he also was forging a nation."[54] Later Irish and Caribbean writers find in this deft blending of the personal and the political something to be both admired and challenged. Even as Milton recognizes the threat to individual human memory represented by Lycidas's drowning, he continues to support and uphold the British Empire. What he fails to recognize, and what postcolonial writers will emphasize in their depictions of drowning, is the fact that the British Empire was itself perpetrating memory loss on a massive scale through its participation in slavery and colonialism.

"Entering the Whirlpool": Drowning in Eliot

The fact that allusions to T. S. Eliot's *The Waste Land* crop up frequently in postcolonial texts about drowning can partly be explained by the poem's own status as a tissue of highly allusive "fragments."[55] *The Tempest* is a frequent intertext, and Ophelia appears throughout *The*

Waste Land in various forms and echoes, most notably as the hyacinth girl. In addition, Eliot indexes other literary drownings not previously mentioned here, including the drowning of Palinurus, the helmsman in Virgil's *Aeneid*, whom several critics have seen as the inspiration for the Phlebas character.[56] Eliot's original title for the poetic work, "He Do the Police in Different Voices," references Charles Dickens's novel *Our Mutual Friend*, one of the most drowning-heavy texts in British literature. Thus some authors who may appear to allude to *The Waste Land* are actually quoting its sources. Eliot, however, does not merely parrot the Shakespearean and other texts he draws on in his depiction of drowning. Instead, he adds a new layer to the literary portrayal of "death by drowning," depicting the sea's effects on human bodies as neither a terrifying threat to memorial traditions, nor as a baptismal image of religious rebirth. While he recognizes and retains some of the anxiety about drowning encountered in Shakespeare and Milton, drowning is more ambivalent for Eliot. Uneasy about water's power over human life and death, Eliot nonetheless emphasizes the sea's forgetfulness as a merciful escape from an often drab and sordid modern world.

The Waste Land's relationship to water may, at first, seem conflicted. The poem's speaker obsessively despairs at the lack of water, most obviously in "What the Thunder Says," where the word *water* appears eleven times in twenty-seven lines, not counting related words like *rain* and *spring*. Throughout the poem water becomes a sign of the hope that is conspicuously absent in Eliot's modern waste land. "If there were water," the narrator groans, "we should stop and drink / Amongst the rock one cannot stop and think."[57] Edmund Wilson titled his 1922 review of *The Waste Land* "The Poetry of Drouth." Yet paradoxically, the one section of the poem where water is plentiful, "Death by Water," emphasizes water's ability to kill. A closer examination of *The Waste Land* shows that these resonances are not opposed, as they might first seem, but that water's ability to erase the human individual is, for Eliot, part of the reason that it brings hope.

The Waste Land, like *The Tempest* and "Lycidas," juxtaposes images of traditional burial with scenes of drowning. The first section of *The Waste Land* is titled "The Burial of the Dead"; the penultimate section

"Death by Water." As in earlier texts, burial and drowning are considered alongside their effects on human memory. However, because of the poem's complex and ambivalent relationship to memory, it does not mirror Shakespeare's or Milton's anxiety about unburied drowned bodies. Instead burial in earth becomes suspect, an attempt to hold on to things that should be released. Drowning, by contrast, is portrayed as an escape from the destructive aspects of human life and the negative and crippling forms of memory.

The first lines of "The Burial of the Dead"—and of the poem as a whole—establish *The Waste Land*'s complex relationship to memory and burial:

> April is the cruellest month, breeding
> Lilacs out of the dead land, mixing
> Memory and desire, stirring
> Dull roots with spring rain.
> Winter kept us warm, covering
> Earth in forgetful snow, feeding
> A little life with dried tubers.[58]

In this famously startling passage, spring rains awaken life and stir up memory, an event conventionally regarded as hopeful and regenerative. Here, however, the rain's reviving effects on memory are "cruel," revealing things that should have remained buried and forgotten. The forgetfulness of winter, by contrast, with the snow that blots out landscapes and landmarks, is comforting and merciful.

The typical association between burial and memory suggests that human beings bury loved ones in order to better remember them. Although the corpse will slowly decay beneath the ground, the coffin slows that process and the headstone provides the illusion of permanence. Eliot's portrayal of burial, however, suggests that he finds something sinister in this attempted preservation of the corpse. After watching the zombie-like hordes crossing London Bridge and musing, "I had not thought death had undone so many,"[59] the speaker sees a friend and calls out:

That corpse you planted last year in your garden,
Has it begun to sprout? Will it bloom this year?
Or has the sudden frost disturbed its bed?
O keep the Dog far hence, that's friend to men,
Or with his nails he'll dig it up again![60]

The last two lines of this passage echo Cornelia's dirge from John Webster's *The White Devil.* A quote by Charles Lamb in the late nineteenth-century edition of *The White Devil* connects the passage to Ariel's song in *The Tempest*, remarking, "As that is of the water, watery; so this is of the earth, earthy."[61] In a poem that is obsessed with the elements, Eliot alludes to songs about both earthy and watery burial. While the human tendency after burial is to focus on the headstone and forget the body decaying under the ground, Eliot insists on the materiality of burial, the fact that a digging dog could uncover a rotting corpse, or flowers grow from its burial site.

The idea of flowers or trees growing on the grave of a loved one is traditionally an image of hope and consolation. In *Hamlet*, Laertes imagines flowers growing from Ophelia's corpse as a sign of her innocence and the eternal rest of her soul:

Lay her i' th' earth,
And from her fair and unpolluted flesh
May violets spring. I tell thee, churlish priest,
A minist'ring angel shall my sister be
When thou liest howling.[62]

Eliot's clever reworking of this common trope emphasizes the irony of the competing ways in which human beings use the earth: as a source of food and growth and life, and as a place to hide our dead. The corpse planted in Stetson's garden, one suspects, will grow into something nastier than violets. This portrayal of the corpse reappearing as vegetal growth is not consoling, but horrifying, much like the subsequent image of the dog digging up the buried corpse "with his nails." Like April's cruel awakening of memory, the return of the dead who have been buried, whether in memory or in a more frightening form, is painful and undesirable.

"The Burial of the Dead" begins the comparison of burial and drowning that will continue throughout *The Waste Land*, in which drowning often comes across as preferable. Madame Sosostris, the comical clairvoyant with a cold, reads the narrator's cards. Although she chooses six cards, she identifies only one as being uniquely his card: "Here, said she, / Is your card, the drowned Phoenician Sailor, / (Those are pearls that were his eyes. Look!)."[63] Later, she returns to the idea of drowning: "I do not find / The Hanged Man. Fear death by water."[64] While Madame Sosostris's words suggest that drowning is something to be feared, her allusions to *The Tempest* complicate her warning. The first allusion, to "Full Fathom Five," reminds readers of Shakespeare's ambivalent portrayal of Alonso's imaginary drowning. In her second comment, about the hanged man, Madame Sosostris recalls a popular saying also referenced in *The Tempest*: "He that's born to be hanged need fear no drowning." In Shakespeare's play, the allusion occurs in the first scene, during the storm that wrecks the ship. Gonzolo comically argues that the ship cannot be wrecked because the insolent boatswain is clearly destined for hanging, not drowning. Thus what may in *The Waste Land* appear to be an injunction to be afraid of drowning could actually be read as a comparison with a potentially worse form of death. It is presumably a relief for the narrator to learn that he is not "born to be hanged." Since hanging is not his destiny, he can expect his death to take another form, and will thus not be protected from drowning by the proverb.

As Eliot remarks perhaps unnecessarily in his notes to *The Waste Land*, Madame Sosostris's prophecy is fulfilled in the penultimate section, "Death by Water":

> Phlebas the Phoenician, a fortnight dead,
> Forgot the cry of gulls, and the deep sea swell
> And the profit and loss.
>   A current under sea
> Picked his bones in whispers. As he rose and fell

He passed the stages of his age and youth
Entering the whirlpool.
            Gentile or Jew
O you who turn the wheel and look to windward,
Consider Phlebas, who was once handsome and tall as you.[65]

The short remnant of what was in Eliot's early drafts a ninety-three-line description of a shipwreck on a New England fishing trip, "Death by Water" has engendered much critical debate both about its relevance to *The Waste Land* and about its intended message. On the one hand, the section's final line sounds an unmistakable warning of mortality. Considered alongside Eliot's note connecting Phlebas to the one-eyed merchant, the sailor's drowning can be read as a caution to the materialistic inhabitants of the waste land, obsessed with "the profit and the loss." In this reading of the passage, Madame Sosostris is correct when she tells the protagonist to "fear death by water."

On the other hand, in a poem that does not shy away from unsavory descriptions, it is hard to imagine a much gentler depiction of death. Martin Scofield observes this in his discussion of an earlier version of the death scene, titled "Dirge," which was vetoed by the poet Ezra Pound. The earlier version is not only anti-Semitic but much more gruesome, with emphasis on the crabs eating the corpse's eyelids and the "bones peep[ing] through the ragged toes."[66] By contrast, the published version, according to Scofield, returns nearer to its Shakespearean source; it "has something closer to the quiet lyric mood of Ariel's song. The ghastly crabs and the grotesque bones of 'Dirge' have been replaced by the only slightly sinister (and even potentially cleansing) image."[67] In the peaceful rise and fall of the "deep sea swell" mirrored in the sibilant sounds of the Phlebas passage, it is easy to lose sight of the central image of the section: not just a drowned body, but a bloated, rotting corpse "a fortnight dead." Despite the gruesomeness of the phrase *picked his bones*, Eliot hurries to assure readers of the gentleness of a current that does not batter or bruise but instead works in soft and subtle "whispers." Phlebas's decomposition seems less like disintegration or decay and more like a careful and deliberate unmaking, reversing the aging process as he passes "the stages of his age and youth."

The gentle lyricism of "Death by Water" has led some critics to read it as a kind of rebirth and thus as a precursor of the Christian hope that appears in Eliot's later works. Paul Lewis writes that "the highly suggestive lines about Phlebas sketch out the process of spiritual rebirth Eliot develops in greater detail in his later poems and plays."[68] There is indeed something amniotic about the work of the whispering current, and it is tempting to read the aforementioned passage as an image of the baptism that marks a Christian as "born again." It is difficult, however, to reconcile the section's final lines with this reading; clearly the handsome young sailors who "turn the wheel and look to windward" are meant to be sobered by Phlebas's fate, not spiritually inspired. Given Phlebas's disappearance after this section and his (easily forgotten) status as a two-week-old corpse, it seems reasonable to conclude that he travels through the whirlpool not toward new life but toward oblivion. Scofield writes that the passage lacks "any suggestion of metamorphosis or transfiguration of Phlebas himself."[69] The tenderness of this section does not derive from "spiritual rebirth" but from the gentleness of the sea that allows Phlebas to forget and be forgotten, unlike the cruel earth that holds on to corpses until they can be dug up again.

Phlebas's watery demise contrasts starkly with the "tumbled graves" and "dry bones" lying among "empty cisterns and exhausted wells" in "What the Thunder Says," the section immediately following "Death by Water."[70] More importantly, Phlebas's cyclical regression through his life and into forgetfulness, contrasts with the cobweb-draped memorials that characterize death on land:

> My friend, blood shaking my heart
> The awful daring of a moment's surrender
> Which an age of prudence can never retract
> By this, and this only, we have existed
> Which is not to be found in our obituaries
> Or in memories draped by the beneficent spider

Or under seals broken by the lean solicitor
In our empty rooms.[71]

Neither obituaries, nor wills, nor the objects left behind in dusty attics or basements, Eliot suggests, can capture our essential identities. No matter our efforts to be remembered, we ultimately leave behind only "empty rooms." We exist instead by what is "not to be found in our obituaries": the unspoken moments of "surrender" to a lover, the impulsive episodes where we forgo "prudence." Phlebas's surrender to the whirlpool, his embrace of watery forgetfulness, seems infinitely preferable to the dry graves and "lean soliciter[s]" of the waste land.[72]

It may seem counterintuitive or simply mistaken to discover a hymn to forgetfulness in the intensely allusive Eliot, in a poem containing the famous line, "These fragments I have shored against my ruin."[73] In "Tradition and the Individual Talent," Eliot will not allow for art that attempts to forget what has gone before: "No poet, no artist of any art, has his complete meaning alone. His significance, his appreciation is the appreciation of his relation to the dead poets and artists. You cannot value him alone; you must set him, for contrast and comparison, among the dead."[74] In their poems and paintings, their novels and symphonies, the dead walk among us and an artist who ignores them is no artist at all. Memory of the literary tradition is vital. But, for Eliot, there is another kind of memory that paralyzes and inhibits: "Poetry is not a turning loose of emotion, but an escape from emotion; it is not the expression of personality, but an escape from personality."[75] In the death by drowning of Phlebas the Phoenician sailor, Eliot imagines a freeing loss of personality. The whispering currents of the whirlpool erase individualities, removing the contingencies of "profit and loss" that drive everyday human life. Unlike the land that attempts to hold on to decaying bodies and crippling memories, the sea allows the individual person to disappear, a possibility that may seem frightening at first but that, for Eliot, is ultimately freeing.

Eliot calls for artists to work among the monuments and fragments of literary tradition while abandoning the constricting ties of personal memory. For the Irish and Caribbean artists discussed in this study, the separation is not always as simple as Eliot suggests. Denied access to personal memory by the ravages of colonialism or alienated from the canons of literary tradition, these postcolonial artists have a much more complicated relationship to memory and tradition. In the drowned bodies that surface in their texts, echoes of Shakespeare, Milton, and Eliot indicate their shared participation in the anxious human negotiation with death and memory. But the ways in which they alter or reimagine these canonical drowned bodies simultaneously signals their rejection of the assumptions and certainties of the earlier authors.

2

The Lost Body

The Author as Mourner in J. M. Synge's Travel Writings and Riders to the Sea

Consoling himself after the death of his young friend by drowning, the narrator of John Milton's poem "Lycidas" imagines the spirit of Lycidas becoming "the Genius of the Shore," a guiding spirit for "all that wander in that perilous flood."[1] "Lycidas" is so concerned with the wandering of the drowned body that the critic Lawrence Lipking describes it as a "rescue mission" in which "Milton tries to locate the body."[2] Milton's anxiety about the "perilous flood" and the wandering of the body is shared by many later authors. The drowned body cannot be located, buried, or given a posthumous resting place. As such, it troubles the meaning-making processes of memory and grief. Milton locates Lycidas's spirit, if not his body, and gives him a place and a purpose both within a Christian narrative of resurrection and as the guiding "Genius of the Shore." Such a satisfying poetic retrieval of the drowned body is not always possible or desirable, however. Within a postcolonial framework, the loss of the body often comes to stand in for other losses: cultural, linguistic, or political. While a drowned body may or may not be recovered, these other losses are often irreversible, sources of deep grief for the postcolonial artist. This chapter examines the lost and wandering bodies in the oeuvre of the Irish playwright and travel writer John Millington Synge.[3] The sea plays a macabre role in Synge's imaginative landscape, seeming at times almost comically overcrowded with drowned bodies.[4] Undoubtedly the most extreme example of this corpse-crowded sea occurs in his 1904 play *Riders to the Sea*, in which one Aran Island woman loses eight men to the ocean. Similarly, Synge's travel narrative, *The Aran Islands*, the result of four months' stay on the islands over the course of four years, records dozens of stories of drownings, and documents at least five separate drowning cases that seem to have occurred during the four years of Synge's visits.[5] While the trope of drowning is especially significant to Synge's Aran writings, given their harsh island setting, drowned bodies also frequently appear in his other travel writings, collected as *Travels in Wicklow, West Kerry, and Connemara*.

Throughout Synge's canon, the drowned body, while often the center of a deeply personal experience of grief, simultaneously signifies a more general sense of cultural loss. Beginning with his travel writings, this chapter examines Synge's tendency to juxtapose stories of drowned or missing bodies with elegies for cultural practices that are dying out. It then highlights the importance of cultural practices of burial and mourning in *Riders to the Sea*, revealing the play's anxiety over individual and communal memory. Finally it returns to Synge's travel writings to demonstrate how Synge's encounters with drowned or missing bodies—in particular his two accounts of attending Aran Island wakes—provide him with the opportunity to interrogate the relationship of the Irish artist to Ireland's various histories. In the process, Synge's own work becomes a kind of keen for cultures that are passing away, whose traditions and ways of life are as besieged by modernity as the Aran Islands are by an often violent sea.

The drowned body in Synge's work has received little sustained critical attention, especially considering its ubiquity in his writing.[6] What attention it has received has tended to focus on the frequency of drownings in Synge's texts less as a deliberate artistic choice than as evidence of his poor—or willfully distorted—ethnography. In 1969 the anthropologist John C. Messenger, reporting the results of a case study conducted on Inis Oírr, the island neighboring Synge's Inis Meáin, attacked Synge, although not by name, for misrepresenting the frequency of drowning deaths on the Aran Islands:

> A recurring motif in writings about [Inis Oírr] is the threatening sea and heavy loss of life among fishermen, with its attendant psychological depression. In the past century, only four sea accidents have occurred in the island with the loss of but 12 lives . . . The claim of one famous writer that each family has lost male members to the ocean reflects not only his psychological outlook, but the breadth and depth of kinship reckoning . . . The motif can be attributed to the projection of a tragic world view into the interpretation of the local culture by some authors, to the nativistic and primitivistic biases of other writers, and to a common sense conclusion reached by observers who have spent little time in the island and have failed to "count noses."[7]

Though Messenger's anthropological statistics may, as Tim Robinson claims in his introduction to *The Aran Islands*, fail to account for Synge's literary project, the criticisms he raises are important ones. A reader of *The Aran Islands* can hardly fail to notice the narrator's "tragic world view," especially as the number of deaths and other tragedies increases dramatically in the latter half of the book. If the looming threat of death in the sea represents less a reality faced by the Aran islanders than a projection of the author's psychological state, then the text must be reexamined, starting with Synge's claim to documentary realism in his introduction: "I have given a direct account of my life on the islands, and of what I met with among them, inventing nothing, and changing nothing that is essential."[8]

One possible response to Synge's apparent exaggeration of the tragic occurrences in the lives of the Aran islanders would be to view it as evidence of his status as an interloper, an Anglo-Irish outsider consumed, at best, with patronizing curiosity about a "primitive" culture; at worst, with the desire to exploit a dwindling folk tradition for his own artistic gain. As Declan Kiberd notes in *Inventing Ireland*, such a view of Synge is common among nationalist critics, who see him as "an unapologetic ascendancy parasite, stocking up his tourist's notebook with self-serving studies in a dying culture."[9] Any exaggeration by Synge of the frequency of drowning deaths among the young male

Aran islanders can be read as part of his case for what he sees as their inevitable cultural demise. In his travel essay "A Landlord's Garden in County Wicklow," Synge links the cultural decline of the Anglo-Irish ascendancy with the dying out of their young men, writing regretfully of "the one or two delicate girls that are left so often to represent a dozen hearty men who were alive a generation ago."[10] Perhaps the least charitable view of this move by Synge would be to suggest that, in emphasizing the death of the Aran culture, he creates a life and a market for his work. Kiberd, although arguing that Synge is aware of the sad irony of his position, describes Synge's writing as the work of a self-aware scavenger: "He himself will feed off the death of the old Gaelic culture, as do all coroners and morticians. The covert desire of his book [is] to *make the present past*."[11] By exaggerating the precariousness of Aran culture, Synge makes his work a last-chance glimpse of a culture on its deathbed, giving it marketability it might not otherwise possess.

A more forgiving, albeit still suspicious, reading of Synge's obsession with the drowned body would take into account his own frequent battles with sickness and his sense of his own impending death. Though not focusing specifically on his fascination with death, Ann Saddlemyer reminds readers of *The Aran Islands* that the work is not merely an anthropological text but also a chronicle of the artist's inner life: "The adventures he records also reflect the contours, emotions and temperament of the author's personality, for this journey to the western world was also an exploration and revaluation of his own consciousness."[12] It is important, of course, when considering the effects of frequent illness on this "exploration . . . of his own consciousness" not to read our knowledge of his early death in 1909, at the age of thirty-eight, into the Synge of 1898–1901, the years of his visits to the Aran Islands. Though his first visit to the Aran Islands in May 1898 was preceded by a surgery in December 1897 to remove a tumor, the doctors seem to have withheld from Synge information regarding the cause of the tumor (Hodgkin's lymphoma, the cancer that, twelve years later, proved fatal). Too much has been made of the sickly, morbid Synge, probably thanks to W. B. Yeats's eulogizing construction of Synge as a pale, unobtrusive martyr, whose "low vitality helped him to be observant and contemplative."[13] By contrast, Jack B. Yeats remembers Synge as "the best companion for a roadway any one could have, always ready and always the same; a bold walker, up hill and down dale, in the hot sun and in the pelting rain."[14] He goes on in the same letter to observe that "Synge was by nature well equipped for the roads. Though his health was often bad he had beating under his ribs a brave heart that carried him over rough tracks."[15] In the narrator of *The Aran Islands*, intensely aware of the beauty of nature and of women, curious about the smallest details of rope-making and about the storytelling traditions of the older islanders, it is hard not to see a young man intensely and vibrantly alive.

Yet Synge's vitality, his sense of the value of a life lived close to nature, is always shadowed by an awareness of his own mortality. In his "Autobiography," assembled from notebook fragments, Synge writes of his childhood that he was "ill continually," and that "this ill health led to a curious resolution which has explained in some measure all of my subsequent evolution . . . I said, I am unhealthy, and if I marry I will have unhealthy children. But I will never create beings to suffer as I am suffering, so I will never marry."[16] Synge's early writings, particularly *Vita Vecchia* and *Étude Morbide*, have an almost obsessive fascination with the suffering of the sensitive artist, expressed both as physical pain and through the emotional travails of love. Yet his Aran Island writings and other travel essays, though they are narrated in the first person, display a curious restraint in dealing with Synge's own sufferings. With a few notable exceptions, *The Aran Islands* is remarkably silent on the topic of the narrator's bodily afflictions. In perhaps the most significant exception, Synge, having caught a cold, worries about what would happen to him if he were to die on Inis Meáin: "I have been walking through the wet lanes in my pampooties in spite of the rain, and I have brought on a feverish cold. The wind is terrific. If anything serious should happen to me I might die here and be nailed in my box, and shoved down into a wet crevice in the graveyard before any one could know it on the mainland."[17] Synge's somewhat hysterical description of being furtively shoved into a wet crack in the rocky island, unmourned by those on the mainland, underscores his awareness of the importance of memorial rituals. This terror that he will disappear into a hole in the ground and be forgotten clearly colors Synge's later depictions of drowning.

Despite this moment of self-pity, Synge's gaze is usually turned outward to the distress of the poor and marginalized people he encounters. Following his complaint about his cold, Synge immediately moves on to discuss the ways in which the islanders handle their medical needs, as if to recognize that the problem of the lack of medical resources on the Aran Islands is far more serious for those who live there full-time than for a tourist. Messenger sees Synge's "projection of a tragic world view" onto the lives of the islanders as evidence of "his masochism," an accusation that seems an unnecessarily simplistic dismissal of a young writer who, though deeply aware of his own frailty, chose to focus on the sufferings of others.[18] It seems almost certain that Synge's illness colored his portrayal of Irish peasant life, drawing him naturally to relate stories of death and suffering.[19] Yet this tendency, rather than revealing a gaping flaw in his art and its relationship to its subject, seems an indication of a serious attempt at empathy. Synge saw in the individual travails of peasant life and the gradual waning of the islanders' culture a kind of tragedy that both echoed and trumped his own personal sufferings.

However significant this empathetic element may be to understanding Synge's work, his attention to the drowned body transcends a purely emotional response to the sight of pain. Drawing on the anxiety, loss, and uncertainty that attend Milton and Shakespeare's depictions of drowning, Synge subtly reshapes the trope for a postcolonial context. While never losing the context of personal grief, Synge uses the drowned body to gesture toward the shifting forms of cultural memories and traditions encountered by the Irish artist. Missing bodies suggest the void that is left when cultures and traditions are forgotten—whether stifled by colonial oppression, suppressed by the monolithic myths of nationalism, or erased by the pragmatic adoption of modern "improvements." The occasional resurfacings of these missing bodies and the reactions of family and friends to their recovery allow Synge to gently examine the relationship of the Irish artist to Ireland's colonial and precolonial past. In some sense, the artist's task is like that of a professional mourner, called to mourn the loss of cultures and traditions that are past or passing. Yet Synge is deeply suspicious of the forgetfulness that can attend or quickly follow the mourning ritual; instead he longs for an art that can confuse straightforward notions of temporality by allowing the quickly decaying remnants of the past to become a thriving part of the cultural wisdom and daily conversation of the modern nation.

Often, in Synge's travel writings, an account of an individual drowned body closely precedes or follows a reflection on cultural change or the loss of ancient traditions. In the Wicklow travel essay "The Oppression of the Hills," a story of drowned or missing bodies becomes tied up with the disappearance or decay of the landed Anglo-Irish class. Toward the end of the short essay, Synge recounts the story of his encounter with a young village girl named Maggie: "That afternoon her two younger sisters had come to see her, and now she had been taken with a panic that they had been drowned going home through the bogs, and she was crying and wailing, and saying she must go to look for them."[20] Although the locals jeer that Maggie simply "likes a walk in the moonlight," and despite the near impossibility of finding drowned bodies in a bog at night, even if it were certain that the bodies were there to be found, Synge accompanies her on her frantic search through the bogs.[21] In fact, he seems to relish the eerie task, and the thrills provided by the sudden noises and movements of the natural world: "The rushes were shining in the moonlight, and one flake of mist was lying on the river. We looked into one bog-hole, and then into another, where a snipe rose and terrified us. We listened: a cow was chewing heavily on the side of a hill and there was a cart far away upon the road. Our teeth began to chatter with the cold of the bog air and the loneliness of the night."[22] They find nothing, and the account ends with the seeming triumph of rationality, with Synge congratulating himself that "the actual presence of the bog had shown my companion the absurdity of her fears."[23] Yet the gruesome night search and the still-missing bodies leave an unfinished gap that shapes the rest of the essay.

In what may initially seem like a typically Syngean non sequitur, the narrator moves on, without resolving the story of the possibly drowned sisters, to discuss the residual affection of older Wicklow inhabitants for "the landed classes."[24] Yet this seemingly disconnected anecdote shares in the tone set by the tale of the missing sisters; it quickly becomes clear that this too is a story of the gaps left behind when people leave or disappear. An old woman recounts to Synge, "with tears streaming on her face, how much more lonely the country had become since the 'quality' had gone away," telling a "long story of how she had seen her landlord shutting up his house and leaving his property, and of the way he had died afterwards, when the 'grievance' of it broke his heart."[25] While Synge is aware of the irony of the woman's tears, calling hers a "curious affection," her sorrow reveals the loss represented by the abandoned houses of the landlord class.[26] This moment could perhaps be read as an attempt by the Anglo-Protestant Synge to foster a sympathetic nostalgia for his privileged and often oppressive ancestors. Yet the sorrow here seems more general, a recognition that all cultures pass away, taking with them not just their failings but also their beauties.

In another Wicklow travel essay, "A Landlord's Garden in County Wicklow," Synge muses on "the innumerable old families that are quickly dwindling away," recognizing that the decline of an aristocratic class represents real political and human gain for Ireland, while mourning the attendant necessity of cultural and artistic loss: "These owners of the land are not much pitied at the present day, or much deserving of pity; and yet one cannot quite forget that they are the descendents of what was at one time, in the eighteenth century, a high-spirited and highly-cultivated aristocracy."[27] While Synge does not seem to regret the loss of the feudal relationship between landowners and their tenants—a relationship he uneasily enacts with the young boy who steals apples from the "landlord's garden"—he laments the passing of their artistic expressions: "Rich bindings, beautiful miniatures and finely-carved chimney-pieces."[28] Lest this regret be simply attributed to high-culture snobbery, Synge is careful to juxtapose the "broken greenhouses and mouse-eaten libraries" with the "four mud walls that are so often left in Wicklow as the only remnants of a farmhouse."[29] Both, Synge writes, are "mournful"; both indicate the passing of a way of life that, however flawed, had its own particular beauties.[30] As P. J. Mathews notes, Synge is not just documenting a loss—he is attempting to recover some of the fleeting beauties of disappearing cultures: "Intermixed with Synge's tacit endorsement of the liquidation of Ascendancy privilege, therefore, is a latent desire that some impulse of cultural vigor might be salvaged and reactivated from the fragments of Anglo-Irish cultivation."[31]

The final lines of "The Oppression of the Hills" juxtapose the old woman's grief over the disappearance or decay of ascendancy culture with the reaction of the "younger people," who "feel differently," and who scrawl the following lines "in pencil on the door-post"[32] of the landlord's abandoned house:

> In the days of rack-renting
> And land-grabbing so vile
> A proud, heartless landlord
> Lived here a great while.
> When the League it was started,
> And the land-grabbing cry,
> To the cold North of Ireland
> He had for to fly.[33]

While these sentiments seem more logical than the old woman's "curious" grief, and while Synge, an occasional writer of bitingly satirical verse himself, cannot have wholly disapproved of this poem or its sentiment, the writing proves as ephemeral as the abandoned house and the missing landlord. "A year later," the narrator passes the house to find that "the door-post had fallen to pieces, and the inscription with it."[34] With this somber line, the essay ends by emphasizing the swiftness with which things fall apart. Though sympathetic with revolutionary ideals, writing that he "wanted to change things root and branch," Synge questions the prudence of attempting to completely banish or erase the past when one's own ideals, values, and artistic tastes are so rapidly fading into obsolescence.[35] Although perhaps ultimately siding with the young vandals and their modernizing project, Synge recognizes the curious appropriateness of the old woman's tears; her grief elegizes the empty spaces left by the passing of a way of life, and the loss of its unique artistic and cultural traditions.

The deaths by drowning that occur so frequently in Synge's Aran Islands writings are likewise tied to anxiety over irretrievable cultural losses. Perhaps the most obvious instance of this connection occurs in the middle of one of Synge's litanies of drowning deaths in part 3 of *The Aran Islands*: "A few years ago three men of a family that used to make the wooden vessels—like tiny barrels—that are still used among the people, went to the big island together. They were drowned on their way home, and the art of making those little barrels died with them, at least on Inishmaan, though it still lingers on the north and south islands."[36] Each death in this small and shrinking society represents not just "the loss of one man" but the likely disappearance of a piece of cultural knowledge—an artistic skill, a folksong, or a story.[37] As the drowned bodies decay in the ocean, losing heads, limbs, and eventually all marks of individuality, so Synge sees the marginalized culture of the Aran Islands blurring around the edges, losing its distinctiveness and color to the inevitable onslaught of modernity.

While Synge's travel writings are full of drowned corpses, the locus for drowning deaths in Synge's oeuvre is undoubtedly *Riders to the Sea*. Only one drowning actually occurs during the play, but through the recounted memories of the grief-stricken Maurya, *Riders to the Sea* packs an incredible eight drownings into its roughly forty-minute running time. Although the play was admired even by its earliest audiences, some reviewers protested against this morbidity, calling it a "corpse-curtain-raiser" or complaining that bringing a drowned corpse onstage was "against all rules of art."[38] The *Irish Times* worried that "the long exposure of the dead body before an audience may be realistic, but it is certainly not artistic."[39] The short play was almost certainly the specific text Messenger had in mind when denouncing "the claim of one famous writer that each family has lost male members to the ocean" as evidence of "the projection of a tragic world view into the interpretation of the local cultures."[40]

Cultural rituals surrounding death feature centrally in Synge's ethnographically focused travel writings, but their recurring, insistent presence in his dramatic work is more surprising, and deserves a closer look. In three of Synge's six major plays—*In the Shadow of the Glen*, *Riders*, and *Deirdre*—a dead body, deathbed, open grave, or some combination of the three spends a considerable amount of time at the very center of the stage. In Synge's earliest play, *When the Moon Has Set*, the dead body is offstage in the next room, but the characters discuss funeral plans at length, mentioning "fine flowers," "white candles," and "grand clothes on the bed," and commenting that "there were so many things to arrange" for the funeral.[41] Even in the plays in which no significant deaths occur, talk of funerals, burial, and the surrounding rituals litter the speech of the characters. *The Playboy of the Western World* contains not only the famous discussion of Kate Cassidy's wake, where the alcohol flows so freely that men are "stretched out retching speechless on the holy stones," but also a debate about whether it was right for Christy, after murdering his father, to bury him secretly, without a decent wake.[42] In the DruidSynge production, which presented all of Synge's published dramatic work in one day, the director Garry Hynes chose to leave the white boards that Maurya has purchased for Michael's coffin in *Riders to the Sea* onstage during all of the plays. Critics were quick to point to these boards as symbols of the omnipresence of death in Synge's work, but the coffin boards also, more specifically, highlight the plays' insistent exploration of the memorial rituals that surround death.

Riders to the Sea depicts a culture that values memory and makes it part of daily experience, but it is threatened by modernity and may soon become little more than a memory itself. In *Realms of Memory*, Pierre Nora describes the turn to modernity as a turn away from memory. Modern, industrialized societies, he argues, have lost the ability to make memory a part of everyday life: "Ideologies based on memory have ceased to function . . . , ideologies that once smoothed the transition from past to future or indicated what the future should retain from the past."[43] Modern societies maintain vestiges of memory in sites Nora calls *lieux de mémoire* ("realms" or "places" of memory). These sites—monuments, archives, museums, graveyards—are invested with the burden of memory once carried by memory-rich cultures and communities, which Nora calls *milieux de mémoire* ("environments of memory"). Nora's description of these environments of memory could easily apply to the Aran Islands culture Synge depicts in *Riders to the Sea*: "Memory is life, always embodied in living societies and as such in permanent evolution"[44] For Maurya, "memory is life," an integral part of her relationship to her community and her family, a powerful force capable of sudden reawakenings. Barbara Misztal's description of the highly social nature of memory certainly applies to Synge's Aran Islands: "While it is the individual who remembers, remembering is more than a personal act; memory exists through its relation with what has been shared with others—through language, symbols, events, and social and cultural contexts. Individual remembering thus occurs in a social context, is prompted by social cues, employed for social purposes, ruled and ordered by socially structured norms and patterns, and therefore contains much that is social."[45] Memory brings lessons from the islanders' past to bear on their present and future, and it keeps the names and stories of lost loved ones fresh on their tongues.

Most readings of *Riders to the Sea* have focused on Maurya's perplexing emotional reaction to the death of her last remaining son.[46] Few, however, have noted her obsession, and the entire play's preoccupation, with the practical business of death: with burial rites, coffin-building, funerals, wakes, and keening. T. R. Henn mentions the emotional significance of burial to Maurya, linking it to the difficulty of finding unoccupied grave space on the rocky islands: "Throughout the play there runs the bitter sense of loss, the importance of ritual burial, that pre-historic man labored so greatly to achieve by dolmen and passage grave."[47] At the center of *Riders to the Sea* is a missing body, the body of Maurya's son Michael, lost in the sea for nine days. Maurya is fixated on her need to find Michael's body, not in order to verify the death, which she and the other islanders seem fairly certain of, but to ensure that her son gets a proper burial.

Initially when Bartley reveals that he is going to the Galway fair, Maurya is more concerned that he stays home to help look for and bury Michael than she is about his safety. As Bartley looks for the new rope, Maurya chides him: "You'd do right to leave that rope, Bartley, hanging by the boards . . . It will be wanting in this place, I'm telling you, if Michael is washed up to-morrow morning, or the next morning, or any morning in the week, for it's a deep grave we'll make him by the grace of God."[48] When Bartley insists that he needs the rope to make a halter for the horse, Maurya warns him about what public opinion will say if he fails to fulfill the culturally appropriate tasks for his dead brother: "It's a hard thing they'll be saying below if the body is washed up and there's no man in it to make the coffin, and I after giving a big price for the finest white boards you'd find in Connemara."[49] It is only after Bartley refuses to be moved by these appeals that Maurya confronts him with the worst case scenario—what if his refusal to stay on the island to help locate and bury his brother results in his own death? She cautions: "It's hard set we'll be surely the day you're drownd'd with the rest. What way will I live and the girls with me, and I an old woman looking for the grave?"[50] By saying that she is "looking for the grave," Maurya means to indicate her age and frailty, but the perhaps unconscious figure of speech indicates how deeply the language of burial and memorialization runs, both in her mind and in the play as a whole.

The fact that Michael has been lost at sea makes Maurya's obsession with burial both more understandable and more poignant. The Aran Islands are tiny specks of land, only approximately two by three miles if she lives on Inis Meáin, the island Synge visited most frequently. On their western shores, the islands face the Atlantic Ocean, with roughly three thousand miles between them and the nearest land, the eastern coast of North America. The idea of losing a beloved son in this vast space, his body floating aimlessly until it eventually sinks to the sea floor to disintegrate unseen, is an unsettling one. Maurya knows what seawater can do to a body in nine days, and worries that it will erase Michael's identity so completely that even she will not be able to recognize him: "There does be a power of young men floating round in the sea, and what way would they know if it was Michael they had, or another man like him, for when a man is nine days in the sea, and the wind blowing, it's hard set his own mother would be to say what man was it."[51] Here, Maurya imagines the sea as a kind of unmarked mass grave for young men, one that denies mothers the consolation of mourning over their sons' bodies. Because of the unpredictability, fluidity, and destructive power of the sea, it is not a suitable burial site; it troubles memory instead of aiding it. According to Daniel Davy, Maurya's statement suggests that the perpetual movement of the sea keeps the young men who drown in it in a weird kind of suspended animation: "The accumulating dead bodies of the sea's victims—'a power'—do not quickly decompose and revert to nature, but remain forever 'young men,' an image which transforms the objective sea into a subjective phantasmagoria of staring eyes of dead faces moving forever in the waves."[52] By contrast, the island grave Maurya imagines creating for Michael is "deep" and secure; his coffin will be a "good" one made from the new white boards.[53] When, at the end of *Riders to the Sea*, Bartley's body is brought in and Maurya learns that Michael's body has been found and buried in "the far north," she responds with relief: "There isn't anything more the sea can do to me."[54] This response is, as has been traditionally recognized, Maurya's acknowledgement that she has no more sons to lose, or to worry about when they go out on the sea. It is also, however, a sigh of relief that both of her sons have been found, that their bodies will be given "clean" burials and not continue to be battered by the unforgiving sea.[55]

Maurya's emphasis on the importance of burial reflects not just a personal preoccupation but the significance that mourning rites played in the lives of rural Irish Catholics of the time period. In their sociological study *The Irish Funerary Tradition*, Nina Witoszek and Patrick Sheeran quote an account of nineteenth-century Ireland by a Mr. and Mrs. Hall: "The most anxious thoughts of the Irish peasant through life revert to death and he will endure extreme poverty in order that he may scrape together the means of obtaining the wake and a 'decent funeral.'"[56] This description of the ultimate importance of the wake and funeral is echoed in other sociological studies focusing on late nineteenth- and early twentieth-century Ireland, including Anne Ridge's *Death Customs in Rural Ireland.* Though Ridge's study focuses on the Irish Midlands, she notes that many of her specific observations apply in Galway, and her general conclusions can be applied across Ireland.

Much of Ridge's study is devoted to examining how Irish funeral rites served to separate the dead from the living, to remove the danger of spirits in transition. She quotes Arnold van Gennep's *Rites of Passage* to describe the threat such transitional states posed to the community: "Danger lies in transitional states, simply because transition is neither one state nor the next, it is undefinable. The person who must pass from one to another is himself in danger and emanates danger to others. The danger is controlled by ritual which precisely separates him from the old status, segregates him for a time and then publicly declares his entry to his new status."[57] Anxiety over transitional states is manifested in many of the folk religious practices described in Ridge's work. Practices such as washing and laying out the corpse, lighting candles around the deathbed, and sprinkling the corpse with holy water, though they have their roots in official Catholic practice, had multiple meanings for the Irish people who observed them. For many of the people interviewed in Ridge's study, a proper funeral and a good burial ensured a clean and unproblematic separation, keeping the spirit of the deceased from wandering or lingering in the house. Though worries over lingering spirits have little basis in Catholic doctrine, they were common; Ridge documents widespread practices, such as leaving the door of the house open at the moment of death to allow the spirit to exit. Such rituals demonstrate concern that the souls of the deceased experience a complete and untroubled transition to the next world.

As a folklorist and amateur anthropologist, Synge would have been aware of at least some of these common beliefs and practices. He demonstrates this awareness in his description of the wake but also in the very construction of *Riders to the Sea.* Ridge emphasizes the central part played by Irish women in the rituals surrounding death: "The role of women in washing, laying out and lamenting the corpse was of paramount importance in ensuring successful separation of the dead person from the community. In Irish traditional society, three women were involved in washing and laying out the corpse and according to one strand of folk tradition they symbolized the three Marys at the foot of the cross and at the tomb of Christ."[58] In keeping with this tradition, *Riders to the Sea* focuses on three women, one whose name derives from the name Mary (Maurya).

While Synge's women do not specifically link the rituals they enact over Bartley's body to a desire to keep his spirit from wandering, there are some hints that such an anxiety may play a role in Maurya's concern with burial. The most obvious of these hints is the fact that Maurya claims to have seen Michael after his death. If we do not simply dismiss her as a hallucinating old woman, and instead accept her world view as the world view of the play, then Michael's spirit may be wandering, unsettled by the days his body spent floating in the sea before being buried. According to Anthony Roche, Michael's spirit is not only unsettled, but bent on revenge: "Not only does [Maurya's] vision at the well confirm that Michael is drowned but also that his spirit has returned to interfere violently in their affairs by drawing the living Bartley with him."[59] Several critics have noted that in Irish folklore the dead do not "countenance the use of their property by survivors."[60] In this reading, Michael's spirit is angered because Bartley is wearing his shirt; Kiberd writes that "it comes as no surprise when the spirit of the dead Michael returns to carry off to death the brother who now wears his fine shirt."[61] When Maurya tells her daughters that she has seen Michael, Cathleen's response carefully negotiates between material and spiritual realms. "It wasn't Michael you seen," she responds, not only because "his body is after being found in the far north" and thus he is proven dead but also because "he's got a clean burial by the grace of God."[62] For Cathleen, a "clean burial" should prevent posthumous dissatisfaction and wandering by ensuring proper separation between the worlds of the living and the dead. As such, funeral and burial rites are not merely coping mechanisms but acts of ultimate importance and meaning. Drowning interferes with these rituals, leaving the dead and their families vulnerable to the difficulties that attend unresolved transitional states.

Viewing *Riders to the Sea* with an eye to the significance of burial and mourning rituals provides new insight into the problem that has traditionally perplexed critics: the difficulty of how to understand Maurya's response to Bartley's death. Even within the play, Maurya's children find her reaction perplexing; her youngest daughter wonders if the disparity in Maurya's grieving over her two lost sons means that maybe she loved Michael more than Bartley. Some have seen Maurya's resignation as evidence of her heroic status; Kiberd reads it as proof of "triumph over . . . selfishness," a victory over "self-absorption in grief."[63] Rather shockingly, Maurya's final speech has led at least one critic, Bert Cardullo, to conclude that Maurya "willed Bartley's death"; that she actually "*wants* him to be drowned."[64] Cardullo, more than other critics, takes note of Maurya's obsession with burial, recognizing that she has "throughout the play desired the retrieval of Michael's body for a proper Christian burial," and exploring how *Riders to the Sea* alternates between the language of darkness and death and the language of "newness" and "whiteness."[65] The latter is connected, surprisingly, not with life as death's opposite, but with burial.[66] Unfortunately Cardullo misreads these helpful insights to conclude, against plenty of evidence to the contrary, that Maurya values Michael's burial over the life of her last remaining son, and that even if Bartley drowns she cares only that Michael's body be retrieved.

What this reading and others like it lack is a close and careful attention to Maurya's final words in the play: "Michael has a clean burial in the far north, by the grace of the Almighty God. Bartley will have a fine coffin out of the white boards, and a deep grave surely. What more can we want than that? No man at all can be living for ever, and we must be satisfied."[67] Plenty of attention has been given to the last two sentences. However, most readings fail to connect these sentences with the two that precede them. In these, Maurya tells us what she is experiencing—not some transcendent tragic heroism, nor a failure to properly love her children—but two conflicting human emotions. She has lost two sons, and she will certainly grieve for them, as she has clearly mourned the six men she has lost previously. Yet Maurya is simultaneously feeling relief, not only that she has no more sons to lose, but that after she has spent nine days "crying and keening, and making great sorrow in the house," her son Michael has been found and given a "clean burial," and that Bartley's body was never lost and she will be able to bury it herself.[68] Most readings of *Riders to the Sea* have assumed that Maurya's response to Michael's death is her norm, and, by contrast, her reaction to Bartley's seems lacking, even unnatural.[69] It seems equally plausible, however, that Maurya's grief over Michael was exaggerated, enhanced by the loss of the corpse that would provide access to cultural methods of grieving and memory.

Maurya is, as her daughters note, a woman who has seen many coffins made.[70] She knows the rituals of mourning and burial so intimately that she is able to lay out her son and anoint him with holy water herself, without waiting for the priest. Bartley's body gives Maurya something to do, a coping mechanism and an active role. While Michael's body was lost, Maurya had been alone in her grief, wandering the beach, "going down to see would he be floating in from the east."[71] Now she has a community of mourners surrounding her: sounding the ritual keen, helping her to build a coffin, legitimizing her grief. Viewed in this light, Maurya's reaction seems neither foreign nor heartless; it is rather the natural response of a woman who has experienced a terrible tragedy but who is deeply invested in a culture that provides her with ritual means for dealing with such inevitable happenings—rituals that will help her to grieve, to heal, and to remember.

For anyone familiar with Synge's other work, *Riders to the Sea* cannot be read only as Maurya's personal tragedy—it is simultaneously a play about cultural loss, about the waning of the kinds of traditions and rituals that Maurya finds so steadying. *The Aran Islands* recounts how keenly Synge felt the tension between the improvements modernization brought to the lives of the islanders, and the equally powerful sense that such improvements heralded the death, or at least the irreversible mutation, of a rich traditional culture. *Riders to the Sea*, with its narrow focus on the inhabitants of one cottage, is less obviously concerned with cultural change, but the signs are there nonetheless. In her article "Synge's *Riders to the Sea*: Island as Cultural Battleground" Judith Remy Leder argues that *Riders to the Sea* "is virtually a textbook case of a folk culture in transition, for the play deals not only with Maurya's grief about the loss of her sons, but also with the conflict between two world views—hers and that of the 'big world.'"[72] The cottage setting in *Riders to the Sea* is a microcosm of this transition, with Maurya representing the traditional culture and its emphases on family, ritual, and storytelling. Bartley, with his focus on economic concerns and his desire to conduct business in the larger world, is drawn to the modernized culture of the mainland, although, as Leder is careful to point out, he is still very much an island man, with all the traditional skills necessary to sustain such a difficult way of life.[73]

Applying Leder's argument to the conclusion of *Riders to the Sea*, which she spends little time on, reveals a poignant and characteristically Syngean paradox. On the one hand, Bartley's death represents a kind of bitter victory for Maurya's traditional point of view—she warned him against going from the first, since all the signs of both folklore and weather were against his going. Bartley exhibits the blindness of the modern world to the wisdom hidden in folklore, superstition, and tradition. As such, his death is, in some sense, satisfactory—ancient wisdom has been proven right, and he was wrong to go against it.

On the other hand, however, Bartley's death also signals the death knell of his mother's traditional culture. Maurya has not lost just one but eight male relatives, a fact that suggests that their way of life, with its heavy reliance on the unreliable sea, is unsustainable. Moreover, Bartley's death leaves a household of three women with "only a bit of wet flour . . . to eat, and maybe a fish that would be stinking."[74] Thus they are faced with a choice: either they must starve or one of the daughters must find work outside the home, striking their own blow against traditional culture. Earlier in the play Maurya had scoffed at the idea of Cathleen doing what she saw as a man's job, asking, "How would the like of her get a good price for a pig?"[75] Maurya is, as she delights in reminding her family, not that far from the grave herself, and the task of keeping her culture alive in her family seems an impossibly tall order with six sons dead and two daughters faced with the choice between starvation and finding work that would take them away from their traditional place at the hearth.

Synge would almost certainly have been torn about such changes. A way of life that resulted in such bleakness and hardship for the islanders was certainly long past due for some change. Yet, as *Riders to the Sea* demonstrates, even in such a necessary transition, much of value can be lost. The culture Synge portrays in the play is a culture of memory. The signs Maurya cites as reasons that Bartley should not attempt a sea journey are the ways her culture has developed to remember how to order the major events of their lives: plantings, harvests, marriages, and voyages. Vital survival skills are not written down, but embodied: learned and passed down from mother to daughter, father to son. Maurya has taught her daughters well, and *Riders to the Sea* is full of these tasks; the play begins with Cathleen kneading bread and, before the first word of the play has been spoken, she finishes the bread and moves on to the spinning wheel. Even the younger and generally more inept daughter Nora is in charge of knitting her brothers' socks and, despite being the play's most forgetful character, she is able to remember her knitting pattern well enough to identify Michael's clothing.

Yet this rich culture of memory is clearly fading even before the play's tragic ending. Michael's shirt is not homespun but store-bought, and even with another piece of cloth to compare it to, his sisters cannot remember it well enough to be sure that it is his. Mass production erases the kind of memory previously encoded in everyday objects; Cathleen asks about the cloth of Michael's shirt: "It's the same stuff Nora; but if it is itself aren't there great rolls of it in the shops of Galway, and isn't it many another man may have a shirt of it as well as Michael himself?"[76] Nora, despite her moment of clarity with the sock, cannot seem to remember where anything is in the small cottage. Leder cites Nora's ignorance of the whereabouts of the new rope, Maurya's walking stick, and Bartley's shirt as evidence of her "modern orientation"—proof that she cares less about the small world inside the cottage than the big world outside.[77] This argument seems fruitful, yet besides a lack of interest, Nora's incompetence indicates a failure of memory. Her inability to recall even the most basic details about their island life stands in stark contrast to Maurya's vibrant and powerful recollections of events long past, marking a troubling decline in a memory-rich culture.

Maurya is the locus of memory in *Riders to the Sea*, and a representative of a culture that recites, rather than writes, the things it wants to remember. She is a storyteller, an adept user of language, a bardic figure. After Maurya returns from the spring well, having seen Michael's ghost following Bartley, she enters the cottage and immediately takes the seat nearest the fire, the traditional place for the storyteller. Maurya's daughters, clearly familiar with this ritual, begin asking her questions designed to elicit a story. Yet for Maurya to tell the personal story of what she saw at the spring well, she must first locate that story in a history of stories, signaling its relevance within the collected experience of the islanders. Thus she begins: "I've seen the fearfullest thing any person has seen, since the day Bride Dara seen the dead man with the child in his arms."[78] The allusion to oral tradition places Maurya's story, telling listeners what kind of story to expect and how to react. Her daughters do not disappoint; at the mention of Bride Dara, both cry, "Uah" and "*crouch down in front of the old woman at the fire*."[79] Maurya recounts her experience at the spring well, and provides her daughters with the interpretation, her certainty that "Bartley will be lost now," and that she will be soon to follow.[80] Instead, however, of ending the story there, weighted down with grief, Maurya continues on, delivering a litany that she must have recited many times before. Believing herself about to die, she enacts a ritual of memory for her daughters, recalling all of the "fine men" that had lived in her cottage and died at sea. In doing so, Maurya tells her own story of grief, but she also names her sons, encouraging her daughters to remember them and to recall the stories of their deaths.[81] Maurya is creating for her daughters an oral history of their family to remain with them after she is gone.

Maurya's tale reveals that while she has been able to bury some of her men, others have remained lost at sea: "Some of them were found and some of them were not found, but they're gone now the lot of them."[82] Here she recognizes that the rituals of mourning and burial are no adequate replacement for a life, that whether or not the body was found, all of her drowned relatives are "gone." Yet in her retelling, the deaths that earn the most specific detail and carry the most emotional weight are the deaths in which the bodies were found. Maurya's first loss was two sons, Stephen and Shawn, who "were lost in the great wind, and found after in the Bay of Gregory of the Golden Mouth, and carried up the two of them on the one plank, and in by that door."[83] Brief as it is, this tale contains a wealth of detail: the names of both sons; the reason for their drowning ("the great wind"); the specific, named location where their bodies were found; and a vivid description of the method by which their bodies arrived home.

By contrast, the next tale of loss receives a much hazier description: "There was Sheamus and his father, and his own father again, were lost in a dark night, and not a stick or sign was seen of them when the sun went up."[84] Neither Maurya's husband nor his father is named, a significant omission for a detail-oriented storyteller. In *The Ethics of Memory*, Avishai Margalit discusses how many victims of the Holocaust were "murdered twice, both in body and in name. This image of the double murder is, I believe, at the core of our attitude toward memory in general, and in particular toward the memory of personal names as referring to the essence of human beings in a way nothing else does."[85] Not only does Maurya omit her husband and father-in-law's names, but the description of the reason for their death is inexact: was it so dark that they got lost and therefore drowned, or did they simply die ("were lost" in a more colloquial sense) on a dark night? Maurya is a careful language user, and this difference in precision must be significant. Without the bodies of her drowned men, without access to the sense-making processes of keening, anointing, and burial, important facets of memory are lost. While both sets of men are equally "gone" in one sense, in another important sense Maurya has lost only one set of them irretrievably. For those whose bodies have been found she has been able to enact the rituals of memorialization, and thus their names and their stories remain fresh on her tongue to be passed on to the next generation.

Maurya's final memory is the clearest, so vivid that it provides one of the theatrical cruxes of *Riders to the Sea.* She not only describes the circumstances of Patch's death—he was "drowned out of a curagh that turned over"—but she distinctly recalls what she was doing when she learned of his death, sitting near the hearth with baby Bartley lying across her knees.[86] Maurya's description emphasizes the presence of the community around her, beginning the mourning rituals, as she sees Patch's body brought up from the sea: "I seen two women, and three women, and four women coming in, and they crossing themselves, and not saying a word. I looked out then, and there were men coming after them, and they holding a thing in half of a red sail, and water dripping out of it—it was a dry day, Nora—and leaving a track to the door."[87] Maurya's memory and retelling of this long-past tragic event is as clear as her memory of the events at the spring well only moments ago. Her telling is so powerful that it seems to conjure up its own visualization; as Maurya gestures "*towards the door,*" "*old women begin to come in, crossing themselves.*"[88] Here Synge's stagecraft and Maurya's memory combine to create a moment so powerful that an audience member may wonder, with Maurya, "Is it Patch, or Michael, or what is it at all?"[89] In this instant, a memory breaks in and threatens to upset the chronology of what has been, up to this point, a realistic, linear play. In so doing, this moment reveals not just the fatalistic cycles of island life but also a culture in which memory is profound and alive. This culture, through its communal rituals of memorialization and its emphasis on storytelling, keeps memory at the center of its daily, lived experience, ever ready to break into the present moment with its wisdom, joy, or grief.

The Aran culture portrayed in *Riders to the Sea* is certainly an environment of memory, and yet it is one on the edge of modernity. On the one hand, Maurya's obsession with burial rites indicates a ritual belief system and a cultural community that help her to process grief and maintain memory. On the other hand, her focus on the tangible, physical elements of these rituals—the dead body, the coffin, the holy water—may indicate a belief system that is gradually becoming empty of content. Pierre Nora writes of the transition from environments of memory to places of memory: "*Lieux de mémoire* exist because there are no longer any *milieux de mémoire*, settings in which memory is a real part of everyday experience."[90] Maurya's fixation on bodies, coffins, and graves, as opposed to funerals, keening, and wakes, looks like the beginnings of such a transition. When read next to the other signs of her culture's decline—Nora's forgetfulness, Bartley's emphasis on earning money on the mainland, and the death of her six sons—these signals seem to indicate that Maurya is also part of the first waves of a major transition. Perhaps one of the clearest evidences of Maurya's movement away from her environment of memory is the fact that upon learning the news of her sons' deaths she does not join the island women in the ritual keen but instead gives a speech detailing her own individual response to the news. Rather than being focused on the communal experience of grief and memory, she is becoming focused on the objects of grief and memory, a shift that may eventually lead to traditions emptied of meaningful content.

Synge highlights the object-focused nature of Maurya's character through his substitution of a few simple inanimate objects for the body of her beloved son Michael. At the end of the play, Michael's corpse has been buried in the north, and Maurya is left only with the shirt and one of the stockings he was wearing when he died. She lays the pile of clothes next to Bartley's body and anoints both with the holy water. The moment draws attention to the fact that Bartley's corpse is now itself an object, with less absolute value and utility than a pile of torn clothing. Maurya suggests this parallel by calling Patch's body "a thing in half of a red sail."[91] Obviously the body of a loved child carries much more emotional weight than a shirt or a sock. However, the striking parallel, as Maurya anoints both "objects" and prays over them, emphasizes the extent to which it is up to her to invest them with significance.

For Maurya, both Bartley's body and Michael's clothing are filled with deep cultural and personal significance, and being able to touch, anoint, and bury them is a meaningful part of her grieving and memorializing process. As Frawley writes, summarizing an insight from

Douwe Draaisma, the reification of memory is a natural part of the human experience: "Memory seems to be something that we need to make concrete, that we need to *realize* in the world. It is so vital an idea to our notions of ourselves as humans, so utterly indispensable to all we do, that memory has been transformed over and over again from an ether, an energy, into a tangibility that we want to see."[92] Yet Synge's substitution of a shirt and sock for Michael's body hints at the fact that as cultures fade, once-meaningful signs can become mere objects. Separated from the keening women, the ritualistic prayers and anointing, the community of men who help to build coffins, Bartley's grave could become a *lieu de mémoire*, an isolated place of memory where once an environment of memory thrived.

Much of *The Aran Islands* is taken up with Synge's attempt to determine the appropriate reaction of the outsider and artist to the kind of cultural change he documents in *Riders to the Sea*. On the one hand, Synge feels the loss of an ancient way of life as an unspeakable tragedy; when witnessing an eviction he notes: "After my weeks spent among primitive men this glimpse of the newer type of humanity was not reassuring. Yet these mechanical police, with the commonplace agents and sheriffs, and the rabble they had hired, represented aptly enough the civilization for which the homes of the island were to be desecrated."[93] Synge, however, is sensitive enough to the islanders' situation to realize that not all of the changes brought by modernity are as insidious as the heartless and mechanical evictions. Instead, he recognizes that the increasing access to a market economy on the mainland and even the fishing industry established in Kilronan by the Congested Districts Board represent hope to a poverty-stricken people. Synge worries over the islanders' restricted access to modern medicine; in the case of illness, the doctor must be brought from the mainland by curragh—a trip that, in the case of rough weather, endangers both the doctor's life and those of the men sent to fetch him. As Kiberd notes in his moving analysis, when faced with the individual travails of the islanders, Synge finds in favor of cultural change, even in light of its devastating costs: "[He] honestly concludes that all these beautiful effects are bound up with a social condition near to penury. He knows that that condition cannot last and so it has, therefore, the added charm of an exquisite, dying thing: and he does not finally oppose the change. He is sufficiently self-aware to admit that his very presence on the islands is a portent of that change."[94] As an outsider, however, Synge, while ultimately supporting changes that will ease the difficult lives of his hosts and friends, is simultaneously able to recognize the losses that accompany such changes, and to observe, appreciate, and mourn the traditions that are passing away.

Read in light of his struggle to determine the place of the artist and outsider on the Aran Islands, Synge's fascination with the practice of keening at funerals, and especially with the role of the keener, becomes more than simply the curiosity of an anthropologist. In the keener, who mediates between the dead body and the grieving community, Synge finds an image of the artist, who stands between the past and passing events he describes and the present and future readers with whom he seeks to communicate. As Synge's understanding and depiction of the keener's role change from his first visit to the Aran Islands to his last, so does his sense of his own role on the islands. Comparing the first extended description of an Aran funeral and the practice of keening in part 1 of *The Aran Islands* with the later description in part 4 reveals a dramatic shift in Synge's sense of the appropriate relationship of an artist to his subject. In his first encounter with the Aran wake and funeral, he maintains a distanced, if sympathetic, documentary realism, while in the second, a drowning, Synge positions himself as both insider and outsider, sharing in the individual and communal grief even as he analyzes its larger significance.

Synge's first description of an Aran funeral largely seems to achieve the purported goal of documentary realism set forth in his introduction to *The Aran Islands*. Concerned with cultural sensitivity, Synge does not attend the wake of an elderly neighbor woman but rather stays in his room, hearing "a faint echo of the keen" and "the strokes of a hammer in the yard, where . . . the next of kin laboured slowly at the coffin."[95] When some mourners bring him poteen in his room he finally joins the funeral procession, but only as a silent observer. The old women lead the mourning ritual, which Synge observes with curiosity:

> Each old woman, as she took her turn in the leading recitative, seemed possessed for the moment with a profound ecstasy of grief, swaying to and fro, and bending her forehead to the stone before her, while she called out to the dead with a perpetually recurring chant of sobs.
>
> All round the graveyard other wrinkled women, looking out from under the deep red petticoats that cloaked them, rocked themselves with the same rhythm, and intoned the inarticulate chant that is sustained by all as an accompaniment.[96]

This is keening seen through a documentary lens—viewed as an example of a common ritual rather than as one specific funeral. The faceless "wrinkled" women in their matching red petticoats keen an "inarticulate chant" that has been carried on for generations, rather than a personalized elegy or heartfelt tears for the deceased woman. Synge makes this point as he goes on to analyze the keen, writing that "this grief of the keen is no personal complaint for the death of one woman over eighty years, but seems to contain the whole passionate rage that lurks somewhere in every native of the island."[97] In the keen, Synge writes, "The inner consciousness of the people seems to lay itself bare for an instant . . . and they shriek with pitiable despair before the horror of the fate to which they all are doomed."[98] In this first of Synge's Aran funeral experiences, the keen is observed and analyzed as a cultural artifact, examined for what it reveals about the "inner consciousness" of a "doomed" people.

When compared to the keeners at Synge's second Aran funeral, who wail out of a rending personal grief, these "wrinkled women" seem almost like professional mourners. While Synge does not mention the existence of professional mourners in *The Aran Islands*, it seems almost certain that he was aware of the practice. Describing Irish funereal practices, Weldon Thornton writes that hired mourners were a common feature of the funeral: "Most of the keening was done by hired, professional keeners, and . . . there were persons who went from funeral to funeral and made their living as professional mourners. It was, in fact, common not only to hire such mourners, but to leave most of the immoderate mourning to them."[99] The position of the hired mourner, the outsider brought in to ritually express the grief of a local community, has suggestive potential for considering the role of the artist in describing and mourning individual and cultural loss. By standing outside of the culture he or she observes, the artist, like the professional keener, has the ability to see through daily losses and individual griefs to the "inner consciousness of the people," to reveal the general, collective truths of sorrow that transcend personal tragedies.

Yet it quickly becomes clear in Synge's second description of an Aran funeral, this time that of a drowned young man, that he is no longer entirely satisfied either with his earlier depiction of the keener's role or with his own position as a cultural outsider intent on documenting ritual practices.[100] Synge attributes the difference in his description of the keen to the different situations of the deceased, writing that "the grief of the people was of a different kind, as they had come to bury a young man who had died in his first manhood, instead of an old woman of eighty. For this reason the keen lost part of its formal nature, and was recited as the expression of intense personal grief by the young men and women of the man's own family."[101] Throughout the funeral, Synge emphasizes the grief experienced by the young man's family; he writes that "the men of his own family seemed too broken with grief to know what they were doing."[102] The keen becomes far more than a ritual expression: "The young women were nearly lying among the stones, worn out with their passion of grief, yet raising themselves every few moments to beat with magnificent gestures on the boards of the coffin. The young men were worn out also, and their voices cracked continually in the wail of the keen."[103] Here the individual and communal experience of deep pain is Synge's main focus, with the cultural ritual providing only a loose format for its expression.

While Synge attributes the differences in his descriptions of the two funerals to actual differences in the situation of the mourners, it is also clear in his second description that his position as an observer and an artist has drastically changed. By the section of part 4 in which the funeral occurs, Synge's narrative has become involved with the sufferings and deaths of the islanders. In part, this involvement is due to the simple fact that he has established personal relationships with the islanders—the story of the young man's wake interrupts the story of a dying woman whom Synge describes as "a young married woman I used often to talk with."[104] As he watches the curragh set off for the doctor and priest for the young woman, Synge notes that "the body of a young man who was drowned a few weeks ago came ashore this morning."[105] The experience is clearly part of Synge's inspiration for *Riders to the Sea.* After wandering for a few weeks, the lost body has been found, and the cultural rituals of consolation and memory can begin. While Synge does not attend the drowned man's wake, neither does he hide himself in his room as he had done previously. Instead, he speaks with his elderly hostess, "keening by the fire," who relates her experience with the newly recovered but long-dead corpse: "'I have been to the house where the young man is,' she said; 'but I couldn't go to the door with the air was coming out of it. They say his head isn't on him at all, and indeed it isn't any wonder and he three weeks in the sea. Isn't it great danger and sorrow is over every one on this island?'"[106] The gruesome detail devoted here to describing the young man's headless and stinking corpse stands in stark contrast to the near invisibility of the dead old woman, whose demise is only suggestively attributed to old age and whose body is never glimpsed. Following this exchange, Synge further demonstrates his engagement in the life of the island by questioning his hostess about the young woman dying of fever and the curragh sent for the priest, and then proceeds to sit "over the fire with the old man and woman talking of the sorrows of the people till it was late in the night."[107]

Synge's increased involvement with the islanders manifests itself not just in his description of the funeral and his behavior in the days surrounding it but also in his interpretive reaction to the experience. The reflective passages following the two funeral scenes seem deliberately parallel: both short paragraphs occur immediately after "the coffin was in the grave," and both involve ruminations about the role of the funeral rite in allowing the islanders to grieve for their collective fate, the death which awaits them all.[108] Yet in the second case, instead of adopting the distanced, factual tone of the anthropologist as he had after the first funeral, Synge expresses his impressions as a part of his personal emotional experience. Whereas in the first passage, Synge attributes the howling, despairing recognition of "the fate to which they all are doomed" to the "inner consciousness of the people,"[109] in the second he recognizes the significance of his own role in transcribing and interpreting the inarticulate keen: "As they talked to me and gave me a little poteen and a little bread when they thought I was hungry, *I could not help feeling* that I was talking with men who were under a judgment of death. I knew that every one of them would be drowned in the sea in a few years and battered naked on the rocks, or would die in his own cottage and be buried with another fearful scene in the graveyard I had come from."[110] This passage, in which Synge acknowledges not just the subjectivity of his impressions but also his own embodiedness, is a far cry from the earlier distant, pseudo-scientific observations. By highlighting his own presence, Synge acknowledges that his physical signs are seen and interpreted by the islanders in much the same way that he observes and "reads" their cultural expressions. By juxtaposing their misreading of his needs ("they thought I was hungry") with his own hyperbolic interpretation of their experience ("I could not help feeling"), Synge admits the fact that this morbid recognition is his own, contingent on his own emotionally charged vision.

Yet, paradoxically, this vulnerability, this admission that Synge's insight into the Aran Islands funeral is filtered through his own "feeling[s]," lends his analysis greater credibility. Rather than musing abstractly about "the fate to which they are all doomed," here he has intimately felt the profound tragedy of an individual death and its ability to spill out and color the life around it. Although Synge is still an outsider, difficult for the islanders to interpret and equally capable of misinterpreting them, still observing the difficulty and danger of their lives from a more privileged position, he has shared a moment of tragedy with them, and allowed that moment to influence his interpretation of their culture. In this moment, Synge, moved by the loss of a young man to the sea, demonstrates the profound way in which the dead or dying can alter the perceptions and behaviors of the living.

As an artist, Synge allowed himself to be changed by the joys and the tragedies he witnessed and participated in on the Aran Islands. He writes in a letter to a friend in 1907 that *The Aran Islands* was his "first serious piece of work," in which by "writing out the talk of the people and their stories," he "learned to write the peasant dialect and dialogue."[111] This conflation of the writing process and the learning process in describing a "serious piece of work" reveals the complexity of Synge's understanding of the role of temporality in the artist's work. A text—even a fixed, published text—can still be a kind of work in progress, representing a process of change and growth on the part of the author. This sense of the potential for writing to change the writer, and perhaps by extension the reader, complicates Kiberd's claim that "the covert desire of his book [is] to *make the present past*."[112] Kiberd writes of Synge's project on the Aran Islands that it participates in the modernizing changes it decries: "Synge knows that he is only an interloper on Aran, a tourist, one of the first and, perhaps one day, one of the most famous among many: and that the more successful is his book called *The Aran Islands*, the more extreme will be the consequent disruptions of tradition by day-trippers who will come in his wake. Indeed he has—though he never quite says this—a vested interest in these disruptions, because after they have had their effect, his book will be even more evocative than ever."[113] This observation, though it seems chiefly and perhaps unfairly the product of hindsight, is perceptive. Synge does frequently seem to recognize his significance as an agent of change on the Aran Islands. Yet Kiberd's assessment ignores the extent to which Synge allows himself to be changed by the culture his book portrays as a dying one. The influence goes both ways—*The Aran Islands*, in narrating the daily life of the islanders for future readers, certainly works to make the present past. Yet in inscribing the beauties of the Aran Islands culture Synge seeks not to archive them, but to demonstrate their living power to alter the vision and voice of a modern Irish artist. Thus *The Aran Islands* simultaneously seeks to make the past present—to demonstrate the ways in which "archaic" or "primitive" cultures can have a positive impact on modernity, even as modernity threatens to stamp them out.

Synge's texts challenge modern understandings of temporality and history by blurring the distinction between folk tales passed down for generations, distant historical facts or memories, and occurrences in the present or immediate past. This running together of time features prominently in the speech of the people he encounters, which often skips from myth, to history, to daily life, with little or no indication of the tense of a given tale. Occasionally this tendency may make their stories seem logically suspect to a modern reader. In his travel essay "In West Kerry," Synge records a conversation with his host on the Blasket Islands in which the man claims that there have been no recent drowning deaths on the island, yet then immediately describes a drowning incident in such detail that it seems to have happened only days before:

> "There has been no one drowned on this island," he said, "for forty years, and that is a great wonder, for it is a dangerous life. There was a man—the brother of the man you were talking to when the girls were dancing—was married to a widow had a public house away to the west of Ballydavid, and he was out fishing for mackerel, and he got a great haul of them; then he filled his canoe too full, so that she was down to the edge of the water, and a wave broke into her when they were near the shore, and she went down under them. Two men got ashore, but the man from this island was drowned, for his oilskins went down about his feet, and he sank where he was."[114]

The simple explanation for this anecdote is that the man is recounting the last drowning death on the island, forty years ago, an incident that he is old enough to remember. Yet the seeming immediacy of the tale, the way in which the teller connects the deceased to "the man you were talking to when the girls were dancing," indicates that, despite the past-tense narration and the uneventful forty years in between, the drowning death has never really become the past. Instead, it remains present in the minds and behavior of the islanders. As the Blasket Islands man goes on to discuss the current mackerel season, he notes, "When we get fish here in the night we go to Dunquin and sell them to buyers in the morning, and believe me, it is a dangerous thing to cross that sound when you have too great a load taken into your canoe."[115] Despite presumably hundreds of successful crossings in the intervening forty years, the death of one islander due to an overloaded canoe has become such an integral part of their cultural lore and wisdom that it seems never to have been relegated to the past.

It is perhaps Synge's adoption of this storytelling technique, which makes ancient myths and past events all part of the present moment, that accounts most fully for the discrepancy between his account of life and death on Inis Meáin and Messenger's anthropological statistics. Aside from the firsthand personal experience of the young man's funeral, the tales of drowning deaths that Synge relates often blend the recent past, history, and myth together in ways that make them almost impossible to separate. The frequent loss of young men to the sea is attributed to the starkly modern problem of alcoholism and specifically to the pub in Kilronan where men from the other Aran Islands come to drink:

> This is the haunt so much dreaded by the women of the other islands, where the men linger with their money till they go out at last with reeling steps and are lost in the sound. Without this background of empty curaghs, and bodies floating naked with the tide, there would be something almost absurd about the dissipation of this simple place where men sit, evening after evening, drinking bad whisky and porter, and talking with endless repetition of fishing, and kelp, and of the sorrows of purgatory.[116]

This is the assessment of a perceptive modern outsider, who sees the problem of unnecessary drowning deaths and attempts to discover its root causes. Yet the language of haunting, lost bodies, eerily empty curraghs, and purgatory is suggestive of the explanation for drownings given later in *The Aran Islands*, where a whole litany of deaths are blamed on the interference of fairy ships, which lure men out in their curraghs to unload their goods, and then disappear. "A while ago," an old man relates to Synge, "a curagh went out to a ship from the big island, and there was no ship; and all the men in the curagh were drowned."[117] The temporal phrase *a while ago* is the same phrase Synge uses to introduce several of the alcohol-related deaths he narrates; yet it is difficult or impossible for the modern reader to determine the relationship between these stories. They may, of course, simply be different versions of the same deaths, or they may be different deaths that both occurred in the recent past with wildly different explanations. Alternatively, the old man's story may indicate the continued resonance of ancient folk tales in the cultural consciousness, an ability to keep old stories alive and present rather than relegating them to the mists of time. If this is the case, than it also seems possible that some of the more naturalistic deaths Synge relates could, like the Blasket Islands man's story, be old stories that continue to carry such tragic weight in the minds of the islanders that they seem to have happened just "a while ago."

Much as the stories told by the islanders seem to have both the authority of ancient tradition and the poignancy of recent grief, Synge's work simultaneously portrays the Gaelic peasantry as members of a dying culture and, paradoxically, as more vibrantly alive than their modernized counterparts. Describing a morning hike to the top of Sybil Head, on the Dingle Peninsula, Synge marvels at the exhilaration of a life lived close to such natural beauty: "One wonders in these places why anyone is left in Dublin, or London, or Paris, when it would be better, one would think, to live in a tent or hut with this magnificent sea and sky, and to breathe this wonderful air, which is like wine in one's teeth."[118] In *The Aran Islands*, Synge uses almost identical language to imagine dying in the middle of the same natural beauty. On a wild curragh ride between the Aran Islands, Synge imagines the experience of drowning: "I thought for a moment that we were likely to be swamped. In a little while, however, I realized the capacity of the curagh to raise its head among the waves, and the motion became strangely exhilarating. Even, I thought, if we were dropped into the blue chasm of the waves, this death, with the fresh sea saltness in one's teeth, would be better than most deaths one is likely to meet."[119] Death and life mingle and overlap in Synge's experience of the Aran Islands, and in the shock of facing one, the other is always imminent. Enthralled by the natural and cultural beauty of life on the islands, Synge is constantly startled by the looming presence of death in the daily experience of the islanders, "Who feel their isolation in the face of the universe that wars on them with winds and seas."[120] Yet as the amateur anthropologist, bitterly aware of the precariousness of the islanders' cultural existence on the edges of modernity, Synge is equally startled by the vibrant life of people whose "archaic" traditions should make them merely the ghostly remnants of a time long gone.

In *The Aran Islands*, Synge documents both the dying of a culture and its extraordinary resiliency and life. Simultaneously, he documents the effects of that culture on his own understanding of the relationship of the artist to his subject, and particularly the difficult relationship of the Irish artist to the various histories he may desire either to uncover and reclaim, or to suppress and erase. In his encounters with drowned bodies, Synge recognizes that part of the artist's role can be to keen, to ritually enumerate the beauties of lives that are past or quickly passing, and to publicly mourn their loss. He shares this focus on the artist as mourner with Milton, whose poem becomes an urn or shroud for the missing body of Lycidas. Yet unlike his poetic predecessor, Synge does not offer a straightforward resolution to grief. He relies neither on the Christian consolation of Heaven, nor Milton's earthly solution of giving the wandering spirit a role as "Genius of the Shore." Instead he worries that the mourning ritual may become a kind of permission to forget and move on. After the funeral of the old woman on the Aran Islands, Synge passes "the old women who had recited in the keen," and notes that "they were still sobbing and shaken with grief, yet they were beginning to talk again of the daily trifles that veil them from the terror of the world."[121] While Synge recognizes that this kind of moving onward, this temporal progression away from the tragedies of the past, is necessary to daily life, he also seems certain that this kind of forgetfulness is not part of the business of the artist. Instead, by carefully documenting the ways in which his experiences on the islands changed him and his artistic vision, Synge demonstrates the profound ability of the dead or dying individual or culture to change the present and future. Thus, while Synge's work does seek in some ways to "make the present past," it also strives to make the past present, to conflate temporality in ways that hold out hope that, through the work of art and literature, the past may change the present even as the present overtakes the past.

3

The Regenerative Body

Creative Amnesia and the New World Author in Derek Walcott's The Sea at Dauphin *and* Omeros

Despite the geographical and cultural particularity that makes Synge's *Riders to the Sea* inseparable from its setting on the Aran Islands, at least four major playwrights with different cultural, national, and linguistic backgrounds have written their own adaptations of or homages to *Riders to the Sea*. While each of the four playwrights—D. H. Lawrence, Federico Garcia Lorca, Bertolt Brecht, and Derek Walcott—maintains Synge's focus on an individual family's response to a personal tragedy and a cultural crisis, only Walcott retains the central image of *Riders to the Sea*, the drowned body, in his adaptation, *The Sea at Dauphin*. Walcott shares Synge's concern with memory and the role of the postcolonial artist, but he ultimately disagrees with the Irish playwright's vision of the artist as mourner. Where *Riders to the Sea* presents the loss of memory as a tragic sign of a waning culture, *The Sea at Dauphin*, while recognizing the real human need for memory, finds more potential in forgetfulness. In its treatment of the drowned body as a site of regeneration and creativity, this early play prefigures Walcott's concept of "creative amnesia" in his later works "The Muse of History" and *Omeros*.

In the drowned body—floating, dissolving, often irrecoverable—both Synge and Walcott find a powerful symbol that captures the human desire for memory in situations where memory is elusive or impossible. Yet Walcott, even in this early play, does not blindly recreate Synge's version of the drowned body. Synge's play focuses on the death of a young man and the waning of a way of life. Maurya mourns over the body of her son, but she also finds peace in the knowledge that he will be buried deep and nearby—that there will be rituals to memorialize him and ways to remember him. *Riders to the Sea* laments the impending doom of the culture that supports such ritualistic ways of remembering. By contrast, Walcott's play mentions the drowning of many young fishermen in order to emphasize the difficulty of their lifestyle, but the only actual death in the play is that of the suicidal old widower Hounakin, who despairs of living after his wife's death. His drowned body becomes a symbol of the dangers of remembering, of dwelling in the past, even as the survivors enact memorial rituals around it. The sea for Walcott is thus deeply ambivalent—both a destroyer of lives and a site of benevolent forgetfulness.

Riders to the Sea is anxious about the loss of memory and cultural meaning. By contrast, *The Sea at Dauphin* has at its center a warning against too much memory. The two plays capture the paradox of postcolonial memory described by Oona Frawley: "Postcolonial memory might thus be said to embody at its extremes two disparate forms of memory . . . the too-much-ness of memory that is nostalgia faced with the too-little-memory that is forgetting."[1] *The Sea at Dauphin*, one of Walcott's earliest plays, was first performed in St. Lucia and Trinidad in 1954, when the playwright was twenty-four years old. Seen by most critics as part of Walcott's juvenilia, the play is little read and less studied.[2] Walcott indicated that *The Sea at Dauphin* is part of a "course of imitations and adaptations" that he undertook as a young writer, citing *Riders to the Sea* as an "obvious model for *The Sea at Dauphin*."[3] He describes being inspired by the way that Synge wrote dialect, the way he "had taken a fishing-port kind of a language and gotten beauty out of it, a beat, something lyrical."[4] Thus in *The Sea at Dauphin*, Walcott "tried to translate the speech of the St. Lucian fisherman into an English Creole."[5] Yet the play is not merely an adaptation or a youthful imitation, and deserves attention for more than its dialect. *The Sea at Dauphin* writes back to *Riders to the Sea*, challenging many of its assumptions about culture and memory. At the same time, the play looks forward to the radical changes Walcott, in his mature poetry, essays, and plays, would make to the image of the drowned body.

Where *Riders to the Sea* stays in the cottage with the Aran women, *The Sea at Dauphin* is set on the beach among the fishermen who risk their lives daily on the sea. The main character is Afa, a fisherman "over forty" and "gritty-tempered," a loner who scoffs at other fishermen for their reliance on women.[6] The play opens in the early morning with Afa preparing his canoe *Our Daily Bread* for a day of fishing. He discusses the bad weather with another fisherman, Gacia, and the two conclude that the sea is at its most dangerous. Yet both agree that they must "work or starve" and decide that they will go out on the sea despite the danger.[7] Afa's younger fishing partner, Augustin, arrives and reveals that last night at the bar Afa got drunk and promised an old man, Augustin's godfather Hounakin, that he could come with them on the sea in the morning. Afa maintains that the sea is too bad to take the old farmer, and accuses Augustin of trying to "drown" his godfather.[8] Hounakin's wife, Rama, has recently died, and he is inconsolable. After some argument Afa finally agrees to take the old man along, but as they are setting out, Gacia returns and claims that going out on the sea in such weather is suicidal. Afa and Augustin begin to suspect that Hounakin actually wants to die, so they pull him out of the canoe, promise to bring him fish, bread, and a "white shell for Rama," and set sail without him.[9] Evening falls, and a "Chorus of Dauphin Women" appear, singing a mourning song. Given the heavy foreshadowing about the bad fishing weather and the precedent set by Synge, the audience assumes one or both of the fishermen have drowned. But Afa and Augustin return, and discover that Hounakin is dead—he has fallen or, more likely, jumped—from some high rocks into the sea. The young French priest's attempt at consolation is met with an angry tirade by Afa. He criticizes the priest for taking the people's money to build the church while around him there is "poverty, dirty woman, dirty children."[10] As the priest leaves, Jules, the young boy who found Hounakin's body, approaches Afa and Augustin and asks to be taught how to fish. Afa reluctantly agrees, telling him that he must be "brave like Hounakin."[11] The play ends with Afa and Gacia sitting on the beach, discussing Hounakin's death and remembering the fishermen who have died in the Dauphin sea.

The Sea at Dauphin is clearly more of an homage to *Riders to the Sea* than a direct adaptation or close imitation. More than the other plays that claim *Riders to the Sea* as their inspiration, however, it maintains the central concerns of Synge's play, exploring the poverty and hardship of life on an isolated island, the tension between outside influence and the local culture, and the way that death in the ocean differs from death on land. Perhaps most significantly, *The Sea at Dauphin* extends and reframes Synge's concern with mourning and memory. In both plays, mourning and memory are integral parts of the daily experience of the characters, who constantly recite the names and the stories of the dead. In *The Sea at Dauphin*, however, memory and the rituals that attend it are treated far more ambivalently—remembering the dead can be a source of valuable lessons but also of crippling and destructive grief.

The most striking difference between *Riders to the Sea* and *The Sea at Dauphin* is that Walcott changes the play's focus from the domestic space of the cottage to the open air of the beach, from the world of the grieving mother to the world of the men who contend daily with the ocean.[12] This is a play about the Caribbean equivalent of Bartley and Michael, not about Maurya and her daughters. Since memory in rural cultures is traditionally connected with women, the hearth, and the storytelling activities that take place around the cooking fire, this change in focus might seem like a move away from memory. Laurence Breiner contends that the play is largely unconcerned with history and memory: "*Dauphin* is especially notable for its calculated avoidance of depth of reference: there is no myth here but threadbare religion, no culture but habit. 'History' here goes no deeper than the few drowned fishermen that are still remembered by name."[13] Although Breiner is correct that among Walcott's early plays, *The Sea at Dauphin* is the least concerned with myth and history writ large, it is a mistake to conclude that the play depicts "no culture but habit." Such a claim ignores not only the extraordinary folk song sung by the women mourning

Hounakin but the fact that in such a spare, short play the talk of the fishermen repeatedly turns to the names and stories of the dead. These repeated litanies may not constitute anything so austere as "history," but they certainly demonstrate the significant role of personal and cultural memory in the lives of the fishermen.

The speech of the Dauphin fishermen is littered with references to the dead. At the beginning of *The Sea at Dauphin*, Afa and Gacia have exchanged only a few words before talk turns to the dead fisherman Bolo; Afa notes that the sea is "white like the time when Bolo drown."[14] This reference is characteristic of the way the fishermen discuss their fallen comrades through most of the play—using them to describe the weather or to warn of the dangers of the sea. Frequently they recall the bravery and skill of their drowned companions; the death of such able fishermen indicates the unpredictability of the sea. For Leif Schenstead-Harris, who also compares *Riders to the Sea* and *The Sea at Dauphin*, the names of the lost become modern, non-Gothic ghosts who haunt the play's language: "In Synge and Walcott's works, ghosts are haunting reminders of loss embodied by the proper names kept current in the plays' circulating, changing, even keening language."[15] In his attempt to convince Hounakin not to come with him and Augustin, Afa says that "the onliest fisherman better than Boileau was Saint Pierre, both of them dead."[16] Remembering the dead is an integral part of how the fishermen understand themselves and their relationship to the sea. Such memories, as a part of everyday life, provide valuable lessons.

For those fishermen who, like Afa and Augustin, are fully aware of the lessons provided by the deaths of their colleagues and yet choose to defy them by risking their lives on a dangerous sea, the names of the dead become something else—a litany of brave men they hope to emulate. When Afa agrees to let Jules ride along in their canoe to learn the trade, he cautions Augustin to initiate the boy by reminding him of the brave men he must follow: "Ask him if he remember Habal, and then Bolo. If he say yes, tell him he must brave like Hounakin, from young he is. Brave like Habal to fight sea at Dauphin. This piece of coast is make for men like that."[17] Deployed in this manner, the memories of the dead become the stories of heroes: heroes whose examples provide validation for a backbreaking and too often fatal way of life. Jules—whose own father, Habal, is among the dead fishermen Afa eulogizes—is excited to be initiated into the company of such men, even when Afa warns him that a fisherman's lifestyle will make him "sour and old and good for nothing standing on two feet" by the age of forty.[18] Here the memories of the dead, their hard work and their bravery, are powerful enough to inspire a new generation to follow in their traditional ways of life, to resist the lure of going to the city "to learn mechanic or work in canes."[19]

It may be tempting to view this type of memory as unambiguously positive, but to do so would be to neglect the more ambivalent nuances in the play. Robert Hamner writes that *The Sea at Dauphin* ends on a note of regeneration and rebirth: "What saves the plot from tragedy and sends it off into yet another cycle is the appearance of young Jules. Jules, the son of Habal, the man who first took Afa out to sea, comes to him for work. At this point Afa, childless, an intractable curmudgeon, begins the initiation of the next generation."[20] Hamner's point is at least partially valid. The end of *The Sea at Dauphin* cannot be read as a complete tragedy, since the memory of the dead fishermen and of Hounakin inspires a young boy to continue the traditional way of life—a way of life that Walcott, at least, believes is worth preserving. Jules's decision represents regeneration for the fishing culture and potentially for Afa, who is bitter and lonely.

Yet to accept this ending as unequivocally positive is to blindly accept Afa's construction of bravery as the most significant thing a man can strive for. At times, Afa seems like the direct antithesis of Maurya, who is so deeply affected by her painful memories that she works to keep Bartley from his necessary and life-sustaining work. By contrast, Afa is so invested in his heroicized version of death in the sea that he seems to lack human emotions. Afa freely admits that his life is, in many ways, a miserable one: "I have no woman. I cannot love woman . . . My head is full of madness. I make my heart hard long."[21] Jules's choice is undoubtedly brave, but it is questionable whether the value of that bravery outweighs the chance of an isolated life and a tragic death. Within *The Sea at Dauphin*, Augustin frequently voices this kind of doubt. He questions Afa's motives, suggesting that constantly valorizing the dead fishermen indicates not Afa's respect but a perversely competitive death wish: "I know you, Afa. All your life is to be better than Bolo. You can't dead better than what is dead. You want Dauphin and the whole coast to say Afa was brave! Is when you drown you brave?"[22] Augustin's doubt makes memory problematic. Rather than indicating a desire to learn from the past or a kindhearted urge to valorize deceased friends, too much memory may indicate an internal deadness, a valuing of the past over the present and the dead over the living.

Though Augustin often accuses Afa of harboring a death wish, it is Hounakin who becomes the center for memory and grief in *The Sea at Dauphin*. His wife of fifty years, Rama, has died an unspecified length of time ago, and he has been immobilized by sorrow. The first detailed description of him occurs when Augustin describes passing Hounakin's house "before daybreak, the house eyes close, and he cannot sleep, he crying in the making dark, making ehhhh like dog, and the dog self watching him, waiting to die."[23] On the one hand, Hounakin's grief over his wife's death is refreshing in a play in which women are rarely named and never appear except as a nameless chorus. The culture of the fishermen is profoundly patriarchal and they almost invariably speak of women as forces holding the weaker fishermen back from their duties on the sea.[24] By contrast, Hounakin's love for his late wife seems deep and genuine; his expressions of grief are touching:

> To dead; what is to dead? not dead I fraid
> . . . For old man that is nothing, wind.
> But when one old woman you loving fifty years,
> That time they dead, it don't like they should have bird,
> And bread to eat, a house, and dog to feed.[25]

This poetic evocation of love and grief provides an important and poignant contrast to Afa's equally poetic anger. For Hounakin, memory is a source of intense emotion; where Afa has made his "heart hard long," Hounakin opens his heart to grief and loss.[26] Edward Baugh writes perceptively about Hounakin that he "stands for the 'weakness' of human love and grief," and that he both "displaces and completes Afa as protagonist in the latter half of the play."[27]

While Hounakin's grief makes him the most sympathetic and emotionally available character in *The Sea at Dauphin*, his memory is most often portrayed as a paralyzing force.[28] Afa, resisting Augustin's plea to allow the old man to join them on the boat, goes so far as to call Hounakin dead: "I not carrying nobody dead in my half the boat, no old man on my shoulder. I know old man, dribbling in bed. Since Rama, his old woman dead, he think everybody must go round their face long like bamboo, the world work must stop because one old woman dead."[29] By this account, Hounakin's grief is neither productive nor healing—it causes him to resent other people's happiness and the "world work." He says that he has "no heart to eat," and hints that he no longer has the desire to live.[30] Part of the killing force of his memory may come from the fact that he feels some guilt over Rama's death; he reveals that he begged "for one whole year" to earn enough money to pay for her medicine, but when she got sick again he was too proud: "I did not want to beg and Rama die."[31] These memories haunt Hounakin and ultimately drive him to his death in the sea.

If Hounakin is the play's center of memory, the sea is its site of forgetting. Even as the fishermen remember their drowned brothers, the sea retains no trace of them:

> GACIA. *Garçon*, to see a next day so like when Bolo . . . [*Shakes his head*] I remember . . .
> AFA. But the sea forget.[32]

This forgetfulness is part of the sea's menace; it does not care how many lives it devours. When Augustin urges Afa to have some compassion toward Hounakin, Afa explodes: "If is compassion you want talk to the sea, ask it where Bolo bones, and Rafael, and friends I did have before you even born."[33] Paradoxically, however, the sea's forgetfulness also makes it seem merciful. For Afa, it offers an escape from a hard life into oblivion: "This basin men call sea never get red for men blood it have. My turn is next. I cannot sleep on land, like Gacia. The land is hard, this Dauphin land have stone where it should have some heart. The sea it have compassion in the end."[34] The sea erases memory; it erects no memorials or tombstones, not even changing color to mark all the men it has swallowed.

Hounakin, laden with too much memory, is drawn to the sea's forgetfulness. He wants to go out with the fishermen in the hope that he may die in the sea, a death he sees as a kind of rebirth: "This sea have many navels, many waves, and I did feel to die in Dauphin sea, so I could born."[35] As a farmer, Hounakin is a man of the land, not the sea, and Afa is skeptical of his desire to risk his life on the sea: "Is land you know, old man, you don't know sea, you know the fifteen kinds of grass this island have, land hard under a old man foot and hard on old woman body, but this sea is no cemetery for old men."[36] This response is typical of the fishermen, who frequently remind Hounakin of burial, graves, and cemeteries, the conventional means of dealing with death on land. When Afa and Augustin discover that Hounakin's desire to go fishing with them is merely a death wish, they leave him behind on land. Augustin attempts to console him by promising to bring him "for Rama grave / A white shell is at the bottom of the sea."[37] This attempt at consolation misses the mark; to a man plagued by too much memory he offers a memorial; to a man who already cannot forget his wife's grave he offers a grave marker.

Hounakin's suicide is his attempt to access the forgetfulness of the sea, but he remains tied in significant ways to land and to memory. Despite promising Afa and Augustin that he will not kill himself, Hounakin jumps from "the high rocks by Point Side" into the sea.[38] Jules, who found the body, says, "I wasn't fraid, he fall and the sea take him."[39] In one sense Hounakin has achieved the death he wanted—the sea takes him and he is presumably no longer plagued by grief and memory. He cannot, however, entirely escape land; without a boat he cannot get far enough from land to ensure that his body will be lost at sea, and it is washed up on land and almost immediately found. Though Hounakin died in the sea he will receive memorial rites and probably be buried next to his departed wife.[40] The women sing a mourning song for him, and Gacia notes that Hounakin's wake will be held in the evening.

While Hounakin's body will receive memorial rites, his death prompts Afa to challenge the efficacy of those rites. In *The Sea at Dauphin*, much more than in *Riders to the Sea*, the priest is presented as an interloper on the island, a foreigner whose bland words of consolation have little to do with the harsh reality of life.[41] Afa blasts the young priest for talking of God when God has been so little help to Hounakin. He accuses the priest of caring more for the dead than the living, for not noticing that the old man was "dying because he will not beg."[42] Afa turns on the women, too, for their empty wailing: "All you can do is what, sing way! way! Hounakin dead and Bolo dead, is all mouth! mouth!"[43] Where in *Riders to the Sea* Maurya longs for burial rituals to help her mourn and remember her sons, Afa finds similar rituals empty of meaning, indicative only of a church that cares more for the dead than the living and a community that makes a show of grief without feeling it deeply. For him, the forgetfulness of the sea is preferable to this kind of memory.

Afa's tirade against the priest can be read as a victory for the postcolonial individual against the imposed rituals of colonial religion, but the play itself ends on a more ambivalent note. The priest and the mourners leave, and Afa is left on the beach with Gacia, securing his canoe for the night. The two men talk through the day's events, and Afa tells Gacia about how he and Augustin had gone looking for Hounakin when they returned from fishing, bringing him half a fish and the white shell for Rama's grave. Despite his angry disdain for memorial rituals, this story is Afa's version of one, and he ends by adding Hounakin's name to his oft-repeated list of dead fishermen:

> Last year Annelles, and Bolo, and this year Hounakin . . . And one day, tomorrow, you Gacia, and me . . . And Augustin . . . And we have only this shell for his old woman is in the *cimetière* behind the church, where Fond River coming down by the canes and making one with the sea at Dauphin.[44]

Like Maurya, Afa ultimately finds meaning in memory, in calling out the names of the dead and those who will one day join them. More surprisingly, he ends this, his final major speech in the play, by admitting that all he can do in the face of certain death is create a memorial, placing the white shell on the grave of the old woman. Yet this is a new kind of memorial, not a symbol of the deadly memory that sapped Hounakin's will to live, nor the traditional gravestone offered by the priest and the women, empty of all but the most perfunctory meaning. Instead, this memorial brings together the importance of remembering the dead with the benevolence of forgetfulness, just as Afa's speech brings together the cemetery and the sea. The shell from the bottom of the sea, itself the empty husk of a once-living creature, is a memorial, but one without even the illusion of permanence; it will quickly decay or be brushed aside. For Walcott, this forgetfulness is a mercy, not a sign of a waning culture but of people moving forward, refusing to be entrenched in past sorrows. Where *Riders to the Sea* presents the loss of memory as a tragic sign of a dying culture, *The Sea at Dauphin*, while recognizing the real human need for memory, finds more potential in forgetfulness.[45]

Even as Walcott's play looks back to Synge's, his depiction of memory and forgetfulness in *The Sea at Dauphin* prefigures the concept of creative amnesia that would become central to his later poems, plays, and essays. One of Walcott's most important and controversial contributions to Caribbean literature—the idea of creative amnesia—is most clearly laid out in his 1974 essay, "The Muse of History." In it, Walcott challenges the tendency of postcolonial literatures to focus on the past, charging that "in the New World servitude to the muse of history has produced a literature of recrimination and despair."[46] Because the Caribbean's past is shaped by the widespread genocide of native populations and the atrocities of slavery and the Middle Passage, Walcott suggests that the amnesia of the slave, his/her memory of his/her origins diluted by the passage across the sea, is the common cultural experience of the New World: "In time the slave surrendered to amnesia. That amnesia is the true history of the New World."[47] For Walcott, the blank slate of the New World should enable the emergence of new political formations that resist isolating nationalisms. As Malouf cautions, "The Muse of History" has been too often read in a vacuum and its context and initial audience ignored. The essay was written for a Caribbean audience and is strongly marked by Walcott's desire for the success of a West Indian federation.

While acknowledging the essay's political context is important, it is also clear that Walcott's primary concern is for the postcolonial artist. Rather than respond to profound loss by attempting to artistically return to a mythologized homeland, Walcott suggests that the postcolonial artist should embrace this amnesia as an opportunity for a fresh start, a new naming of the world. Describing those whom he calls the "great poets of the New World," Walcott writes that they share an "Adamic" sensibility: "Their vision of man in the New World is Adamic. In his exuberance he is still capable of enormous wonder. Yet he has paid his accounts to Greece and Rome and walks in a world without monuments and ruins."[48] In this renaming the artist should renounce the "muse of history" in order to move more freely in and among literary traditions and languages, openly embracing whichever literary ancestors he finds most enabling, regardless of race. George Handley, who writes extensively about Walcott's version of the sea in *New World Poetics*, accurately describes Walcott's poetry as a "rechristening that sees the New World as palimpsest and poetry as the adamic task of turning away from the allure of fading names, history, and meanings in order to keep language fresh and alive to the demands of the natural present."[49] For Walcott, the authors of the New World do not forget the past entirely, but they begin a "new naming of things"—a naming that marries the bitter wisdom of the past with a keen joy at nature's renewing processes.[50] In Walcott's imagined Caribbean, according to Maria McGarrity, "The traumas of history are not elided but integrated into the islands, thereby enriching their generative, creative soils."[51]

Though the idea of creative amnesia recurs in a number of different guises throughout Walcott's prolific oeuvre, it never strays far from the ocean and the bodies drowned in it. For Walcott, Hounakin's drowned body and the white shell Afa retrieves from the ocean to place on Rama's grave represent a new kind of memory, memory that shapes the present and future but does not paralyze the living. In the forgetfulness of the sea, a forgetfulness that had caused so much anxiety for Synge's Maurya, Walcott finds hope and a new direction for Caribbean art. This new direction, this move toward creative amnesia, would prove both controversial and productive for Walcott and the Caribbean artists that followed him.

For many Caribbean writers and theorists, both Walcott's contemporaries and his followers, the millions of slave bodies discarded into the Atlantic, while representing an unspeakably tragic past, have become the site for new understandings of identity that challenge the unitary, bounded subject of Western and Judeo-Christian tradition. In his *Caribbean Discourses* (1981), the Martinican writer and theorist Edouard Glissant explores how the Caribbean sense of historical identity has developed in the face of the drastic displacement of African slaves—a displacement that separated them not just from their homelands but from any connection with their own languages, religions, and cultural practices. Glissant writes of what Kamau Brathwaite calls the "submarine unity" of the Atlantic, describing the trail of African bodies strewn across the Atlantic by slave ships as the source of a new, more fluid concept of cultural identity: "They sowed in the depths the seeds of an invisible presence . . . Submarine roots: that is floating free, not fixed in one position in some primordial spot, but extending in all directions in our world through its network of branches. We, thereby, live, we have the good fortune of living, this shared process of cultural mutation, this convergence that frees us from uniformity."[52]

For Glissant, the slave bodies drowned in the Atlantic signify cultural fluidity, the development of identities that are neither uniform nor predictable but extend "in all directions." This symbolic use of drowned bodies—individual bodies that are free-floating and yet immersed in a greater whole—challenges a notion of selfhood characterized by boundaries and thus threatened by mutation and convergence. Yet it simultaneously resists the tendency, in the face of cultural displacement and a loss of historical identities, to subsume individual differences in a monolithic and hence more politically effective whole.

By rooting this new notion of identity in specific, physical bodies, Glissant indicates the importance of recognizing and maintaining difference. Yet by choosing floating, disintegrating bodies, he rejects the construction of fixed, impermeable boundaries around individual subjects; it is convergence, not separateness, that frees them from uniformity.

In Walcott's work, as in the passage from Glissant, the sea often functions as a space that enables a kind of rebirth through the construction of new cultural and cross-cultural identities. Even where, realistically, the sea appears as an ever-present threat to human life on small Caribbean islands, its force is frequently depicted as being simultaneously creative. Although Walcott's sea is a complex and multivalent symbol, this sense of its enabling forgetfulness is one of its most frequently recurring valences.[53]

This claim that Walcott's sea is a site of forgetfulness may seem initially odd given that one of his best-known poems is titled "The Sea Is History." Despite its unequivocal title, however, the poem combines creative amnesia with a selective memory. Asked for the "monuments" "battles," and "martyrs" that signify "History" to Westernized minds, the Caribbean narrator responds, "The sea / has locked them up. The sea is History."[54] The poem continues by narrating the events of the Middle Passage through a kind of marine archeology; the narrator takes the skeptical Western "Sirs" diving in search of Caribbean history. Their expedition reveals painful artifacts of Caribbean history, but these artifacts are being transformed by the sea into "gothic windows" and "those groined caves with barnacles / pitted like stone," which "are our cathedrals."[55] "The Sea Is History" does not allow readers to forget the tragic remnants of the Caribbean past, and in fact implicates that past in the difficult present in which "each rock" has broken "into its own nation."[56] However, it allows the sea to complicate history, to erase certain elements of the past and transform others.[57]

Omeros, Walcott's majestic 1990 epic poem, a Caribbean reimagining of *The Iliad* and *The Odyssey*, is set mainly among the inhabitants of one fishing village, Gros Îlet, in Walcott's native St. Lucia, but picks up subplots in Europe, Africa, and North America. The poem intertwines several main narratives: the struggle between the fishermen Hector and Achille for the love of one woman, Helen; the journey of the wounded Philoctete toward healing; the attempts of the British Major Plunkett to write a history of the island; the death of Plunkett's wife, Maud, an Irishwoman in exile; and the travels of the Walcott narrator in his search for poetic inspiration. Though these stories overlap in fascinating ways, to discuss them all would be the work of a lengthy book, thus this chapter focuses on only one of *Omeros*'s many narrative threads in detail.[58] This thread follows Achille, spurned lover of Helen, who throughout the poem undergoes a journey of self-discovery that involves a kind of reversed Middle Passage, a mystical trip back across the Atlantic to visit his African ancestors and attempt to discover his true name. On this voyage, which takes place not only on but underneath the Atlantic, Achille has several encounters with the drowned of the Middle Passage, encounters that demonstrate his changing relationship with memory and the past, ultimately leading the narrator to an almost euphoric moment of creative amnesia.

Unlike *The Sea at Dauphin*, *Omeros* bears little direct relationship to Synge, but it maintains the earlier play's connection to Ireland. In *Transatlantic Solidarities*, Michael Malouf traces Walcott's shift from his early Caribbean phase toward a transatlantic cosmopolitanism: "The geography of Walcott's cosmopolitanism is not limited to the Caribbean islands but also 'opens out' to include a transatlantic relationship with Ireland."[59] Walcott's narrator visits Ireland, encountering not just Syngean curraghs, tinkers, and wells, but the more urban ghost of James Joyce.[60] But *Omeros*'s most sustained engagement with Ireland occurs through the Plunketts, the retired English major and his Irish wife, who yearns for her distant island home. As Maria McGarrity documents in her article "Cataloguing Ireland: Exile and Indigeneity in Derek Walcott's *Omeros*," the Plunkett name carries with it a wealth of Irish history, from the family of museum managers mentioned in *Ulysses* to the revolutionary Joseph Mary Plunkett, executed for his part in the Easter Rising.

Interestingly, this Irish connection also provides one of the poem's first discussions of drowning. In his research on the island's history, the childless Major Plunkett comes across an ancestor, the nineteen-year-old Midshipman Plunkett who drowned fighting for the English during the Battle of the Saints. In one of *Omeros*'s frequent reversals of temporality, the major begins to think of the midshipman as a missing son. On finding the record of his drowned ancestor, the major enacts a brief and private memorial service:

> This was his search's end. He had come far enough
>
> to find a namesake and a son. *Aetat xix.*
> Nineteen. Midshipman. From the horned sea, at sunrise
> in the first breeze of landfall, drowned! And so, close
>
> his young eyes and the ledger. Pray for his repose
> under the wreath of the lilac ink, and the wreath
> of the foam with white orchids.[61]

This prayerful moment and the major's interest in his own history and family tree draws attention to the fact that the vast majority of the drowned in *Omeros* cannot be remembered and prayed for by name. Despite dying at a young age in relative obscurity, Midshipman Plunkett's life and death are recorded; the opening of the poem's final chapter refers to St. Lucia's "amusing museum," containing "a log with its entry, *Plunkett*, in lilac ink."[62] Though after his wife's death Major Plunkett is focused on learning to forget, his ancestor's name remains inscribed in the museum for other historians or family members to encounter.

By contrast, Achille's first encounter with his ancestors who drowned in the Middle Passage is characterized by anger and despair. Broken by Helen's abandonment of him for the wealthier Hector, Achille goes diving in search of a rumored sunken ship, hoping to find enough coins to win back Helen. He ties a cement block to his heel and begins to sink; the narrator notes that "the stone heart inside / his chest added to its poundage."[63] As he sinks, Achille ponders the death of Helen's love and feels "the cold of the drowned entering his loins."[64] As he reaches the sea floor Achille discovers not only the sunken ship but an eerie dead world:

> This was not a world meant for the living, he thought.
> The dead didn't need money, like him, but perhaps
> they hated surrendering things their hands had bought.
>
> The shreds of the ocean's floor passed him from corpses
> that had perished in the crossing, their hair like weeds,
> their bones were long coral fingers, bubbles of eyes
>
> watched him, a brain-coral gurgled their words,
> and every bubble englobed a biography
> no less than the wine-bottle's mouth, but for Achille,
>
> treading the mulch floor of the Caribbean Sea,
> no coins were enough to repay its deep evil.[65]

In this, Achille's first vision of the sea floor, it is a haunted place. The traumatic memory of the Middle Passage leads Achille to see corpses in every coral. The dead of the Middle Passage have undergone a sea change, but it is less a transformation into something rich and strange than an imprisonment. They haunt Achille, but are inaccessible to him, their words reduced to the gurgles of a "brain-coral," their life stories entombed in bubbles. For Achille, the Caribbean Sea becomes an agent of the "deep evil" that erased the memory of millions of his ancestors.

It is perhaps this first vision of the inaccessible but traumatic Caribbean past that prompts Achille to go in search of memory—memory that would help him establish his own identity. His search for memory takes place during a fishing trip with an unnamed mate. Initially, echoing *The Sea at Dauphin*, Achille's remembering takes the form of a litany of dead fishermen, each name accompanied by a story of drowning:

And these were the noble and lugubrious names
under the rocking shadow of *In God We Troust*:
Habal, swept in a gale overboard; Winston James,

commonly known as "*Toujour Sou*" or "Always Soused,"
whose body disappeared, some claimed in a vapour
of white rum or l'absinthe; Herald Chastenet, plaiter

of lobster-pots, whose alias was "*Fourmi Rouge*,"
i.e., "Red Ant," who was terrified of water
but launched a skiff one sunrise with white-rum courage

to conquer his fear. Some fishermen could not swim.
Dorcas Henry could not, but they learnt this later
searching the pronged rocks for whelks, where they found him,

for some reason clutching a starfish. There were others
whom Achille had heard of, mainly through Philoctete,
and, of course, the nameless bones of all his brothers

drowned in the crossing, plus a Midshipman Plunkett.
He stood like a mast amidships, remembering them,
In the lace wreaths of the Caribbean anthem.[66]

This naming ritual allows Achille access to short-term memory—the memory of his friends and contemporaries who have been swallowed by the sea. Yet in the midst of all these names Walcott leaves a yawning gap, two lines positioned appropriately on either side of the stanza break: "And, of course, the nameless bones of all his brothers / drowned in the crossing."[67] While Achille can "murmur name upon name," enacting a poetic ritual to remember his lost Caribbean brothers, he has no way to recall the nameless African dead.[68]

As the sun beats down on Achille and he begins to succumb to sunstroke, he is haunted by his inability to appropriately remember the unnamed dead of the Middle Passage. Drowned corpses begin to rise up from the water, beginning with Midshipman Plunkett and followed quickly by hundreds of faceless corpses, the bodies of drowned slaves:

> Out of the depths of his ritual
> baptism something was rising, some white memory
>
> of a midshipman coming up close to the hull,
> a white turning body, and this water go fill
> with them, turning tied canvases, not sharks, but all
>
> corpses wrapped like the sail, and ice-sweating Achille
> in the stasis of his sunstroke looked as each swell
> disgorged them, in tens, in hundreds, and his soul
>
> sickened and was ill.[69]

These dead cannot be adequately remembered but neither can they be escaped; they are signs of "the tribal sorrow / that Philoctete could not drown in alcohol."[70] Achille begins to pull in his fishing line, and is horrified to find at the end of it "the ghost / of his father's face."[71] It is this ghost that forces Achille to recognize his crisis of memory as a crisis of identity:

> Achille stared in pious horror at the bound canvas
> and could not look away, or loosen its burial knots.
> Then, for the first time, he asked himself who he was.[72]

The amnesia of the New World is seen here as a profound tragedy for Caribbean individuals; denied access to the names and stories of their ancestors, they are unable to truly know themselves.

Succumbing to sunstroke, Achille begins a dream journey, his pirogue towed by the sea swift, back to Africa and back in time, to his father's village before it was ravaged by slavers. His trip is primarily a quest for names: the names of his ancestral gods, the name of his father, and his own forgotten African name.[73] As Martin McKinsey notes in his article exploring naming in *Omeros*, "Achille's dreamed voyage to Africa represents 'the journey back': that symbolic return to the ancestral homeland that figures prominently in postcolonial and diasporic discourses of origins."[74] Such journeys are often characterized by a powerful nostalgia that turns the half-forgotten homeland into a pastoral idyll. Initially it seems that Walcott's narrative will give in to this temptation: Achille discovers in Africa a quiet village on an ancient river, peopled by a friendly tribe who welcome him as a returning warrior into their rituals of chewing kola nuts, drinking palm wine, and storytelling.[75] He meets his father, Afolabe, and recognizes "himself in his father."[76] Despite these initial hallmarks of the nostalgic idyll, however, Achille feels out of place in the African village. He sits on his own, brooding "in discontent," partly troubled by his knowledge of the village's tragic future, partly disappointed in his father's inability to tell Achille his true name, to grant him access to his original identity.[77] Achille is not the only one who has forgotten, his father tells him: "I have forgotten the [name] / that I gave you," and calls him "only the ghost / of a name."[78] Despite the fact that Achille is "home" in Africa, he finds himself thinking of his home in St. Lucia with tears in his eyes.[79]

Eventually Achille begins to realize that the truth of his identity lies neither fully in Africa nor completely in the Caribbean, but in some mixture of the two. As the African warriors perform a dance on a feast day, Achille realizes that the dances and the drumming are familiar: "Achille saw the same dances . . . The same, the same."[80] His hybrid identity, McKinsey argues, is written into his name. Achilles, *Omeros* tells us, is the name given to his enslaved ancestor by a British admiral grateful for his help in a naval battle. It is also, of course, the name of his parallel character in *The Iliad*, a name deliberately chosen by Walcott for its resonance in the literary tradition of the West. As McKinsey notes, however, Achille's name is not the same name given to his ancestor by the white soldier, nor the name of the ancient Greek; rather, "The colonial repetition is marked by an elision . . . the *s* that drops out in the process of creolization."[81] In creating this hybrid character who bears some similarity to the Greek Achilles but refuses to fully mimic him, McKinsey argues, Walcott begins the important work of changing the canon, adding new layers to the signifier *Achille(s)*.

As Achille begins to recognize his own hybrid nature, he is forced to face its traumatic origins. Walcott retells the story of the enslavement of Africans and their forced transport to the New World. His retelling, though filled with grief, is clearly the product of hindsight, of Walcott's knowledge that some of the slaves would survive to create new, hybrid cultures and identities in the New World. As Achille walks around "the barren village," its people stolen by the slavers, "the doors were like open graves."[82] The image is typically Walcottian—simultaneously suggestive of extreme desolation and of hope. An open grave can signify either a raw, unhealed wound or the promise of resurrection, and Walcott sees both in the tragic history of slavery. As Walcott depicts the Africans aboard the slave ship, he does so in similarly mixed language; the village griot sings:

> There were seeds in our stomachs, in the cracking pods
> of our skulls on the scorching decks, the tubers
> withered in no time. . . .
>
> When inspected,
> our eyes showed dried fronds in their brown irises,
> and from our curved spines, the rib-cages radiated
>
> like fronds from a palm-branch.[83]

The language here is dry, desolate, marked by sorrow and rupture. Yet the song speaks of seeds and plants, an image made explicit in its final stanza, where each slave is pictured as the seed of a new nation:

> So there went the Ashanti one way, the Mandingo another, the Ibo
> another, the Guinea. Now each man was a nation in himself,
> without mother, father, brother.[84]

As the griot's song ends, the narrator remarks, "But they crossed. They survived. There is the epical splendor."[85] Without minimizing the trauma, the physical and psychic devastation of the Middle Passage, Walcott marvels at the resilience of the African slaves, many of whom survived and went on to create new nations and new identities across the Atlantic from their original home.

As Achille comes to recognize his own hybrid identity, *Omeros*'s depiction of the sea and its drowned denizens changes sharply. Achille "returns" from his sunstroke-inspired trip to Africa, newly appreciative of the Caribbean culture around him. Yet late in *Omeros*, well after Achille is safe on the shores of St. Lucia, the poem's longest depiction of the undersea world occurs, in which the narrator imagines the corpse of Achille lying on the sea floor. The episode is chronologically ambiguous; the reader cannot be certain whether the narrator's vision is analeptic, revisiting the corpse of one of Achille's slave ancestors killed during the Middle Passage, or proleptic, anticipating Achille's own death, which does not occur in the poem, but of which the narrator later writes, "When it comes, will be death by water."[86] Thus the vision occurs in a liminal realm of simultaneity, becoming, like the earlier song of the griot, a "prophetic song / of sorrow that would be the past."[87] In this submarine realm, the corpse is gradually being transformed into a coral reef:

> Why waste lines on Achille, a shade on the sea-floor?
> Because strong as self-healing coral, a quiet culture
> is branching from the white ribs of each ancestor,
>
> deeper than it seems on the surface; slowly but sure,
> it will change us with the fluent sculpture of Time,
> it will grip like the polyp, soldered by the slime
> of the sea-slug.[88]

The coral growth on the body creates an underwater city, "A parodic architecture" of "porous / temples" and "spiked minarets."[89] The narrator pictures the city giving birth to a new race: "From that coral and crystalline origin, a simply decent / race broke from its various pasts."[90] This new "race" resists the temptation to erect memorials or religious temples; it has "no needling steeple," because, the narrator notes, "This is the true element, / water, which commemorates nothing in its stasis."[91]

This vision of Achille's corpse opens up a number of compelling possibilities for the creation of a shared sense of artistic promise enabled by a new understanding of Caribbean identity. By rooting the coral city and its "simply decent race" in the dead black body, Walcott does not dismiss the past and its tragedies. Yet by depicting the process wherein the body ceases to be a decomposing corpse and becomes "a patient hybrid organism," *Omeros* also resists the temptation, frequently denounced by Walcott as one of the paralyzing features of negritude, to become fixated on past wrongs.[92] Instead, it creates a space where the past no longer requires memorialization because it has become an integral, organic part of the present and future.[93] This collapsing of temporality enables cultural convergence; freeing the postcolonial subject from the artistic compunction to voice only the pain of history, and the descendent of colonizers from dwelling artistically in the corresponding historical guilt.

The "quiet culture . . . branching from the white ribs of each ancestor" suggests a remaking of cultural identity similar to the one Walcott describes in "The Muse of History." The sea's transformation of the individual bodies submerged in it suggests the possibility of a space where the Caribbean artist can be freed from history to reimagine and rename his world, freed to "walk . . . in a world without monuments and ruins."[94] In an interview with David Dabydeen, Walcott emphasizes the lack of monuments in the Caribbean, finding freedom in the absence of these physical reminders of the past: "In the Caribbean we have something around us that you can't make a mark on—which is the ocean. There are no memorials on land, there is this continual sense of an isness that happens."[95] Walcott goes on to argue that the lack of written and memorialized history in the Caribbean may be one of its greatest strengths: "What Europeans call a sense of history is something that we may not need to have."[96] In the uncertainties and gaps of Caribbean history, Walcott suggests, lie true freedom for the Caribbean artist. Echoes of *The Waste Land* and *The Tempest* in the description of Achille's corpse indicate that, for Walcott, the amnesia of the Atlantic never erases literary narratives. Rather, it erases the historical narratives that would grant or deny certain authors access to certain literary traditions, enabling an open, cross-cultural intertextuality.

Walcott's vision is undeniably exhilarating, providing an important warning of the temptation faced by postcolonial movements like negritude to make an aesthetic out of anger. However understandable and necessary such rage may be, dwelling in it for too long could prove paralyzing to a young artistic movement, and, finally, may only serve to reify the expectations of white audiences, for whom "the anger of the black is entertainment or theater."[97] Caribbean art must, Walcott warns, move beyond a dangerous entrenchment in the past, transcending and transforming it as coral does a drowned body. In order to accomplish this, a new Caribbean cultural and artistic identity must exist in a more fluid space, open to hybridity.

Yet for the authors and critics who come after Walcott, this reformation of cultural identity contains its own dangers and oversimplifications. Malouf points to the "basic contradiction that has persisted throughout Walcott's career: his emphasis on Caribbean 'nothingness' and 'newness' that mixes uneasily with his profligate use of literary sources and tradition."[98] More troublingly, Walcott's Adamic myth of the Caribbean artist suggests the existence of a unified, authorial sensibility that has both the authority and the desire to rename the world.[99] In her article on gender and hybridity in Caribbean writing, Jana Gohrisch suggests that Walcott, despite his emphasis on racial hybridity, sets up the authorial mind as a stable, singular force; he "resort[s] to the literary imagination to forge a new wholeness out of the hybrid multitude of Caribbean languages and cultures."[100] Gohrisch links this understanding of the artist, although only in passing, to Walcott's reliance on "gendered metaphors," noting that he "display[s] a perhaps involuntary affinity to the almost stereotyped images of female fertility and inspiration as devices to describe the creativity of Caribbean society and its people."[101] His "Adamic" artist refigures understandings of race, but he does so while remaining firmly connected to a traditional, gendered conception of artistic creativity. Handley notes that "Walcott's definition of a New World community . . . disappointingly lacks women" but argues that since Walcott's poetry resists the neocolonial urge to possess and exploit the environment, it undermines its own gendered metaphors.[102] This argument seems like a stretch, and it may miss the real danger that such an exclusionary poetics poses, regardless of its stance toward the natural environment.

It is important not to diminish the significance of Walcott's disruption of binary constructions of race.[103] Jahan Ramazani writes that Walcott's embrace of the intercultural artist was both powerful and prescient: "Decades before the academic dissemination of such concepts as hybridity, creolization, cross-culturality, postethnicity, postnationalism, *métissage*, and *mestizaje*, Walcott argued vehemently for an intercultural model of postcolonial literature. Against a 'separatist' black literature that 'belligerently asserts its isolation, its difference,' he counterposes a vision of the Caribbean writer as inevitably 'mixed.'"[104] It seems regrettable, however, that this radical refiguration of the postcolonial artist relies so heavily on simplistic narratives of gendered creativity for its authority.

By generally avoiding complex or unexpected triangulations of race, gender, and creativity, Walcott opens his work to some of the same criticisms that have been leveled at the Africanist movements he reacts against. Criticizing the same movements that Walcott has accused of dwelling in the past, Carole Boyce Davies points out that their prioritizing of racial concerns subsume other kinds of difference, thus creating a one-sided and exclusionary understanding of identity: "Pan-Africanism, Black/African nationalism and Afrocentricity are 'totalizing discourses' which can tolerate no different articulation and operate from a singularly monolithic construction of an African theoretical homeland which asks for the submergence or silencing of gender, sexuality or any other ideological stance or identity position which is not subsumed under Black/African nationalism."[105] Ironically, Walcott's refiguring of Caribbean cultural identity to resist these monolithic discourses has come under similar criticism. Claiming that Walcott's portrayals of women reinforce patriarchal constructions of gender has become a critical cliché.[106] Yet it seems that, far more importantly than any antifeminist leanings on the author's part, the frequent resistance to gender complications in Walcott's work points to his desire to maintain a stable identity for his artist figure, whose unique power derives from his racial hybridity, but for whom multiple layers of difference would threaten fragmentation and incoherence.[107]

Walcott's focus on the sea's amnesia and the artist's Adamic task of renaming combine to create an image of the artist that, despite its cultural specificity, is in many ways reminiscent of the Romantic concept of the artistic genius. Paula Burnett addresses this question when she writes that "although [Walcott] may at times seem to lay hieratic claim to the special position of artist, that status is defined as valid only through the artist's role as shaman to the people, as their servant."[108] This is a valuable insight into Walcott's conception of the artist's purpose; however, it does not explain Walcott's tendency to make the authorial voice the only fixed point in an otherwise fluid narrative, and to suggest that the author's voice confers significance on the world around him. While Walcott's work is, on the one hand, deeply invested in the world around him, it simultaneously allows the authorial vision and voice to overpower that world, seeing in its fluidity and heterogeneity an inviting space for inscription. In his 1970 essay, "What the Twilight Says: An Overture," Walcott depicts a moment in which the sight of a young female actor after a performance inspires the author, not through her individuality, but through her vacuity: "A shawled girl caught in that gesture which abstractly gathers cloth to shoulder, her black hair lightly lifting, the tired, pale skin flushed, lost in herself and the breaking camp. She was white, and that no longer mattered. Her stillness annihilated years of anger. His heart thanked her silently from the depth of exhaustion, for she was one of the small army of his dream. She was a vessel caught at the moment of departure of their Muse, her clear vacancy the question of a poem which is its own answer."[109] The woman, like the sea in *Omeros*, enables a kind of amnesia. Her individual identity is erasable; she serves only as a vessel whose emptiness reifies the power of the author's gaze and voice to fill the moment with significance.

Walcott's triangulation of femaleness, fluidity, and vacancy in this passage, a move repeated frequently throughout *Omeros*, is more complicated than it may seem at first glance. In his insightful article "Encomium of Helen: Derek Walcott's Ethical Twist in *Omeros*," Victor Figueroa argues that Walcott's emphasis on the opacity of the Other is a self-aware ethical move, since "the epistemic violence par excellence is to imagine the other as adequately defined by a closed, faultless narrative or the perfect metaphor."[110] By paralleling the narrator's attempts to write the St. Lucian epic with the fumbling if well-meaning attempts of Major Plunkett to write a history of Helen/St. Lucia, Walcott flags the dangerous and almost inescapable desire to dominate the Other through metaphor and rhetoric. Figueroa claims that both men are aware of the danger of their rhetorical strategies, and "both acknowledge Helen's resistance to their representations of her."[111] As such, Helen, despite being the focus of both narratives, ends up being "the character about whom, tellingly, we end up knowing the least."[112] In the end, however, neither man can resist the allure of domination through metaphor, and Figueroa concludes that *Omeros* is, on this level, a failure, but one whose "success, then, is to clarify the terms of its failure."[113]

Figueroa's reading is a compelling one, and provides an important reminder of the need to read *Omeros* in all of its complexity. A too-dismissive reading of gender in *Omeros* might overlook characters like Ma Kilman, whose careful healing of Philoctete's wound makes her one of the poem's most powerful and sympathetic characters. A reading that insisted too strongly that Walcott's artist figures are unitary and stable might miss the fact that they are also portrayed as wounded, vulnerable men. Yet there are difficulties with Figueroa's reading as well. Most significantly, he links Walcott's seeming respect for Helen's opacity to her race and class more than her gender, claiming that Walcott's treatment of Helen is an examination of Spivak's famous question of whether the poet can "speak for the subaltern."[114] This is misleading, given that Walcott's narrator seems fully willing to speak for male characters who share Helen's race and class—Achille, Hector, Seven Seas, Philoctete. In fact, the character Walcott treats the most like Helen is not from the Caribbean at all, but a white European woman, a Polish waitress he meets in chapter 42. The narrator stares at the beautiful young waitress, hoping "that adoration unnerved her."[115] As Walcott muses on the suppressed violence of her past as a Polish immigrant he approaches the issue of her name several times, noting that on her immigration form, "Her name ran over the margin." Later Walcott notes that "her name melted in mine like flakes on a river," and tries to read "the glow / of brass letters on her blouse."[116] The narrator's attempt or his memory fails, however, and in the final stanza of the section he calls her "Nina Something."[117] Instead of pursuing her identity further Walcott ends the stanza by listing three Polish surnames, not Nina's but rather the names of three male Polish poets who he seems to decide are more important than the pretty waitress: "Zagajewski. Herbert. Milosz."[118]

This encounter demonstrates the difficulty of separating a proper respect for the opacity of the Other from a more insidious equation of femaleness with a kind of erasability and namelessness that requires the writing of the male author to give it meaning. Figueroa's assumption that respect for the Other's opacity is an ethical move may be problematic in itself, since asserting that the Other is unknowable could easily result in a kind of dehumanizing language of difference, a refusal to listen to the Other and attempt meaningful communication. Handley worries, for example, that Walcott's focus on the sea's "oblivion" may actually be a form of resistance to the ways nature does communicate to human beings: "To speak of oblivion, of course, is risky business. Categorically refusing to believe nature's communicability renders us indifferent to what it might seem to say to us."[119] Similarly, depicting women as opaque others may be a sign not of respect but of a refusal to listen.

The focus on naming in the passage with the Polish waitress seems to flag it as an instance of the dangerous equation of femaleness with namelessness—the narrator cannot or will not read the waitress' name and so writes over her identity with the names of male authors.

Helen, who the narrator also lusts after from a café table, is also in a sense nameless; her name is written over by the Greek myth that provides Walcott's framework and by her island's nickname, "the Helen of the West Indies." Though as Figueroa notes, Walcott repeatedly points out that "the two Helens cannot and should not be conflated," she is given no other name, no alternate identity to separate her from her mythical namesake—the archetypal object of male desire.[120] By contrast one need only remember Achille's quest to relearn his African heritage and name, through which he gains a kind of dual identity despite never learning his original name. By giving Achille multiple identities, by creolizing his name instead of directly replicating the Greek original, and by allowing his African name to remain unspoken, the narrative respects his opacity and otherness while still allowing him a voice and a story.

By comparison with Achille, Helen functions in *Omeros* as an elusive, unknowable object of male desire, one whose individual identity and particular humanness are erasable, and can be overwritten by the male artist. The few brief moments in which Helen's consciousness takes over the narrative are also the moments in which she is most sexualized for the male gaze. When she removes her hotel costume in protest and walks out naked, the narrative slips from the third to the first person:

> Take off her costume, and walk straight out the hotel
> naked as God make me, when I pass by the pool,
> people nearly drown, not naked completely, I
> still had panty and bra, a man shout out "Beautifool!
> More!" So I show him my ass.[121]

Later in *Omeros*, the poem does not allow Helen a first-person voice but enters her innermost thoughts as she pleasures herself, revealing that she is imagining not Hector's but "Achille's hand" touching her.[122] Though Helen is ostensibly alone, the scene is palpably voyeuristic as she slowly undresses and sprawls on the bed, exposing her naked body to the narrator's voice and the reader's gaze.

In *Omeros*, the sea is almost invariably female, its amnesia creating a blank space requiring the writing of the male artist. "*Mer* was both mother and sea in our Antillean patios,"[123] the narrator notes in the midst of his description of *Omeros*'s moment of inspiration, a sexual encounter with a woman whose body he describes using marine language:

> I write, it returns—
> the way she turned and shook out the black gust of hair.
>
> I saw how the surf printed its lace in patterns
> on the shore of her neck, then the lowering shallows
> of silk swirled at her ankles, like surf without noise . . .
> She lay calm as a port, and a cloud covered her
> with my shadow; then a prow with painted eyes
> slowly emerged from the fragrant rain of black hair.[124]

Here, both the woman and the sea are depicted as possessing a fluidity that erases individual identity, allowing them to be written on and about by the male artist, whose authorial voice emerges as the only fixed point in the encounter. Fluidity and heterogeneity thus become the express characteristics of the object, on which the author's gaze confers a temporary fixity, just as the narrator's description of Achille anchors the corpse to the sea floor.

Edward Baugh writes that "*Omeros* is monumental, but not monolithic."[125] While this is indisputably true about the rich, multilayered poem, there remains something monolithic about Walcott's image of the regenerative drowned body. Achille's body is neither lost nor wandering; the coral fixes it to the sea floor and becomes a kind of gravestone, with Walcott's poem serving as an epitaph. Despite his vocal opposition to European "places of memory" and the histories they encode, Walcott uses Achille's drowned body to construct his own Afro-Caribbean monument. Its fixed resistance to the ocean's fluidity can be seen as analogous to the masculine stability of Walcott's artist. The only differences between Achille's resting place and a traditional gravesite are its bizarre location and the fact that the coral reef will continue to grow and change long after Achille's body has disappeared.

Yet perhaps these small differences are more significant than they initially seem. In slightly altering a traditional Western "place of memory"—the graveyard—Walcott subtly challenges accepted notions of how history and memory ought to operate. The *Omeros* passage is suggestively similar to the Middle Passage Monument (which it predates), conceptualized by Wayne James, a native of St. Croix, and designed by the American artist Michael Walsh. The monument, an aluminum arch, was conceived as a memorial to the dead of the Middle Passage, and in July 1999, after receiving funeral rites in New York City, it was placed on a replica slave ship and submerged 427 km from New York Harbor, where it rests on the floor of the Atlantic.[126] Though replicas of the sculpture exist on land, there is a certain irony to the fact that the original is an inaccessible, invisible memorial. As Renée Ater observes in her essay on slavery memorials, the monument's "memory work in New York appears finished; it offers no consolation in a public space in the city and it cannot serve as a gathering place for commemorative activity there. The burden of remembering rests with those women and men who witnessed the dedication ceremony or the lowering of the monument and those who continue to read about it."[127]

A monument that does not aid memory is a bizarre contradiction. It seems logical to worry that in creating an unreadable, invisible gravestone for the dead of the Middle Passage, the creators of the Middle Passage Monument have simply perpetuated the Western tendency to ignore or gloss over an unpleasant history of slavery. Ater cites the art historian James Young, who asks about Holocaust memorials: "How does a nation memorialize a past it might rather forget?"[128] The answer would not seem to be to submerge memorials of that past deep in the Atlantic Ocean. Yet Ater gestures toward a more sophisticated reading of the monument; it may, she suggests, serve "as a counter-monument . . . one that undermines the permanent materiality of its form and even the memorial idea attached to it."[129] Though Ater does not follow up on this observation, it seems a productive one for understanding both the Middle Passage Monument and Walcott's depiction of the drowned slave body. The monument is pulling in two directions: toward the necessary memory of great atrocities and great heroism, and toward the kind of selective forgetfulness that may be necessary if the ancestors of slaves are to heal and move forward. It is, in this sense, a counter monument, a memorial both for and against memory.

In his depiction of the drowned Achille, Walcott similarly constructs a counter monument. The coral reef growing out of the drowned body is a memorial, but one that advocates forgetfulness as much as memory. The coral transforms Achille's body: "Where coral died / it feeds on its own death, the bones branch into more coral, / and contradiction begins."[130] Soon this memorial will be illegible, unrecognizable as the product of a human death. In Walcott's version of the drowned body, past tragedy blooms into a new ecosystem, a fertile environment for the creative imagination. His vision of the drowned body as counter monument suggests the need to combine memory and forgetfulness, to move away from the confining monoliths of history and to create new, hybrid stories about the past and the future.

4

The Disintegrating Body

The Unstable Author in David Dabydeen's "Turner"

The drowned body in *Omeros*, fixed to the sea floor where it hosts the growth of a coral "city," defies the anxieties that commonly surround Western depictions of the drowned body. For cultures in which a burial plot and an engraved headstone are the appropriate means of dealing with death, one of the most terrifying aspects of the sea is its ability to disintegrate and disperse the bodies drowned in it. The battered, unidentifiable drowned body, limbless or even headless, haunts literary portrayals of drowning even when the images are sanitized for a general audience. For Synge, the artist's role is to name and to mourn those lost at sea and, more significantly, the waning cultural traditions they represent. Walcott denies the sea its disintegrating force, choosing instead to emphasize its transformative, regenerative power. Yet his Caribbean successor—the poet and novelist David Dabydeen—embraces, even revels in, the gruesome image of the disintegrating drowned body. Dabydeen's work clearly engages with Western literary tradition and its anxieties about bodily dissolution, yet he is more profoundly concerned with writing back to Walcott, challenging his unified and hopeful image of the drowned body and the Caribbean future.

The fate of bodies "buried" at sea creates a fascinating and problematic set of questions for the Judeo-Christian religious tradition and the literary and cultural traditions inflected by it. While the dissolution of the body to dust is presumed as the inevitable end of conventional burial services, traditions of interment and memorialization attempt to give order to the entropic process. Headstones or other grave markers symbolically demarcate where one individual's dust ends and another's begins, while coffins physically reinforce those boundaries. Besides fulfilling a desire for memory on the part of the friends and family of the deceased, such rituals reinforce impermeable boundaries of selfhood concomitant with the religious idea of the resurrection of individual bodies. If the afterlife entails a reunion of each individual soul with its body, the entropy of the decaying corpse is a source of concern. On cremation, for example, the pre–Vatican II *Catholic Encyclopedia* states that while the practice does not threaten the resurrected body, it is generally inadvisable. The article tellingly concludes by simultaneously claiming that cremation is not against the church's teaching and calling its practitioners "sinister": "It must be remembered that there is nothing directly opposed to any dogma of the Church in the practice of cremation, and that, if ever the leaders of this sinister movement so far control the governments of the world as to make this custom universal, it would not be a lapse in the faith confided to her were she obliged to conform."[1] The palpable unease in this ostensibly reassuring statement demonstrates the extent to which, in Judeo-Christian cultures, bodily dissolution is a cause for apprehension.

Given this concern for maintaining the boundaries of the deceased body, it is unsurprising that most Christian traditions have historically discouraged sea burials.[2] Burial at sea denies the illusion provided by the headstone or memorial that the individual corpse can be marked off from other bodies. The seawater hastens the process of decomposition, quickly bleaching and disfiguring individual bodies beyond recognition. Additionally, the sea's tides and currents ensure that decayed particles of such corpses will not, like the dust of buried bodies, remain relatively sedentary, but will instead flow and mingle unpredictably. While most sea burials mandate that the body be weighted, storms and predators combine with the natural buoyancy of decaying bodies to make resurfacing a real threat (a fact that has provided many a denouement for murder mysteries). Thus, while Christian tradition allows for sea burials in cases of absolute necessity, they are clearly sources of anxiety, threatening the boundaries of the individual body in ways that have disconcerting implications for the unity of the individual soul.

Such anxieties haunt the seventeenth-century English poet George Herbert's poem "Doomsday," which pictures the dust of human remains rising from graves on Judgment Day, and concludes with the prayer:

> Come away,
> Help our decay.
> Man is out of order hurled,
> Parceled out to all the world.[3]

While Herbert's poem expresses faith that God will reunite the scattered bits of bodies on Doomsday, it simultaneously suggests a religious responsibility to resist disorder as far as possible. Dead human bodies are returned to dust and scattered—"parceled out to all the world"—but humankind is "out of order" in a spiritual sense as well. In lines such as "thy flock doth stray," Herbert clearly links the physical dissolution of bodies with the sinful wandering of God's people.[4]

Dabydeen's scholarly and creative work has been deeply influenced by Western literary traditions. Born in Guyana in 1955, he spent his first thirteen years there, but moved to the United Kingdom as a teenager and studied eighteenth-century British art and literature at Cambridge and Oxford. Though Dabydeen's novels and poems most often deal with Caribbean, Indian, or African characters and themes, they also draw heavily on British art and literature. In his fourth novel, *A Harlot's Progress* (1999), loosely based on the Hogarth engravings by the same name, Dabydeen's narrator describes the scene belowdecks a slave ship in terms that directly recall the worries expressed in Herbert's "Doomsday": "It was difficult to count [the slaves] accurately, for there were hands sans arms wedged in the iron restraints, feet sans legs, stumps of necks. It was like a resurrection gone gruesomely wrong, for they were without benefit of the sacramental. One woman, torn from her chains, sans head and feet, rolled endlessly about, according to the rhythm of the waves battering the ship."[5] Dabydeen's depiction of the slavehold as a gruesome resurrection scene echoes Herbert's anxiety regarding physical dismemberment. "Without benefit of the sacramental," the dead slave bodies are, like the woman "torn from her chains," doomed to wander within the slave ship at the mercy of the waves until their bodies are thrown overboard, only to dissolve and disintegrate further. Yet while the mentions of the resurrection and "the sacramental" demonstrate Dabydeen's engagement with Western culture and literature, the content and historical context of this scene reveal that he is reinflecting, not simply embracing, those traditions.

While poems such as Herbert's evince a concern over the relationship between the decaying body and the individual soul, this same concern was not extended to slaves who died during the voyages of the transatlantic slave trade. Between one and two million Africans died during the Middle Passage, and their bodies were thrown into the sea, "without benefit of the sacramental," with no memorials or tomb markers.[6] In addition, as Dabydeen notes in the preface to his 1994 poem "Turner," slaves who were sick or weak were frequently drowned so that the captain might claim their insurance value as "goods lost at sea."[7] If African bodies were understood to be simply goods that had lost their value, the sea's dismemberment mattered little. These bodies were presumed to have no eternal souls that would require their preservation.

While Dabydeen's language of Christian resurrection hearkens back to the Western literary preoccupation with the relationship between body and soul, his placing of this language in the hold of the slave ship, among bodies that were treated like soulless goods, challenges Western models, revealing their latent hypocrisies. The narrator of *A Harlot's Progress* describes the dismembered slave woman as the waves toss her around the ship: "Eventually when the ship lurched massively she was flung to the far end of the hold. She landed alongside her son and he recognized her even in her acephalous and fractured state. He yanked at his chains in a bid to embrace her. It was in such a bizarre manner that families were separated, then united, on board the slaveship."[8] Ironically the woman's physical dismemberment serves to reunite her with her son—to undo, if only momentarily, the dreadful separation wrought by the slave trade. Here the institution of slavery is revealed as a far more terrible dismemberer than the impersonal force of death; it separates families and tears apart human lives. Thus Dabydeen, while sharing with Herbert a concern over the deeper ramifications of bodily decay, a worry that "man is out of order hurled / Parceled out to all the world," emphasizes the fact that white Westerners separated families, destroyed cultures, and dismembered human bodies in pursuit of profit.[9] In the face of literary and religious anxieties about the inevitability of physical dissolution, Dabydeen creates a horrific scene of an unnecessary dismemberment, of the rampant and brutal destruction caused by human greed.

Though Dabydeen's work clearly interacts with the Western canon, the author has also emphasized the importance of responding to a Caribbean literary tradition. In an interview with Kevin Davey, Dabydeen emphasizes the need for young Caribbean authors to engage with their own tradition: "There is a younger generation of Caribbean writers who should be responding to and reworking these [Caribbean] masters . . . and avoiding an obsession with *The Tempest* and Conrad and canonical texts which have encapsulated us in way [*sic*] which are negative or brutish."[10] For this generation of Caribbean writers, the task of positioning their writing in relation to colonial history and discourses has been in some ways eased, in others complicated, by the relative success of the previous generation. Now, besides choosing to evade, embrace, ignore, or reinterpret the long shadow of the Western literary tradition, Caribbean writers must also consider their relationship with their own: with Frantz Fanon and the politics of negritude, with V. S. Naipaul's vast success and unapologetic Eurocentrism, with Jean Rhys's rewriting of the Western classic *Jane Eyre* from a West Indian perspective. For Dabydeen, the work of earlier Caribbean writers is both enabling and daunting.[11] When asked by Mark Stein about the influence of this earlier generation on its successors, he was quick to acknowledge the positive effects of the older writers' pioneering achievements: "The fact that they achieved meant that it was relatively easier for us to publish because there was already Derek Walcott, there was already

George Lamming, there was already Sam Selvon, there was especially V. S. Naipaul."[12]

Yet the stature of these literary ancestors can simultaneously intimidate young writers; in the same interview Dabydeen goes on to ask: "When you're following Walcott and when you're following Lamming, certainly when you're following Naipaul, how can you achieve excellence? . . . You had a sense that there was a body of writing to which you had a certain responsibility and which also presented a challenge."[13] Dabydeen's own writing takes this responsibility and challenge seriously, intertextually engaging with his predecessors' texts in ways that both affirm and complicate them.[14] His poem "Turner," though written in response to a European art object—J. M. W. Turner's painting *Slavers Throwing Overboard the Dead and the Dying—Typhoon Coming On*—also engages indirectly with a Caribbean precursor, Derek Walcott's *Omeros*.[15] In its wide-ranging depiction of the inhabitants of a St. Lucian fishing community, *Omeros* creates a sense of Caribbean cultural identity that is fluid and hybrid, grounded not in memory or history but in the "amnesiac Atlantic,"[16] whose transformation of the slave bodies drowned in it metaphorically frees an artistic space for "the new naming of things."[17] Where Walcott's drowned body is stable and regenerative, in "Turner" the bodies jettisoned from a slave ship float, dismembered and disintegrating, unable to recall their origins, yet doomed to dwell in the pain of their past. For Dabydeen, memory loss is involuntary and destructive, and the artist's role is complicated and unclear. Dabydeen's much darker poem thus illuminates the creative power of Walcott's vision of the drowned body and the Caribbean artist, while exposing both to questions about the fragmentation of all subjects.

Walcott's and Dabydeen's use of the sea as a creative site and enabling metaphor parallels the contemporaneous political and theoretical concern with fluidity expressed in a variety of poststructuralist discourses. In attempting to articulate the relationship between poststructuralist theory, identity politics, and poetic representation, the theorists Carole Boyce Davies, Stuart Hall, and Homi K. Bhabha have each grappled with the difficulty of constructing a politics based on difference—one that, in Hall's words, could "build those forms of solidarity and identification which make common struggle and resistance possible . . . without suppressing the real heterogeneity of interests and identities."[18] Such a construction depends on the simultaneous assertion and erasure of individual identities, as depicted by Bhabha's essay on Fanon. It must seek a common ground, "a generalized purpose of resistance to domination,"[19] while always questioning that space; recognizing that any sense of shared identity, one based on race, to use Hall's example, "Always appear[s] historically in articulation, in a formation, with other categories and divisions and [is] constantly crossed and recrossed by the categories of class, of gender, and of ethnicity."[20] As Bhabha writes, "The political must always pose as a problem, or a question, the *priority of the place from which it begins*, if its authority is not to become autocratic."[21]

Metaphorically, the impracticality of creating a productive structure that must continually question and shift its own foundations suggests the need for common ground that is not, in fact, ground at all, but is instead fluid, capable of constant change and flux without violent upheaval. As Elizabeth DeLoughrey perceptively observes in *Routes and Roots*, a study of Caribbean and Pacific island literature through the lens of the sea, the fluidity of the sea is a suggestive source for more flexible understandings of history, nationality, and politics: "Focusing on seascape rather than landscape as the fluid space of historical production allows us to complicate the nation-state, which encodes a rigid hierarchy of race, class, gender, religion, and ethnicity for its representative subjects. Because the surface of the ocean is unmarked by its human history and thus cannot be monumentalized in the tradition of colonial landscapes, a turn to the seas as history can produce an equalizing effect."[22] In searching for new, less rigid ways of imagining the nation and the postcolonial subject, postcolonial artists such as Walcott and Dabydeen have turned to the sea, finding inspiration both in its fluidity and in its resistance to the marks and monuments of human history.

For Walcott and Dabydeen, the sea encapsulates the theoretical potential of fluidity and flux, while simultaneously embodying a variety of inescapable historical resonances. On the one hand, it represents a powerful resistance to colonizing forces. The sea cannot be claimed or possessed in any real sense—it complicates human attempts to extend national borders beyond shorelines. On the other hand, the sea is a poignant reminder of the history of colonialism, saturated with memories of events such as the Middle Passage that leave no visible traces on the sea surface but litter the submarine world with the bodies of drowned slaves. In both *Omeros* and "Turner," the sea and the bodies in it symbolically suggest each of these nuances.

In Walcott's poem, as in "The Muse of History," the sea is most significant as a place that erases history, enabling the postcolonial artist to rename his world from a space where cultures and traditions converge. Dabydeen draws heavily on Walcott's concept of creative amnesia in his own work, frequently citing it as a useful way for the Caribbean artist to approach history. In an interview with Kwame Dawes, Dabydeen opposes England's memorials and statues to the almost history-less landscape of the Caribbean:

> So if you live in England where the English have a very powerful concrete (or stone/marble) sense of their histories and you as a Caribbean person come to a sense that your history is nebulous and shifting, it means that you have a tremendous capacity for a new kind of freedom . . . We are free, not because it was the British intention to make us free, but in a peculiar way we became free, we were freed of certain traditions, knowledges, and so on, and while we have sorrow about the loss of those, nevertheless, we are always on the threshold of originality.[23]

Like Walcott, Dabydeen recognizes that the painful histories of the Caribbean have the potential to paralyze artists, to freeze them in a literature of anger or despair. In an interview with Davey, Dabydeen cites Walcott's creative amnesia as a way to escape: "There is a desire for a kind of emptiness from which one could emerge creatively. Derek Walcott calls it 'creative amnesia.'"[24] Dabydeen is openly drawn to the freedom represented by Walcott's vision of the Caribbean artist as a figure unencumbered by the burden of the past, free to invent, rename, and to draw on any literary or artistic tradition openly.

Besides receiving frequent mentions in his interviews and critical work, creative amnesia plays an important role in Dabydeen's literary oeuvre. As critics have recognized, a driving force behind Walcott's emphasis on creative amnesia is his desire to write in traditional European poetic forms, to borrow from the Western canon, to engage with British literary figures, without being accused of mimicry or of pandering to white audiences. Dabydeen shares this desire, as his work continually engages with European intertexts, and it is in this guise that creative amnesia appears in his first novel, *The Intended* (1991). The semi-autobiographical novel tells the story of a Guyanese teenager growing up in London, tracing his journey from Guyana to South London to Oxford University. The narrator receives his first poetic commission when his landlord's sister, a Pakistani peasant woman, dies, and he is asked to compose her epitaph. Drawn to all things English, the narrator recognizes the role of tombstones and monuments in preserving English history, and hopes to earn his own place in history by his inscription: "I fancied that my own immortality was secured by the verse on her tombstone."[25] As he attempts to gather the woman's biographical details from his landlord, Mr. Ali, however, his poetic ambitions are thwarted by her unmemorable life: "Either death had blanked his memory or she was truly ordinary. Perhaps he did not care to remember. Still I persisted, seeking to uncover the slightest clue which would lead me to hidden bounties and inspire a treasury of words. But there was no landmark, no strangely lopsided rock, no scratchings in the soil which would suggest secret burials. Her life was as plain as the ground in which the village stood, an expanse of neatly tilled earth."[26] Where Englishness is signified by the "immortal" verse on the tombstone, Mr. Ali's unnamed sister is represented by a field of unmarked earth, its details and stories plowed under in the relentless cycle of agricultural life.

Faced with the inscrutability of the woman's history, the narrator sits down and attempts "to fabricate verse with an exotic flavor."[27] Despite his Indian roots, the narrator is at two removes from the woman's home in Pakistan: born in Guyana and raised in England, he cannot imagine her world except as a cliché of monsoons and man-eating tigers. His tiger, "its stripes burning bright in the forest of the night," is more indebted to William Blake than to the Indian subcontinent, and he wonders whether he will ever be able to "rival Conrad and other white writers when it came to jungle scenes."[28] The narrator's second attempt, a generalized elegy for the human condition, is not much better, and as he reads it to his friends he realizes it is "all wrong, even silly."[29] He pulls out Milton's "Lycidas" instead and begins to read it out loud, "as if to drown out the banality of what I had written."[30] His friend Shaz rejects the poem, deriding it as "old-fashioned white-people expression," inapplicable to a Pakistani peasant woman.[31] By contrast, his other friend Joseph, an uneducated but mystically insightful Rastafarian boy, is enchanted.[32] In response to Shaz's claim that "black people have to have their own words,"[33] Joseph retorts: "Lycidas dead and gone to a world where nowaday-things don't matter nothing, like white people against black people, like thieving and hustling and pimping and rioting, like slavery and all that kind of history. The man turn pure spirit, pure like flowing water, that's why it's all water talk, the theme thing is water. His body bathe and the spirit come out clean—clean and clear—not white or black but clear."[34] For Joseph, the "water talk" in "Lycidas" erases the world of "white people against black people," eradicating the notion that a certain kind of expression or experience is the sole property of one race. As in Walcott's "The Muse of History," here the erasures of the ocean, working on the submerged body, gesture toward the freedom of the poet to choose his or her own literary ancestors. Creative amnesia frees Joseph to find meaning and inspiration in "old-fashioned white-people expression," just as it frees Dabydeen to draw on both Milton and Walcott as literary models—this despite the provocative title of one of Dabydeen's essays, "On Not Being Milton."[35]

Critics have made much of Dabydeen's use of creative amnesia. Lars Eckstein describes how the narrator of *A Harlot's Progress* attempts to banish the "ghosts of the past" through "acts of *creative* forgetting."[36] Erik Falk, in a rather surprising moment of critical amnesia, writes of

"David Dabydeen's 'Creative Amnesia,'" relating the concept to Western sources, but cutting Walcott out of the picture entirely. Writing of "Turner," Falk claims that "on all levels, it may be argued, the poem is concerned with, and engaged in attempting, a 'creative amnesia.'"[37] While such statements are true on one level, they fail to recognize the ways in which Dabydeen's work complicates Walcott's version of creative amnesia. His poems and novels are haunted by the past; his narrators wounded by their inability to remember. Even as Dabydeen's oeuvre represents creative amnesia as tempting ideal, it remains skeptical, questioning both whether it is possible to forget and whether it is ultimately desirable. Briefly examining *A Harlot's Progress* before turning at greater length to "Turner" will demonstrate both Dabydeen's interest in creative amnesia and his rejection of Walcott's regenerative vision of forgetfulness.

Published in 1999, five years after "Turner," *A Harlot's Progress* is in many ways a novelistic retelling and expansion of the earlier poem, which Dabydeen called in a 1994 interview with Dawes, "The only thing that I have written so far which I feel comfortable with."[38] Set in London and narrated by an elderly former slave—alternately known as Mungo, Perseus, and Noah—the story is filtered through the lens of Mr. Pringle, a member of the Abolition Committee who wants to write down Mungo's story in the traditional slave narrative format.[39] He bribes the poverty-stricken Mungo with coins and food, withholding payment until the elderly man has produced a suitable number and type of memories. But Mungo is recalcitrant, aware that by telling his story to Mr. Pringle he is selling himself as surely as the titular harlot. The story he tells refuses to bind together in a coherent narrative, constantly contradicting itself and denying Mr. Pringle the narrative structure and familiar tropes he desires. In his meandering story, it is impossible to tell truth from fiction, memory from fantasy or nightmare.

Mungo's resistance to Mr. Pringle's narrative control can certainly be read as a victory for a Walcottian form of creative amnesia. Instead of remembering, Mungo forgets, and from that forgetfulness he creates a surprisingly rich tale that thwarts the designs of the white listener.

Mungo asserts creative control over memory; he boasts: "Memory don't bother me, that's why I don't tell Mr. Pringle anything. I can change memory, like I can change my posture, fling the blanket away, spring out of bed, dance a step or two of a cotillion, and babble into his blank pages the most lively of syllables."[40] As Eckstein has demonstrated, the revisionary power of Mungo's narrative is evident in the ways in which his tale challenges the prejudices of the novel's European intertext: William Hogarth's series of popular engravings, also titled *A Harlot's Progress*. Eckstein persuasively argues that Mungo's tale subverts the engravings, notably in the way that the Jewish doctor is changed from a racist caricature to a "messianic figure."[41] Such politically potent retellings highlight the power of creative amnesia to challenge the official narratives of the past, to complicate and trouble sanctioned canons and accepted ways of remembering.

At times in the novel, Mungo's forgetfulness and creative revision of the past seem not only subversive but potentially healing, even life-giving. Separated from any environment of memory, he nonetheless refuses to conform to the modern European fascination with places of memory; he will not be turned into a monument. Dabydeen highlights this resistance by noting that in Mr. Pringle's estimation, "Mungo is a ruined archive."[42] By refusing to release his memories, to allow them to be written down and cleaned up by Mr. Pringle, Mungo retains a part of himself in privacy: "In Mr. Pringle's society, expression is vaunted, and a book is deemed the highest achievement of man. But, for me, the book is no more than a splendidly adorned memorial and grave. To speak is to scoop out substance, to hollow out yourself, to make space within for your own burial, so I have kept in things as bulwarks against death. I have kept silence before the nib and gravedigger's spade of Mr. Pringle."[43] Resisting the modern Western tendency to replace living memory with a memorial or a grave, to thereby render it monolithic and certain, Mungo instead keeps things in. Creative amnesia becomes a means to keep Mungo whole, to avoid writing his own epitaph before he is dead.

Despite Mungo's recalcitrance about Mr. Pringle's memoirs, he does briefly toy with the idea of creating an archive. Tellingly, this archive is not singular and personal, but wide-ranging and multivocal. He saves newspaper clippings relating to the African presence in England, musing that "no such comprehensive compilation on the Negro exists in one place (though hidden under my bed in no more than two or three fish-boxes, such is the scantness of our history)."[44] Mungo imagines donating the archive to the Abolition Committee and earning a small measure of personal fame, a plaque bearing his name, though he cannot settle on which of his many names the collection should bear. Ultimately he decides against donating it, and instead of a monolithic memorial bearing one personal name, the collection becomes an access point to the communal, multifaceted experiences of African slaves, allowing Mungo to speak in a voice that is multiple, containing the voices of all of his fellow slaves: "In the faraway plantations of the West Indies, in the barracoons of the African coast, I have rebelled, stabbed, poisoned, raped, absconded, and sought escape by killing myself and my offsprings. In return I have been strangled, flogged to death, roasted alive, blown away and lynched. Truly I have made havoc in the hearts and minds of white people, compromising their civility, sharpening their Christian principles to breaking-point."[45] Even as Mungo recognizes the value of a kind of archival memory, he shows how history, like his own shifting narrative, can speak in multiple voices. The voices of his fellow slaves refuse to be consigned to a dead archive but instead retain the power to disturb and subvert, to reveal the lies embedded in the traditional narrative of Western "civilization" and its "Christian principles."

While critical consensus has generally confirmed a positive reading of Mungo's creative amnesia, there remains something troubling about his forgetfulness and about the ways in which he chooses to reimagine his own story. Readings like Falk's, which see Dabydeen's work as a straightforward vindication of creative amnesia, ignore or gloss over these nuances. One problem with such readings is their tendency to exaggerate Mungo's agency. In an understandable enthusiasm for the way in which Mungo's tale thwarts Mr. Pringle's purposes, critics have neglected the important fact that much of Mungo's forgetfulness is not of his own choosing. At times, Mungo does not care to remember or to share his memories, but more often it seems he simply cannot remember; his past is as inaccessible to him as it is to Mr. Pringle or the reader. "I remember nothing," Mungo notes, "but I pity Mr. Pringle's solicitousness, and I am in need of his charity, so I must create characters."[46] Neither Mungo's amnesia nor his creativity are deliberate choices; his forgetfulness is a scar left from the unspeakable traumas of the slave ship, and his creative storytelling is his only means of obtaining food and money. Despite Mr. Pringle's general unreliability as a narrator, it is worth taking him at least somewhat seriously when he suggests that Mungo may be experiencing "the initial stages of dementia, brought on by the tribulations of a Negro's life as much as by his advanced years."[47] Whether or not dementia is the correct diagnosis, Mungo's memory is certainly damaged; Sofia Muñoz-Valdivieso correctly observes that Mungo's "memories are fractured by the traumatic events he has experienced."[48] Celebrating Mungo's fractured and circular narrative wholly as an act of resistance neglects the fact that his repetitions, elisions, and confusions are also the marks of the great trauma he has experienced. To read Mungo as a whole, unscathed narrator fully in control of his story, mischievously delighting in manipulating Mr. Pringle, is to practice a dangerous kind of readerly amnesia.

Of course Walcott's concept of creative amnesia is itself intended as a deliberate response to trauma. In "The Muse of History," he writes that "in time the slave surrendered to amnesia"—that amnesia caused by the conditions of slavery—the violent removal of Africans from their homelands; the conditions of the slave ship; the deliberate separation of families, tribes, and language groups; and the renaming of slaves.[49] For Walcott, creative amnesia is the choice to embrace this forgetting, a refusal to excavate the painful past and dwell in it. At times, however, Walcott's sense of the powerful potential of creative amnesia for the Caribbean artist fails to account for the fracturing power of inherited trauma, the way in which a horrific event can haunt families or communities for generations. His assumption that the Caribbean artist can be free of the past is exhilarating and inspiring, but it can also occasionally seem naïve. A less forgiving reading of Walcott might even see his creative amnesia as a calculated move, designed to make his work appeal to the widest possible audience. By acknowledging the painful past of slavery but at the same time choosing to forget it, Walcott avoids alienating either the descendants of slaves or those of slave owners.[50] Dabydeen's portrayal of Mungo suggests his awareness of these problems and his discomfort with any idealized version of creative amnesia; even his deliberate act of forgetting and rewriting cannot erase the destructive effects of the past.

Besides the traumatic past that haunts Mungo's subversive storytelling techniques, other features in his narrative trouble any romanticized vision of creative amnesia. In Mungo's reimaginings of his past, he works to thwart the bland liberal expectations of Mr. Pringle, who wants a story that will prey on the sympathies of white Christian readers, moving them to support abolition. In his resistance to this formulaic narrative, Mungo creates stories that often come dangerously close to other, more insidious racist narratives about Africans and the slave trade. In seeking to undermine the standard abolitionist stories, Mungo occasionally slips into the kind of stories told by those who would deny that the atrocities of the slave trade ever occurred. Though it changes in his various retellings, Mungo's imagined Africa is often a savage, brutal place, where barren widows are raped, mutilated, and sent to the wilderness to die. In his resistance to the idyllic childhood in Africa often represented in the slave narrative, Mungo goes to the opposite extreme, uttering the rhetoric of those proponents of slavery who claimed that the savagery of Africans warranted their capture and removal to a more "civilized" world. The tension between these two versions of the past becomes evident as Mungo imagines a conversation with Manu, the village shaman. Mungo asks, "And what was our land but widows scavenging in the wilderness?"[51] Manu replies, "There were no such women, only in your imagining. Our tribe was content, each with each. There were ceremonies of love by which we lived, each with each and in communion with the gods of earth and sky."[52] Clearly both "memories"—the nightmare and the idyll—are simplified and fictionalized versions of the past, each dangerous in its own way.[53]

Mungo's invented recollections become even more troubling when he describes his relationship with the slave ship's captain, Thomas Thistlewood. Though he describes his sexual and physical abuse at the hands of the notoriously brutal captain, his descriptions are disturbingly couched in the language of love. Mungo rarely mentions the captain without a kind of anguished reverence, and defends him to Manu in the aforementioned conversation. When Manu claims that "Captain Thistlewood will try to kill you," Mungo retorts: "He has saved me and has baptized me, . . . and when he beats me, it is that I too must know the suffering of the Cross."[54] Mungo's feeling for Captain Thistlewood is bound up with the captain's role as the purveyor of Christianity, the English language, and a utopian pastoral vision of England that he presents to the boy through paintings and stories. Through Mungo's unsettling imagining of his rapist as teacher and lover, Dabydeen points to some of the problems with the concept of creative amnesia. Mungo is free to forget his past and to invent new stories to replace his memories. He cannot, however, escape the prison of language. In avoiding one kind of familiar narrative, he merely reverts to others. Through Mungo's disturbingly familiar retellings of the past, Dabydeen suggests that even if it were possible to forget the traumas of the past, the stories we could invent about the past would never truly be new, but always marked by stories that have been told before, with their prejudices and elisions. While Walcott's creative amnesia frees him to allude freely to whatever literary ancestor he chooses, for Dabydeen, allusions to Western stories can also function as insidious and inescapable traps.

Drawn to the suggestive potential of Walcott's creative amnesia, Dabydeen is simultaneously suspicious of the regenerative promise with which the older author invests the concept. In Walcott's privileging of the stable authorial voice, able to speak with confidence and rename the world, Dabydeen senses a dangerous fiction, one that fails to fully account for the still-damaging force of the traumatic events that caused "the amnesia of the slave," while also ignoring the tendency for the past to haunt the present through language and familiar narrative tropes. This unease is most pronounced in "Turner," in which Dabydeen's depiction of the disintegrating body drowned in the sea allows him to question the stability of individual identity and the extent to which anyone's memory is really his or her own. Seen next to the drowned body as coral reef in *Omeros*, Dabydeen's disintegrating bodies highlight the ways in which Walcott's work often challenges its own fluidity and heterogeneity in order to foreground the creativity of the individual artist, thus making his work susceptible to an "authority" that may "become autocratic."[55] Unlike *Omeros*, "Turner" offers little hope for a true creative amnesia; its narrator is haunted and fractured by the past even as he struggles to reinvent it.

In some ways, Dabydeen's depictions in "Turner" of the sea and the bodies in it adhere quite closely to Walcott's figuration of the ocean as the site for a new formation of Caribbean identity—a site whose amnesia empowers the artist to undertake an imaginative project of re-creation. Dabydeen clearly views Walcott's seascapes as a positive influence on his own; in an interview with Mark Stein, Dabydeen asks admiringly: "I mean how can you write the sea in the way that Walcott writes it? . . . When you're following Walcott . . . how can you achieve excellence?"[56] In an earlier interview with Heike Härting and Tobias Döring, Dabydeen expressly states his appreciation of Walcott's depiction of the fluid, hybrid Caribbean character: "I come back to Walcott's statement that if you look for Caribbean history, look for it in the pages of the sea. This means that the Caribbean character has been subjected to endless transformations, so that it is in a constant state of flux."[57] Like Walcott, Dabydeen values the transformative flux of the sea, its power to erase histories and thus make room for new stories. His narrator, the drowning slave visible at the bottom of Turner's painting, longs to create a new story for the stillborn child thrown overboard from a passing ship:

> I wanted to teach it
> A redemptive song, fashion new descriptions
> Of things, new colours fountaining out of form.
> I wanted to begin anew in the sea.[58]

Like Walcott, Dabydeen here depicts the sea as a place to "begin anew," to redeem the past through creative expression.

In the initial lines of "Turner," it seems as though Dabydeen, in his appreciation for Walcott's reimagining of Caribbean cultural identity, may likewise accept his depiction of the artist figure as racially hybrid but otherwise unitary, able to speak with authority from a secure position of male privilege. The poem's first image is of a woman aboard a slave ship giving birth to a stillborn child:

> Stillborn from all the signs. First a woman sobs
> Above the creak of timbers and the cleaving
> Of the sea, sobs from the depths of true
> Hurt and grief, as you will never hear
> But from a woman giving birth, belly
> Blown and flapping loose and torn like sails,
> Rough sailors' hands jerking and tugging
> At ropes of veins, to no avail. Blood vessels
> Burst asunder, all below-deck are drowned.[59]

The metaphorical linking of the woman's body and the ship would seem generally reminiscent of Walcott's persistent feminization of seascapes, even without the presence in *Omeros* of a more directly similar passage, in which Achille imagines the pregnant Helen in nautical terms:

> The sail of her bellying stomach seemed to him
> to bear not only the curved child sailing in her
> but Hector's mound, and her hoarse, labouring rhythm
> was a delivering wave.[60]

Despite this similarity, Dabydeen's poem sets up the *mer/mère* connection so prevalent in *Omeros* in order to challenge it, allowing the sea to erode the constructions of gender and sexuality that give Walcott's narrator his authorial stability.

While Walcott's author figures are often racially hybrid and physically wounded, their identities are more or less fixed, their gender certain and unshifting. By contrast, Dabydeen sets up race and gender as continua along which each of the characters move; their identities not fixed but fluid. Certainly it is worth pointing out that Dabydeen has not been an exemplary feminist in contrast to Walcott's old-fashioned chauvinism. One has only to browse through Dabydeen's earlier collections of poetry, *Slave Song* and *Coolie Odyssey*, to note a troubling tendency to reduce women to one of two types. The first is the unapproachable, unfathomable object of sexual desire, almost always a white woman, seen in "Caliban" or "The Canecutters' Song," who often becomes the target of a rape fantasy or a sexual epithet. The second is the elderly mother, hardworking but crude and shrewish, of "Day's End," whose complaint about her daughter's promiscuity is described as "one long wife-wailing and a hollering."[61] Where Walcott's women often lack voices or artistic agency, many of Dabydeen's women represent even more dangerous stereotypes. Benita Parry writes perceptively of Dabydeen's early poems that their portrayals of women simply reinforce the lies that justify male sexual violence against women: "As the cut, chop, hack and stab of 'the savage ceremony of cane' takes possession of the imagination of male canecutter and slave, the rage against their condition is spent in fantasies of abusing and mutilating the white woman. This implicates the poems in a discourse shared by the master's culture and beyond, one that represents rape as what woman wants."[62] This troubling tendency continues to haunt Dabydeen's more recent work. In his 2008 novel, *Molly and the Muslim Stick*, the protagonist, while still a young teenager, is repeatedly raped by her father, who then forces her into prostitution, selling her body to his friends and clients while he looks on. Though she is eventually driven mad, presumably by this abuse, she is mostly portrayed as enjoying these rapes, calling her rapists her "pals."[63]

Dabydeen defends these passages of extreme sexual violence as his attempt to reveal that slavery was an erotic undertaking as well as an economic one. In his essay "*On Not Being Milton*: Nigger Talk in England Today," Dabydeen describes his collection *Slave Song* as a group of poems "dealing with the Romance of the Cane, meaning the perverse eroticism of black labor and the fantasy of domination, bondage, and sado-masochism."[64] He goes on to argue that "the British Empire . . . was as much a pornographic as an economic project."[65] This interest in what Wilson Harris calls "the pornography of Empire" is one that has gained recent attention among postcolonial and British writers alike; Elizabeth Kuti's 2005 play, *The Sugar Wife*, serves as a clear example.[66]

In exploring the erotic underpinnings of the colonial enterprise, Dabydeen often uses sexual violence as a metaphor for colonial violence. As the captain of the slave ship in "Turner" rapes the young boys aboard his ship, he simultaneously teaches them the English language:

> Each night
> Aboard ship he gave selflessly the nipple
> Of his tongue until we learnt to say profitably
> In his own language, *we desire you, we love*
> *You, we forgive you.* He whispered eloquently
> Into our ears even as we wriggled beneath him,
> Breathless with pain, wanting to remove his hook
> Implanted in our flesh.[67]

Dabydeen has written that rape is a paradox—a destructive, violent act that can potentially result in new life.[68] In the context of slavery, this paradox becomes even more complex as rape becomes a kind of economic transaction; if a sailor rapes a slave woman aboard ship and she becomes pregnant, the value of the ship's cargo increases. In *A Harlot's Progress*, the narrator recounts of the slave ship: "Rape was allowed, not only for necessary manly recreation, nor because it calmed their craving for a shore, but because it promised to increase the stock of slaves."[69] Dabydeen's 1987 academic study, *Hogarth's Blacks: Images of Blacks in Eighteenth Century English Art*, recounts similarly, "The female slaves were 'breeder women'; the slave owner had his fun of them secure in the knowledge that his sexual recreation was profitable since it led to an increase in the stock of slaves."[70] Seen in this light, Dabydeen's tendency to portray the victims of sexual violence enjoying or being thankful for their exploitation can be viewed more as a comment on colonialism than a statement on gender relations. Imperialism was often justified under the guise of giving: the colonizers claiming to bring civilization, government, religion, education, language, health care, and advanced technology to the "savage" or "primitive" peoples whose lands they stole. In the metaphor of the rape that brings new life, Dabydeen explores the unique psychological position of many postcolonial peoples who have adopted—even embraced—the language and culture of the very Europeans who destroyed their own native languages and cultures.

In spite of his tendency to sensationally dwell on sexual violence, Dabydeen's portrayal of gender is unquestionably more complex than Walcott's. In "Turner," Dabydeen allows his characters to slide between genders and races, destabilizing the authorial voice and flagging the flexibility and uncertainty of individual identity. Where the sea's amnesia allows Walcott's artists to speak with authority, to rename the world from a secure position of male power and privilege, the sea's disintegrating power troubles Dabydeen's artist figures, erasing the certainties of race and gender.

In the previously cited interview with Härting and Döring, Dabydeen expresses his desire to write "the absence of the body," to complicate individual identity by making its boundaries porous or invisible, a goal that he says can be accomplished by poetically placing bodies in the sea: "What you really want to do now is not to write the body—because to write the body is to write those grievances—but to write the absence of the body. That is why one creates ghostly figures, figures that want to disappear, figures that aren't actually born. Now you place them in the sea, so you don't need to give them a land. You are trying to escape from landscape, body, history, by having a kind of unborn foetus in the sea."[71]

Dabydeen's poetic move toward an elusive invisibility is one that Bhabha has pointed to in postcolonial writing as evidence of the overlapping of poststructuralist theories of subjectivity with the postcolonial experience. Briefly examining Bhabha's essay on Fanon before turning back to Dabydeen's work suggests how "Turner" stages the intersection between a poststructuralist fragmented subject and Caribbean cultural identity as formulated by Walcott.

Bhabha's work on Fanon has been widely criticized for its imposition of poststructuralist ideology on Fanon and on the broad swath of postcolonial writing. As Neil Lazarus explains, Bhabha and those who have followed him portray Fanon as "a post-structuralist *avant la lettre*" and an opponent of "all notions of fixed identity and all forms of identitarian politics—including those organized under the banners of 'race' and class and nation."[72] To anyone familiar with Fanon's life and passionate commitment to anti-colonial and nationalist causes, this representation rings patently false. If Bhabha's essay is taken less as a commentary on the historical figure of Fanon and more as a general comment on the postcolonial condition, it has some important insights to offer but also some significant distortions and misrepresentations. As Lazarus argues, Bhabha assumes that there is a unitary condition of postcoloniality that all postcolonial authors write from, and that they all embrace fragmentation, hybridity, and negation as tools to express that condition. Simply examining the works of Synge and Walcott demonstrates that Bhabha's conclusions are not true of all postcolonial authors. Importantly, as Lazarus writes, "They do not fail to write from this perspective by omission or default, but on the basis of the strictest conviction. Put baldly, their assumptions about identity and community and cultural value and politics are quite different" from Bhabha's.[73] For the two younger authors in this study, however, there is some value to be gleaned from Bhabha's essay. In particular, Dabydeen's work is heavily impacted by the poststructuralist ideas of fragmentation and hybridity. While expressing his skepticism of academia and theory, in an interview with Abigail Ward, Dabydeen admits to using both to achieve his own ends: "You can chuckle, not maliciously, about your academic past and at a type of pretentiousness; getting up to read Foucault, Derrida, and Lacan, and trying to impress your students with your knowledge of theory, when deep down you really did not care a damn, but you had to do it to inspire them to study and write their essays."[74] He goes on to say, "I was certainly an Anancy character," surviving on his "wits," while pretending to be something he wasn't.[75] This slippery, tongue-in-cheek use of poststructuralism pervades Dabydeen's work, clearly echoing the disruptive moves of the postcolonial artist as described by Bhabha.

Bhabha's essay interprets Fanon as revealing the ways in which colonial and postcolonial experience may entail the fragmentation of both black and white subjects. Fanon describes how the white gaze dismembers the black body—an act that, Bhabha argues, in the ambivalent mixture of alienation and desire involved in confronting the Other, reveals the instability of the white body: "The white man's eyes break up the black man's body and in that act of epistemic violence its own frame of reference is transgressed, its field of vision disturbed."[76] By creating images of their own bodies as invisible, fading, or otherwise elusive, postcolonial artists similarly challenge any conception the reader may have of a unitary or bounded selfhood: "What these repeated negations of identity dramatize . . . is the impossibility of claiming an origin for the Self (or Other) within a tradition of representation that conceives of identity as the satisfaction of a totalizing, plentitudinous object of vision. By disrupting the stability of the ego, expressed in the equivalence between image and identity, the secret art of invisibleness of which the migrant poet speaks changes the very terms of our recognition of the person."[77] Bhabha's description of these disruptions of subjectivity provides an instructive model for reading Dabydeen's writing, after Walcott, of the body in the sea. As Dabydeen's sea dismembers and dissolves the bodies in it, it refuses to provide a "totalizing, plentitudinous object of vision," and so dramatizes the changing "terms of our recognition of the person."

The depiction of black bodies in "Turner" cannot be separated from the white gaze. By selecting the fragments of black bodies barely visible at the bottom of Turner's painting as the speakers of his poem, Dabydeen chooses characters who are refracted and dismembered through the gaze of the white artist. Painted following the abolition of the slave trade in the British colonies, *Slavers* depicts a slave ship jettisoning its human cargo into the sea, most likely in order to claim the insurance value of sick and dying slaves as goods lost at sea during the oncoming storm.[78] Despite this unequivocal choice of subject material, Turner's methods and the responses of white museumgoers have made the painting the center of much debate.[79] The majority of the canvas is taken up with the dramatic sea and sky, with the slaves whose murder is ostensibly being condemned confined to the bottom third, away from the twin focal points of the blindingly white sun and the ghostly ship. The few visible slave bodies are disembodied fragments: an arm here, a leg there, the suggestion of a head or a hand sinking beneath the waves. Surrounded by the eyes and gaping mouths of fish, they seem less than human, somehow a fitting part of the bizarre natural scene.

John Ruskin, who owned *Slavers*, famously devoted a long section of his *Modern Painters* to a description of its sea, which he called "the noblest sea that Turner has ever painted."[80] Conspicuously absent, however, from Ruskin's analysis, is any direct mention of the slave bodies submerged in this "noble sea"; the only acknowledgment of the subject of the painting occurs in a terse footnote: "She is a slaver, throwing her slaves overboard. The near sea is encumbered with corpses."[81] Ruskin's pointed dismissal of the black bodies that make Turner's painting so poignant has been seen as emblematic of the white viewer's refusal to read race as a central element of English culture and history. Paul Gilroy writes that *Slavers* illustrates "the extent to which race has been tacitly erased from discussion of English culture."[82] Dabydeen's poem, by giving voice to the black bodies in Turner's painting, intervenes in this discussion, resisting the erasure of race while acknowledging the destructive effects of the white gaze on his poem's speakers.

In his preface to "Turner," Dabydeen writes of its two main "characters"—the floating head of the male slave in Turner's painting, who narrates the poem, and the stillborn child of the white captain and

Slave Ship (Slavers Throwing Overboard the Dead and Dying, Typhoon Coming On). 1840. By: Joseph Mallord William Turner, English, 1775–1851. Oil on canvas. 90.8 × 122.6 cm (35 ¾ × 48 ¼ in.). Henry Lillie Pierce Fund. 99.22. Photograph © 2020 Museum of Fine Arts, Boston.

the black slave woman tossed from the slave ship: "Neither can escape Turner's representation of them as exotic and sublime victims. Neither can describe themselves anew but are indelibly stained by Turner's language and imagery."[83] The speaker, floating in the sea, longs to undertake a Walcottian project of "naming"; he writes, when first encountering the child's floating corpse:

> Such was my bounty
> Delivered so unexpectedly that at first
> I could not believe this miracle of fate,
> This longed-for gift of motherhood.
> What was deemed mere food for sharks will become
> My fable. I named it Turner
> As I have given fresh names to birds and fish
> And humankind, all things living but unknown,
> Dimly recalled, or dead.[84]

While Dabydeen's enthusiasm to name nature clearly echoes Walcott's enthusiasm for the Adamic artist, his choice of a name for the child challenges his claim to be giving "fresh names" to humankind. "Turner" is a Eurocentric and patrilineal choice in two senses, the name of both the child's white artistic creator and his white biological father, the captain of the slave ship.[85] Yet the narrator attempts to invent an African childhood for the stillborn child, thereby foregrounding its hybridity and refiguring the white, masculine name. The speaker's attempts to name the child and give it a new story turn on him, however, as the child's voice echoes back and perversely names the speaker. The only word the child speaks in answer to the narrator's fabricated memories of Africa is *nigger*, effectively and violently condensing the search for origin and identity into a single epithet, reminder of the reductive, dismembering white gaze.[86]

As this reciprocal exchange of names, repeated several times throughout "Turner," demonstrates, the boundaries between Self and Other in the poem are complex, their permeability making any notion of a unified authorial identity deeply problematic. Any act of naming as an attempted assertion of power, whether by black or white beholders, is troubled by the extent to which names reveal not only the properties of the object but the preoccupations of the subject. Thus naming, which can be an insidiously violent form of colonialism, simultaneously endangers the speaker, whose fears of and desires for the Other the names inadvertently expose. "Turner" enacts this process through the progression in the narrator's reaction each of the five times the stillborn child speaks.

The first time the infant speaks its sole epithet, the narrator treats it as a straightforward recognition of his own racial identity, which remains visible beneath the sea's bleaching effects: "'Nigger!' it cried, seeing / Through the sea's disguise as only children can."[87] Despite the offensive nature of the "name" chosen, the narrator portrays this identification as fairly straightforward, an attempt on the child's part to recognize and verbally express some quality in the Other. Naming is, in this case, linked to "seeing," to visually distinguishing the Other as a unique, bounded being, separate and different from oneself.

By the second such encounter, however, the naming has become more sinister, a thinly disguised assertion of power and access to knowledge: "'Nigger,' it cries, naming me from some hoard / Of superior knowledge, its tongue a viper's nest / Guarding a lore buried by priests, philosophers."[88] Here the speaker sees the epithet as evidence of the child aligning itself with its white half, taking on the language and the lore of the colonizer in order to distance itself from blackness and slavery. The infant speaks from residual cultural or linguistic memory, the kind of memory that troubles any idealized version of creative amnesia.

Although the narrator does not explicitly make the connection, this recognition of the child's complicity in the colonial project entails a similar recognition of his own adoption of Western literary language, tradition, and forms to tell his supposedly new story. Thus while the child's adoption of a nasty racial slur indicates that it is "guarding a lore buried by priests, philosophers, / Fugitives," the narrator similarly lays claim to that lore

> which I will still ransack
> For pearls and coral beads to drape around
> Its body, covering the sores that the sea
> Bubbles on its skin.[89]

Despite being drowned and forgotten in the sea, neither the narrator nor the child (nor, the implication is, Dabydeen himself) can forget the language and stories that have been imposed on them by colonialism. This recognition seems to double as Dabydeen's tacit allusion to his decision to write "Turner" in standard English, using mostly pentameter, while many of his other poems are written in a Guyanese creole. Dabydeen underscores this point by referencing in these lines Ariel's famous song from *The Tempest*: "Full fathom five thy father lies; / Of his bones are coral made; / Those are pearls that were his eyes."[90] Dabydeen's dissolving bodies may be free of the monuments and markings of Western tradition, but their minds have been colonized in profound and inescapable ways.

Dabydeen suggests this reading in an interview with Dawes in which he compares himself to the discarded infant in "Turner": "I feel like the stillborn child in 'Turner,' definitely. Or even worse than that, I feel like an abortion, messy and bloody and unborn, and that's partly because of a racism, where other people are trying to reduce you to nothing all the time and erase everything that you brought with you, or else they remind you of what you could have brought with you had they not taken it away."[91] Here forgetfulness is not a hopeful gateway to a new kind of creativity but an inescapable wound of the past, a mark of all that has been taken away from the colonized. Unable to avoid the reductive gaze of racism, Dabydeen mourns the loss of languages and stories that have led him to "ransack" the language and lore of the colonizer.

In "Turner," the recognition that both the child and the narrator are relying on the tools of European language to name each other, albeit with what seem like markedly different intentions, leads, a few lines later, to the realization that any attempt to name the Other entails an act of self-revelation:

> "Nigger,"
> It cries, sensing its own deformity.
> I look into its eyes to see my own coves,
> My skin pitted and gathered like waves of sand.
> I have become the sea's craft and will so shape
> This creature's bone and cell and word beyond
> Memory of obscene human form, but instead
> It made me heed my distress at being
> Human and alive, its anger at my
> Coaxing it awake.[92]

The child's name for the speaker is a mark of "its own deformity." Similarly, the speaker's authorial desire to shape words and stories reveals the way in which the sea has altered his own body and sense of identity. As aspiring author, he is not just shaper but shaped, unable to escape a body that has been penetrated and deformed by the sea.

This passage, in which the narrator becomes aware of "my own coves, / my skin pitted and gathered like waves of sand," provides an important contrast to *Omeros*, in which the body described in similar marine terms belongs to the woman lying "calm as a port" under the male author.[93] In "Turner," the sea, besides challenging unified understandings of race, is also a site for a kind of gender "hybridity." Jana Gohrisch's statement that "Turner" "deals neither with hybridity nor with issues of gender" seems unnecessarily dismissive.[94] Whether or not Dabydeen's explorations of gender are seen as positive or helpful, there is no question that they permeate "Turner."

The infant is deliberately left androgynous, referred to only as "it." For most of the poem, however, the sea's distortions of the gendered body do not result in an androgynous voice or vision but rather one in which any assertion of gendered identity is immediately suspect and often quickly reversed. The speaker is male, yet his ideas of gender are complicated by the sea, so that his attitude toward the stillborn child seems alternately maternal, paternal, and pedophilic. Nor can the speaker's authorial attempts be linked exclusively to either gender. At one moment, he links authorship to the female body and the act of breastfeeding, asking: "Shall I suckle / It on tales of resurrected folk"?[95] Later, his attempt to "teach it / A redemptive song" is linked to the phallus, as the child resists his advances with its characteristic response: "'Nigger,' it cries, loosening from the hook / Of my desire, drifting away from / My body of lies."[96] "Turner" alternately attributes authorial desire to the male and the female body, thereby locating the act of writing in a fluid space where gender identifications are neither easy nor straightforward. Authorship is at one moment linked to the comforting, nourishing act of suckling—the next to an image of violent male desire. It would certainly be possible to read Dabydeen's use of maternal images for authorship as simply forming another link in a long chain of male authors who appropriate maternal language to naturalize their artistic creativity. In fact, part of the fascinating complexity of "Turner" lies in the fact that this reading remains present even to the reader who suspects that something more intriguing may be going on. The poem reveals its own complicity, its unavoidable tainting by thousands of years of patriarchy.

Yet even as it discloses its own patriarchal authorial moves, "Turner" refuses to allow gender to become a stable binary, to allow the language of one gender to occupy a position of privilege. The contrasting metaphors of authorship, the male image a depiction of authorship as sexual exploitation, may seem at first glance to privilege the view of authorship as breastfeeding. Yet Dabydeen complicates the issue by linking the suckling image to "tales of resurrected folk." This phrase recalls the beginning lines of "Coolie Odyssey," a poem deeply suspicious of the Barbarian poetry movement exemplified by Seamus Heaney:

> Now that the peasantry is in vogue,
> Poetry bubbles from peat bogs,
> People strain for the old folk's fatal gobs
> Coughed up in grates North or North East
> 'Tween bouts of living dialect[97]

"Coolie Odyssey" ironically observes how images of folk cultures are framed, sanitized, and sold to "congregations of the educated," who greet the poems rife with images of slavery and torture with polite applause, "Fluttering from their white hands / like so many messy table napkins"[98] In this context, the image of authorship as suckling becomes suspect, a suggestion that postcolonial authors too often pander to the tastes of the white and the educated. Thus gendered images in "Turner" are always complex; as the language of one gender seems to be privileged, it is simultaneously undercut.

This slippery sense of gender extends equally to the poem's depiction of the sea and the drowned body. The sea penetrates all of the human bodies in it, whatever their original race or gender. Referring to Turner's painting *Fire on Board*, in which a shipwreck fills the stormy sea with drowning women and children, this time mostly white, the narrator describes the sea's effects on the bodies of the women:

> The sea decorates, violates.
> Limbs break off, crabs roost between their breasts
> Feeding. The sea strips them clean. I am ashamed
> To look upon the nakedness of my mothers.[99]

Though this description seems to depict the female body as particularly vulnerable, the sea has the same effect on the male body; the narrator writes that it has "painted me gaudy, dabs of ebony / . . . I have become the sea's whore, / Yielding."[100] Although it could perhaps correctly be remarked here that *whore* is traditionally a feminine word, and that the speaker simply feminizes his body whenever he wishes to express vulnerability, the poem's deliberate emphasis on the sexual exploitation of boys seems to underscore the vulnerability of all human bodies. Yet this focus on the sea's penetration is balanced by a more Walcottian attention to its maternal qualities: "The sea / Has delivered a child sought from the moon in years / Of courtship."[101] While the sea "decorates" and "violates" the bodies in it, it also surrounds and cradles them, its gender simultaneously inescapable and uncertain.

Situated in this realm of constantly sliding gender, the patriarchal maneuvers in the narrator's stories of an African childhood are revealed as part of his desire for a unified sense of identity, a clear and uncomplicated story of the past. He imagines two sisters, emphasizing his ability to "name" them and "endow" them with qualities and histories.[102] By foregrounding this myth of a male authorial subjectivity, able to poetically create and control female objects, "Turner" highlights the connection between such a myth and a nostalgic longing for a unified self. Thus the authorial voice that "creates" his childhood and two sisters is directly implicated in the peevish reactions of his younger self to his sisters' meddling:

> Girls are stupid, they know only how to wash
> And cook, my father will marry them off
> Soon, two goats each for bride-price. That will teach
> Them not to tamper with my things and thieve.[103]

By layering a childish reaction to gender difference with the more powerful voice of culturally enforced patriarchy and the masculine voice of the author, "Turner" here powerfully encapsulates the dangers inherent in any binary understanding of Self and Other, while also not denying the nostalgic allure of such constructions. In his essay on Fanon, Bhabha describes postcolonial art as a particular threat to unitary conceptions of subjectivity. He argues that the poems he quotes enact a "doubleness or splitting of the subject" indicated by their simultaneous assertion and erasure of identity and "articulated in those iterative instances that simultaneously mark the possibility and impossibility of identity, presence through absence."[104] Dabydeen's poem attempts to stage precisely these paradoxes through its placement of human bodies in a sea that permeates their boundaries, revealing their interconnectedness and allowing their gender and racial identifications to cross and recross.

Dabydeen's marking of "the possibility and impossibility of identity, presence through absence" is perhaps clearest in the poem's final lines, the last "naming" encounter between the narrator and the child:

> "Nigger"
> It cries, naming itself, naming the gods,

The earth and its globe of stars. It dips
Below the surface, frantically it tries to die,
To leave me beadless, nothing and a slave
to nothingness, to the white enfolding
Wings of Turner brooding over my body,
Stopping my mouth, drowning me in the yolk
Of myself. There is no mother, family . . .
No savannah, moon, gods, magicians
To heal or curse, harvests, ceremonies,
No men to plough, corn to fatten their herds,
No stars, no land, no words, no community,
No mother.[105]

The string of negations is at least partially a dark and agonized riposte to Walcott's too-positive vision of creative amnesia. Amnesia here is revealed as a painful and gaping wound, separating the narrator from any true knowledge of himself or his origins. Dabydeen has called "Turner" "a great howl of pessimism about the inability to recover anything meaningful from the past."[106] The "howl" climaxes in this final statement of loss, losses which can never fully be forgotten or redeemed.

Despite the undeniable pain of these last lines, the cries of "no stars, no land, no words, no community" nonetheless enact a reverse kind of naming. Thus "Turner" powerfully stages a "presence through absence." Döring writes of these final lines that they both create and erase: "The paradoxical effect of such a strategy arises from the fact that it must always name what, at the same time, it tries to negate. For the negative in language cannot erase without also creating something to erase; it [*sic*] doing so it gives life to what it tries to kill."[107] This elusiveness, this refusal to either claim an origin and erect a unitary self—or, conversely, to allow the poem to descend into linguistic fragmentation to match the fragmented self—both holds and confuses the reader's gaze. It seems to maintain the possibilities of artistic creativity in its final negations, while revealing the danger and ultimate impossibility of a unified authorial subject. In so doing, it points out the fragmentation of all subjects—black or white, female or male—and the extent to which all such identifications are constantly slipping and crossing. Simultaneously, it reveals the real complexity and difficulty of any attempt at creative amnesia. Neither amnesia nor memory are possible in "Turner"; the speaker is haunted by the traumas of the past even as he cannot access his own memories consciously.

Even as Dabydeen's speakers emphasize the instability of human identity, his poetry refuses to descend fully into fragmentation. Later poetic treatments of the *Zong*—such as M. NourbeSe Philip's *Zong!* or Douglas Kearney's "Swimchant for Nigger Mer-Folk (An Aquaboogie Set in Lapis)"—take fragmentation a step further by deconstructing language and poetic form. Kearney uses the layout of "Swimchant for Nigger Mer-Folk" to mirror the ship, the water, and the downward movement of the sinking bodies. Yet intriguingly, he rejects the idea of the sea's amnesia. Though the refrain "can't remember; c'ant remember," appears twice in the short poem, "Swimchant for Nigger Mer-Folk" also twice emphasizes the blood stains on the sea that will never wash out, once in a tragicomic note from "Thee Management": "Attention: Nigger mermaids, mermen & merninnies chained like hooked & sinked sardinnies:/ Do not bleed in the sea. The stains won't wash out. We ain't'nt responsible for your mess."[108] Philip's book-length poem *Zong!* uses the text of the *Zong* legal case *Gregson v. Gilbert*: cutting; reorganizing; even fading, erasing, and overlapping the words to create her poem. She writes, "I mutilate the text as the fabric of African life and the lives of these men, women and children were mutilated,"[109] emphasizing the appropriateness of her method to the subject material, "The poems resist my attempts at meaning or coherence and, at times, I too approach the irrationality and confusion, if not madness . . . of a system that could enable, encourage even, a man to drown 150 people as a way to maximize profits."[110] In contrast to Philips and Kearney, Dabydeen keeps language and poetic form mostly intact, while deconstructing memory and individual identity.

Critics have been quick to accept Dabydeen's claim that, as a writer, he is more interested in aesthetics than ethics. Indeed, many elements in his work seem ethically problematic: notably his penchant for portraying sexual violence and his tendency to render suffering in lush, eroticized tones. Eckstein notes that Dabydeen does not share "Adorno's ethical scruples about the forbidden consequences of making 'sense' of the suffering by rendering it accessible to the 'senses,'"[111] adding that "Dabydeen's poetics of memory is, if anything, provocative, given the discussion . . . of what is possible in writing about inhumanity and suffering."[112] Dabydeen insists on unrestricted imaginative access to the past, on his artistic right to represent whatever he wants in any way he sees fit; Eckstein cites Dabydeen's claim that for any event "you can remember it in a different way, even though it never happened like that. You can remember its potential for happening like something else."[113] This refusal to tread carefully on the great traumas of history understandably makes readers and critics uneasy, and makes many of Dabydeen's novels and poems almost physically uncomfortable to read.

Yet Dabydeen's "politics of memory" is not without its own ethical stance. Recognizing, and gesturing toward, the healing power of Walcott's "creative amnesia" as an enabling goal for the Caribbean writer, he nonetheless resists the temptation to set himself up as a stable authorial voice, outside history. Dabydeen's speakers reveal their brokenness, the ways in which they are fragmented by the past and cannot escape its haunting. They yearn for the kind of amnesia that would allow them to create new, hopeful stories, but more often find themselves dealing with the kind of amnesia that is not a choice, the crippling amnesia left in the wake of colonialism:

> I wanted to begin anew in the sea
> But the child would not bear the future
> Nor its inventions, and my face was rooted
> In the ground of memory, a ground stampeded
> By herds of foreign men who swallow all its fruit
> And leave a trail of dung for flies

To colonise; a tongueless earth, bereft
Of song except for the idiot witter
Of wind through a dead wood. "Nigger."[114]

The speaker here recognizes that, because of the "foreign men" who have rendered his homeland "tongueless," he cannot remember. Yet he is simultaneously imprisoned by memory, "Rooted / In the ground of memory," aware that his mind and his words have been tainted by the hiss of prejudice and hatred that lurks behind the language and stories he has been taught.

Stef Craps sees in these kinds of moments a unique ethical stance, one that resonates with Derrida's concept of mid-mourning; she writes of "Turner" and D'Aguiar's novel *Feeding the Ghosts*: "Dabydeen's poem and D'Aguiar's novel both resist the temptation to leave the reader with the sense that the story has been told, consigned to the past; that it has been taken care of and can therefore now be forgotten. Instead of clearing away the dead, they permit this traumatic history to live on as a haunting, troubling foreign element within the present."[115] "Turner" neither dwells in the past nor escapes it; its narrator reaches toward the future and its new stories even as he is irremediably fragmented by the traumas of the past. Craps goes on to argue that both Dabydeen and D'Aguiar refuse to separate the past and the present, demonstrating in their work how the two are interwoven: "Their works conjure the ghosts of victims of racial violence without, ultimately, conjuring them away in the name of a supposedly redeemed present, free from the burdens of the past. Rather than affirm a clear distinction between the past and the present, they demonstrate how those two are imbricated in one another, as the past continues to structure the present."[116] This refusal to conjure away the pain of the past even while recognizing, with Walcott, that amnesia is the unique burden and gift of the Caribbean writer, forms Dabydeen's ethical response to the problem of memory. His characters yearn both for forgetfulness and for memory; unable to fully attain either, they instead reveal their own fragmentation. If Synge uses the drowned body to position the artist as cultural mourner and Walcott embraces the creative amnesia of the Atlantic, Dabydeen presents a more complicated vision of drowning and its relationship to memory. In his work, the trope of the drowned body reveals the artist's ultimate lack of control. Desiring forgetfulness, the artist confronts the gendered and racialized violence of the past (and the present). Desiring memory, the artist finds only elusive hints, wavering between the nightmare and the idyll.

5

The Ghostly Body

Gender and Memory in Marina Carr's The Mai *and* Portia Coughlan

If drowning, as I have argued, is a literary trope used by authors to explore the postcolonial relationship with memory, a number of other recurring concerns tend to surface in its wake. Questions about the role and authority of the artist accompany the lost body, as Synge's work reveals. The disintegration of the drowned corpse, in turn, raises questions about the stability of identity and of gender, with Walcott and Dabydeen coming to very different conclusions. By placing gender at the center of her examination of drowning, the Irish playwright Marina Carr reconsiders what memory means for postcolonial women. By investigating what happens when the drowned postcolonial body is a female one, Carr complicates her predecessors' use of the drowned body as a postcolonial place of memory, suggesting that memory itself may be an inescapable trap for women.

Reading Marina Carr's *The Mai* (1994) and *Portia Coughlan* (1996) alongside the other texts in this study, a number of striking differences emerge. The only female-authored works of the lot, they are also the only ones to prominently feature female drowning victims. Besides Walcott's *The Sea at Dauphin*, they are the only texts to explore drowning as a means of suicide. They also feature different bodies of water: the protagonists drown in a lake and a river, respectively, rather than the ocean. Finally, although the bodies of both women are found and given appropriate burial rites, the plays suggest that their ghosts will linger, haunting the landscapes they loved and the families they left behind.

Given these significant differences, it may seem like a stretch to include Carr's work in a book focused on postcolonial explorations of drowning. For Carr's heroines, drowning is unquestionably an attempt to escape the limitations imposed on them by their gender. A straightforward reading of the plays suggests that both the Mai and Portia drown themselves for the love of an absent man; the Mai grieving her wayward husband, Robert; Portia, her dead twin, Gabriel. However, Carr overdetermines her protagonists' deaths: gesturing toward mental illness, postpartum depression, genetic defects, domestic imprisonment, fate, and ghostly intervention as possible contributing factors to the suicides. It is impossible to provide a final, fully satisfying causal explanation of either death. Because of this uncertainty, Carr's plays encourage intersectional thinking as one factor and then another comes into focus for the audience. Carr's protagonists die because they are women, but also because they are Irish, and these overlapping identities threaten their relationship to the past and to memory. As postcolonial characters they long for access to an idealized, precolonial past. But as women they can neither escape the past nor dwell in it comfortably, and as a result they are doomed to remain behind as ghosts even after their drowned bodies are found and buried.

Any attentive reader has probably noticed, and may be puzzled by, the predominance of male authors and male drowning victims in this study. As Helen Emmitt writes, "Drowning in literature is gendered."[1] From Ophelia to Edna Pontellier, Maggie Tulliver to Virginia Woolf, female characters and writers drown in unusual numbers. The sense of drowning as an easy or peaceful death may go some way toward explaining the prevailing linkage of women and drowning. Of Maggie Tulliver, George Eliot's heroine in *The Mill on the Floss*, Mary Jane Lupton writes, "Drowning becomes the 'good death,' sensuous, lyrical, erotic."[2] In his creative nonfiction essay titled "Famous Drownings in Literary History," Kevin Haworth writes, "Women perceive the water as feminine, seductive: a friend with open arms. For men, the water is also a woman, one who yearns to grab him and pull him down and away from other men. Thus men fear the water and women seek it out."[3] His musings accurately reflect the cultural myths that surround drowning, if not the actuality.

In fact, the vast majority of drowning victims are male. The "Irish Water Safety Report on Drowning in the Republic of Ireland, 1988–2012," found that 79 percent of drowning victims were male.[4] This gender disparity, partly attributable among adolescents and adults to alcohol and risk-taking behavior, persists, despite the fact that most drowning victims are young children. While it is impossible to extrapolate such statistics backwards into the heyday of British colonialism, it seems only logical to assume that given the much higher number of men than women involved in travel or high-risk professions—fishermen and sailors, to name just two—the disparity would have been similar or even larger. If drowning in literature is gendered female, drowning in reality is, and has probably always been, a predominantly male experience.

Literature is, of course, not bound to reflect the statistics of the Irish Water Safety Board, and authors have a variety of reasons for choosing to feminize death by drowning. Notably, despite the much higher overall numbers of male drowning victims, the report found that nearly twice as many women than men died of intentional drowning (suicide). However, the connection between drowning and women in literature may have more to do with literary critics than authors themselves. For example, at least four of George Eliot's male characters drown, compared to one drowning and one failed attempt for her female characters. Maggie Tulliver's brother Tom drowns with her, locked "in an embrace never to be parted," and yet critics refer almost exclusively to Maggie's drowning, seeing Tom's death merely as the fulfilment of her wish for union with her brother.[5] Emmitt writes, "The flood makes possible what she wants,"[6] emphasizing the kinship between Maggie and the water and the extent to which this is really Maggie's death, in which Tom just happens to be caught up. Nor is Eliot criticism unusual in this regard. Of the relatively few critical articles and chapters on literary drowning, nearly all take gender and sexuality as their primary interrogative frameworks.

Psychoanalytic theorists, gender theorists, and French feminists have posited the existence of a unique connection between femaleness and fluidity. In "The Laugh of the Medusa," Hélène Cixous famously connects *écriture féminine* with breast milk; the female author "writes in white ink."[7] Yet the equation of femaleness and fluidity has not always been positive; as Elizabeth Grosz writes: "The female body has been constructed not only as a lack or absence but with more complexity, as a leaking, uncontrollable, seeping liquid, as formless flow; as viscosity, entrapping, secreting . . . a formlessness that engulfs all form, a disorder that threatens all order."[8] Women, whose bodies experience "tides," have been thought to possess a unique kinship to the uncontrollable, threatening, formless sea. This sense that fluidity is female may partly explain the cultural association of women and drowning.

Read negatively, fluidity implies mutability, even erasability. To choose death by drowning is to willingly disappear, to submerge oneself completely in a larger whole. In Eliot's *Daniel Deronda*, Mirah Cohen describes her attempted suicide by drowning in terms that foreground her loss of self: "The more I thought, the wearier I got, till it seemed I was not thinking at all, but only the sky and the river and the Eternal God were in my soul. And what was it whether I died or lived? If I lay down to die in the river, was it more than lying down to sleep?—for there too I committed my soul—I gave myself up. I could not hear memories any more: I could only feel what was present in me—it was all one longing to cease from my weary life, which seemed only a pain outside the great peace that I might enter into."[9] While suicide is often depicted as giving oneself up, Mirah's language here is specific to the act of drowning. She imagines her thinking self being replaced by "the sky and the river and the Eternal God," and pictures herself committing her soul to the river. This connection between drowning and the disappearance of the self may explain both the persistent connection of women and drowning and the intense anxiety about memory that often follows literary drowning deaths, particularly those in which the drowning victims are male. Traditionally, women in Western culture have been used to having their identities erased: their names and legal status changed through marriage, childbirth, and widowhood.

For men, such experiences are far less common and thus much more threatening. Being submerged suggests a loss of legacy, a failure to have made a mark on the world.

Writing in the 1990s, Carr is certainly aware of the gendered resonance of drowning. Both of her protagonists chafe under the restrictive expectations and domestic burdens culturally imposed on women: childbirth and rearing, cooking and cleaning, sexual monogamy, and the pressure to submerge their own interests and desires in their husband's. Both women defy these mandates but ultimately are drawn to the water for its alluring freedom and fluidity, seeing it as a means of escape. Maria Doyle is correct when she observes that the Mai and Portia "opt for a mode of suicide often considered particularly feminine," going on to note drowning's supposed passivity and its symbolic connection with "sexually transgressing women."[10] Doyle notes that drowning deaths also raise "the question of agency": "A woman found drowned might be understood as a victim whose apparent lack of conscious intent removed any meaning from her death (save that of her own fragile inability to save herself) or as a sinner who in choosing to drown herself opts for a passive death that might symbolically wash away her gender-related fault."[11] Intriguingly, *The Mai* and *Portia Coughlan* each contain a male drowning victim in addition to the female protagonists: Grandma Fraochlán's nine-fingered fisherman husband, who drowned in a fishing accident sixty years before the play, and Portia's twin brother, Gabriel, who drowns himself at fifteen. The Irish-speaking nine-fingered island man lost at sea stands out from the others, an undeniably masculine death and a deliberate homage to Synge. By contrast, Gabriel's death underscores the feminization of drowning as a means of suicide; the play's characters comment that he "looked like a girl" and "sang like one too."[12] Damus Halion, Portia's lover, remarks that he couldn't tell the twins apart.[13]

Carr's embrace of the traditional feminization of drowning raises some problems for her frequent identification as a feminist writer. Margaret Higonnet, writing about historical representations of female suicide, identifies one of the typical problems that occur when writers depict suicidal women: "The insistent representation of women—rather than men—who commit suicide for love complements the familiar assumption that woman lives for love, man for himself. If Brutus commits suicide for the nation, Portia commits suicide in order not to live without Brutus."[14] Carr's women, who despair of living without their male counterparts, seem initially to feed into this connection of female suicide with love, not politics. Yet Carr's careful overdetermination of her heroines' drownings complicates the assumption that female drownings are apolitical. As postcolonial subjects, Carr's characters, like Synge's or Walcott's, long for a return to a precolonial past. Yet as women, the structures that imprison them run deeper than colonial occupation. Even in a magical return to a precolonial idyll, a dream journey like the one undertaken by Achille in *Omeros*, the Mai and Portia would find themselves trapped by their gender, forced into the same restrictive roles that they have come to loathe in the present. Thus they find themselves both longing for the past and unable to escape it; even after they drown their bodies are found and buried, and their spirits continue to haunt the living. By investigating what happens when the drowned postcolonial body is a female one, Carr complicates her predecessors' use of the drowned body as a postcolonial place of memory, suggesting that memory itself may be an inescapable trap for women.

The Mai (1994), the first of three plays that have come to be known as the Midlands Trilogy, is widely considered to have begun Carr's rise to her current position of prominence in Irish—and world—theater. Like the other two plays in the trilogy, *Portia Coughlan* (1996) and the wildly successful *By the Bog of Cats . . .* (1998), *The Mai* tones down the Beckett-inspired absurdism of Carr's early plays, combining a mostly straightforward narrative and realistic—though larger-than-life—characters with a penchant for the supernatural and mythic. Set in 1979 on Owl Lake in the Irish Midlands, *The Mai* focuses on four generations of women: the Mai and her sisters, Beck and Connie; their grandma Fraochlán; and the Mai's daughter, Millie, the play's narrator.[15] The Mai's mother, Ellen, died giving birth to her, but she remains a ghostly presence during the play. The Mai has built a house overlooking Owl Lake in an attempt to draw back her husband, Robert, who abandoned her and their four children five years earlier. The play opens with Robert's return, and although their reunion is passionate, the Mai's family is skeptical of Robert's intentions. The often tense but mostly comic banter of act 1 ends with a surprising revelation from the future: Robert appears in a "ghostly" vision, carrying the Mai's body in his arms, as Millie narrates the "legend of Owl Lake," in which a fictional Irish goddess, abandoned by her lover, cries a lake of tears and dissolves into it.[16] Act 2, set "the following summer," finds Robert taking a weekend trip with his mistress on the Mai's birthday.[17] After a vicious fight, the Mai attempts to reconcile by taking Robert to a ball, where he ends up dancing with his mistress. The play ends on the night of the Mai's suicide. When Millie asks her mother why she doesn't leave Robert, the Mai responds: "I can't think of one reason for going on without him."[18] She turns and walks from the room toward the lake, and the play ends with the "sounds of geese and swans taking flight, sounds of water. Silence."[19]

Of the Midlands Trilogy, *The Mai* is the play most likely to feed into the stereotype of women who drown themselves because of love. Clare Wallace writes of the trilogy: "Carr's recent work, if regarded in terms of its capacity to represent contemporary women's voices, proves somewhat frustrating. She offers her audience/readers little of the assertive self-empowerment of, for example, the drama of Ibsen, to which some of her work has been likened. Carr's heroines in these plays seem to abdicate from a confrontation with patriarchy, or if they do engage they, disappointingly, throw in the towel by committing suicide."[20] Wallace has a point. Despite its unusual cast list of seven women to one man, *The Mai* almost fails to pass the Bechdel test.[21] Its women—though strong, intelligent, fiery, rebellious, and funny—return obsessively to discussions of their husbands and lovers. The Mai is educated, hardworking, and successful. Even though she gave up her position in the college orchestra to marry her composer husband, the play suggests that she is a more naturally gifted musician than he is. Mid-argument, the Mai touts her educational achievements:

THE MAI. I'll have you know I came first in every exam I ever sat!
ROBERT. Degrees, degrees, you collect them like weapons![22]

Yet this intelligent, assertive woman, able as a single mother to earn (or borrow) enough to build a beautiful new house, is unable to imagine life without her philandering husband.

The Mai is not the only woman in her family who attempts to drown herself for love, though she is the only one who succeeds. Woven throughout *The Mai* is the love story of Grandma Fraochlán and the man she calls the "nine-fingered fisherman." Grandma Fraochlán's name comes from the name of her small island, "north of Bofin."[23] She bore seven children with her Irish-speaking sailor but neglected them to fulfill her all-consuming passion for her husband: "There's two types of people in this world from what I can gather, them as puts their children first and them as puts their lover first and for what it's worth, the nine-fingered fisherman and meself belongs ta the latter of these. I would gladly have hurled all seven of ye down the slopes of hell for one night more with the nine-fingered fisherman and may I rot eternally for such unmotherly feelin.'"[24] When the nine-fingered fisherman drowns in a fishing accident, Grandma Fraochlán attempts to throw herself into the sea. Her daughter Julie relates: "Several nights I dragged her from the cliffs, goin' to throw herself in, howlin' she couldn't live without the nine-fingered fisherman, opiumed up to the eyeballs. She was so unhappy, Mai, and she made our lives hell."[25] Like her granddaughter, Grandma Fraochlán is smart, funny, and tenacious. Yet even at the age of one hundred, sixty years after her husband's death, she has no life apart from him, carrying his curragh oar everywhere with her and even sleeping with it in her bed. She is frequently visited by his ghost and requests that, when she dies, she be thrown into the Atlantic, where his curragh went down.

It is possible to read *The Mai* as a play about the paralyzing dangers of romantic love, and the women as weak-willed characters whose lives revolve around men. Carr's plays, according to Kelly Marsh, "Sit uneasily among other plays by Irish women to which they have been compared because, although hegemonic power structures are exposed in the plays, they are not presented as the root cause of the heroines' extremity."[26] Indeed, it is difficult to blame the Mai's suicide on anything other than her own choice to give in to her unhealthy obsession with Robert. When she tells her daughter that she cannot find any reason to live without Robert, Millie retorts, "Mom, you've never tried."[27] Yet it is too simple to say that *The Mai* is a play about a woman who dies for love. Into this small play, focused on a private family in a provincial rural area, Carr deftly weaves hints of the postcolonial context of the Mai's story. Simultaneously, the characters' conversations quietly but insistently connect Owl Lake to the transatlantic world, suggesting a broader and more intriguing context for the Mai's suicide.

A play set in rural Ireland in 1979 may feel very far removed from Ireland's colonial past. The Mai's Owl Lake house is not the globalized, Americanized Celtic Tiger setting of some of Carr's contemporaries, but neither do the characters seem consciously aware of the ways in which colonialism has shaped their nation and their lives. Yet through the character of Grandma Fraochlán, Carr reminds audiences of J. M. Synge's Ireland, an Ireland yearning for independence and mourning the loss of its languages and cultural traditions under British rule. An interview with the *Irish Times* notes Carr's "special affection for *Riders to the Sea*"; she remarks, "I think that's Synge's great play."[28] Born and bred on a tiny island near Bofin and married to a fisherman who works from a curragh, Grandma Fraochlán could almost be Carr's version of Maurya. In fact, before she appears onstage, Carr announces her approach with a comic nod to Synge: "A huge currach oar moves across the window with a red flag on it."[29] For connoisseurs of Irish drama, the curragh is inextricably tied up with Synge, and the red flag recalls the red sail in which Patch's drowned body is carried to Maurya. In fact, it is almost tempting to read Grandma Fraochlán as Carr's imaginative version of what happens to Maurya after *Riders to the Sea*. She has had seven children (Maurya had eight), and yet any male children are curiously absent.[30] While it is hard to imagine that all of her sons were lost at sea like Maurya's, it is clear that Grandma Fraochlán is making her way in the world with the help of her daughters and granddaughters, as Maurya will be forced to after *Riders to the Sea* ends. The most significant difference between the women, of course, is that Maurya is the quintessential Irish mother, grieving the loss of her sons. In her litany of lost men, Maurya does not even name her husband, but calls him Stephen's father. Grandma Fraochlán, by contrast, shatters the stereotype of the selfless Irish mother by neglecting her children and grandchildren to mourn her drowned husband.

By making Grandma Fraochlán exactly one hundred years old, Carr draws attention to her age and to the relative recency of colonial rule; she would have already been in her forties by the time Irish independence was achieved in 1922.[31] In so doing, Carr makes Grandma Fraochlán's obsession with the past not just a personal love story but a eulogy for the things that were lost under colonialism. Grandma Fraochlán's tragic love story also depicts the demise of the Irish language and of traditional ways of life. In a conversation about her granddaughter Beck's "new man," Grandma Fraochlán reveals the ways in which Ireland has changed since her youth:

> GRANDMA FRAOCHLÁN. What does he do?
>
> CONNIE. I told you I didn't ask her.
>
> GRANDMA FRAOCHLÁN. Well what does his father do or did ya not think of axin' that aither?
>
> THE MAI. These things don't matter any more.
>
> GRANDMA FRAOCHLÁN. I remember the first time I met the nine-fingered fisherman. "*Is mise Tomás, scipéar, mac scipéara*," he said. I knew where he was comin' from, one sentence, one glance of his blue eyes and me heart was in his fist.[32]

While the modern audience member may initially side with The Mai's contention that "these things don't matter any more," especially given Grandma Fraochlán's already apparent snobbery and prejudice, it is clear in this exchange that something has indeed been lost. The ability that Tomás had to identify himself fully in "one sentence" containing his name, his profession, and his father's profession is no longer possible. Ancestry is no longer considered important, and professions are no longer passed down from father to son. Without these markers to understand Beck's new husband, Grandma Fraochlán is adrift, and the man remains a vaguely unpleasant cipher throughout the play. When the Mai asks Beck why she married Wesley, she replies simply, "Ah I don't know," a response that contrasts starkly with Grandma Fraochlán's claim that she "knew" her husband on their first meeting.[33]

The unspoken loss that haunts Grandma Fraochlán's love story is the loss of the Irish language. This retelling of her first encounter with the great love of her life contains the only full Irish sentence in the play. Other than a few sprinkled endearments such as "*a stóir*" and "*a chroí*," the play's dialogue takes place entirely in English. Despite the fact that she obviously spoke Irish with her beloved husband, Grandma Fraochlán speaks English with her children and grandchildren, and even speaks to the ghost of Tomás in English. Like Brian Friel and Synge before him, Carr is making a calculated decision to write in English based on the limitations of audiences and perhaps on her own facility with the Irish language. Yet, like Synge's characters, Grandma Fraochlán's speech patterns retain the stamp of her first tongue; Anthony Roche notes that "Grandma Fraochlán is as old as the century and Synge's drama; she resembles his characters in the closeness of her speech to Gaelic."[34] Like the nine-fingered fisherman, who Beck says she'd "love to have known," the Irish language haunts *The Mai*, a lovely memory for the older characters that remains inaccessible to the younger.[35]

Like her predecessor Synge, however, Carr is not inclined to sentimentalize the past or to accept the nationalist myth of the western islands as the home of pure Irishness. Although the gaze of the play is personal and local, Carr complicates these notions by insistently connecting her characters to a much wider world. Though in some ways the most Irish character in her speech and origin, Grandma Fraochlán is also mysteriously and nonspecifically "exotic": "She was known as the Spanish beauty though she was born and bred on Inis Fraochlán, north of Bofin. She was the result of a brief tryst between an aging island spinster and a Spanish or Moroccan sailor—no one is quite sure—who was never heard of or seen since the night of her conception. There were many stories about him as there are about those who appear briefly in our lives and change them forever. Whoever he was, he left Grandma Fraochlán his dark skin and a yearning for all that was exotic and unattainable."[36] By making this ancient, Irish-speaking character not only "the only bastard on Fraochlán in living memory" but also possibly biracial, Carr takes Synge's complication of the pure West of Ireland one step further.[37] Grandma Fraochlán's mother, who called herself the Duchess, encouraged an outward-looking, oceanic focus in her daughter: "The Duchess told me me father was the Sultan of Spain and that he'd hid The Duchess and myself on Fraochlán because we were too beautiful for the world. But in the summer he was goin' to come in a yacht and take us away to his palace in Spain. And we'd be dressed in silks and pearls and have Blackamoors dancin' attendance on us and everyone on Fraochlán'd be cryin' with jealousy—and I believed her and watched on the cliffs every day for the Sultan of Spain."[38] This outward focus, damaging though it was for the Duchess's young child, seems to have continued in her female descendants, from Beck's sojourn in Australia to Ellen's distinctly non-Irish choice of names for her daughters: "Mai, Connie, and Beck. Didn't she pick lovely names for ye at a time in Connemara when everyone was called Máire or Bridgín or Cáit. Oh she was way ahead of her time—."[39] Time and again, Carr resists the myth of pure Irishness; even the cello music that plays as Grandma Fraochlán dances with the ghost of her husband is "*Irish with a flavour of Eastern.*"[40]

Despite the fact that the family's hereditary connections extend beyond Ireland, their attitudes to those people and places they consider Other are often markedly provincial. Conversations about the outside world swing between a gushing Orientalism and a thinly veiled racism. Grandma Fraochlán does not know her father's actual ethnicity; at one point she claims in defiance of mathematical possibility to be "quarter Tunisian, half Moroccan and half Spanish!"[41] As a result of this uncertainty, she tends to lump together all of her stereotypes about the "East" when discussing her father; after visiting with his ghost, "She'd banish him back to his tent in the desert or to his palace in Morocco or his villa in Spain or to the exotic ghost section of her ancient and fantastical memory."[42] In one of *The Mai*'s funniest scenes, Grandma Fraochlán and Beck, high on opium, plan a trip to Zanzibar, travelling by curragh since Beck reveals to her grandmother that traveling in an airplane is like sitting "in a can of beans":[43] "Jay, we'll go be the currach so. What d'ya think, Beck? Down the Atlantic Ocean, through the Straits of Gibraltar, on into the Arabian Gulf, the hills of Kilimanjira to the left, down be Mogadisha, a little more to the left or is it the right, anyway there we are in Zanzibar!"[44] This portrayal of the Other as exotic and glamorous persists in Grandma Fraochlán's granddaughters and great-granddaughters; Millie tells the story of her mother's job at an Arab hairdressing salon where the women are either spoiled royal princesses or "docile, shrouded mother[s]."[45] Connie and the Mai both admit to longing for a one-night stand with "a black man or an Arab," and Millie's lover and the father of her son is an unnamed "El Salvadorian drummer who swept [her] off [her] feet."[46]

The flip side—or the logical extension—of the family's exoticization of Otherness is revealed in the Mai's Aunt Julie, one of the pair of comic elderly aunts who descend on the house in an attempt to convince Beck not to get a divorce. While Aunt Agnes is old-fashioned but good-hearted, Aunt Julie reveals a nasty racist streak. She blames her mother's unladylike language on her "dirty Arab tongue."[47] Perhaps most tellingly, she finds herself unable to believe, despite Beck's testimony to the contrary, that indigenous Australian peoples are human beings just like herself and her family:

> AGNES. And did you meet any aborigines?
> BECK. Several.
> AGNES. And what're they like?
> BECK. Well they're like ourselves I suppose.
> JULIE. Indeed'n they are not! They live in caves, don't they, and they're black, black as ravens with teeth of snow. Sure didn't I see them on the telly![48]

Later, Julie asks the Mai if Beck's husband is "an aborigine," adding defensively, "Not that I've anythin' against them. It's just these mixed marriages rarely work."[49] While Julie's offensive pronouncements provide the play with a bit of off-color comic relief, they also point to something deeper and more disturbing—the ongoing presence of past structures of oppression and prejudice in the supposedly enlightened world of the present. Julie's assumptions about aboriginal peoples come not from completely uninformed ignorance but from the fact that she saw a program on television. This combination of one of *The Mai*'s few mentions of modern technology with the most racist comment in the play indicates that racism and sexism are as inescapably part of the present day as they were of the past.[50]

Victor Merriman has been one of the few critics to consider Carr's work through a postcolonial lens, and also one of the few to be highly critical of the Midlands Trilogy. In "'Poetry Shite': Towards a Postcolonial Reading of Portia Coughlan and Hester Swane," he asserts that "not all plays staged in Ireland at this time may be understood as the products of postcolonial consciousness. Not all plays are culturally useful, in the sense that they enable spaces for transformative dreaming, for thinking otherwise."[51] Merriman considers Carr's work and its popularity as a product of the economic conditions of Celtic Tiger Ireland in the 1990s. Fueled by foreign investment, the economic boom of the Celtic Tiger and the flourishing Irish tourism industry helped to launch the career of artists such as Carr and her contemporary Martin McDonagh. Yet according to Merriman, plays like Carr's become popular precisely as a result of their failure to critique the neocolonial reality of 1990s Ireland: "Ireland is a neo-colonial state, in which coercive narratives of identity interact to marginalise experiences, events, persons, and groups whose defining quality is difference from an assumed norm, or dominant consensus."[52] For Merriman, Carr's theater is itself "neo-colonial" in its tendency to mock the recent past or the rural poor and leave the contemporary, globalized reality of Irish life unexamined.

The broad contours of Merriman's argument are fascinating and helpful in understanding Carr's historical and artistic context. He reveals the tendencies of bourgeois neocolonial theater to deny or actively deride Otherness. As a nation emerges from colonialism, he writes: "The exigencies of struggle forge a powerful sense of group solidarity. Building on this base, the resultant independent state further legitimises itself as the embodiment of popular liberty. In proclaiming common cause in liberty, the new entity actually enforces a denial of difference as a condition of inclusion in its orthodoxy."[53] These historical realities certainly shape Carr's work, and Merriman is right to indicate that they must be grappled with. Yet his specific readings of Carr's plays are less convincing. In "Decolonisation Postponed: The Theatre of Tiger Trash," Merriman asserts that Carr, like her contemporary Martin McDonagh, places the poor and rural Irish on the stage to elicit the mockery of the urban elite:

> Such stagings populated by violent child-adults repeat the angriest colonial stereotypes as a form of communal self-loathing. The dramatis personae of these plays specifically mark out figures of the poor which are overdetermined in their Irishry. Gross caricatures with no purchase on the experiences of today's audiences, their appeal to the new consumer-Irish consensus lies in their appearance as ludicrous Manichaean opposites—the colonised simian reborn. In each belly laugh which greets the preposterous malevolence of its actions there is a huge cathartic roar of relief that all of this is past—"we" have left it all behind.[54]

Merriman's assertions, like his article titles, are certainly provocative. In fact, they correspond usefully to the feminist unease with Carr's suicidal heroines. Is Carr, as Merriman suggests, embracing and exploiting stereotypes of the Irish past for the amusement of upper-class urbanites? Or is there something more complex going on in her plays?

Merriman seems certain that the laughter of Carr's audience is at the expense of her characters, expressing a sense of "relief that all of this is past." Because of this, Merriman contends, Carr's plays fail to acknowledge the neocolonial reality of present-day Ireland and thus become complicit in Ireland's failure to fully decolonize. I contend, however, that Carr is quite aware of the ways in which a supposedly independent Ireland has denied freedom to those it considers Other, and that her plays, in subtle ways, enact the postcolonial critique Merriman desires. It would take a singularly inattentive audience member at one of Carr's plays to feel comfortably certain that "all of this is past." Instead, *The Mai* and *Portia Coughlan* trouble any easy separation of the past and the present, especially in the lives of women. Carr's women long for a kind of precolonial past but are forced to recognize that the structures of oppression they experience in the present are part and parcel of the past, and probably of the future as well. There is no escape for these women, whether in nostalgia or hope, and even suicide proves unfulfilling as they remain trapped instead in a ghostly purgatory. Their freedom is deferred as surely as the decolonization of which Merriman writes.

The Mai and her sisters' crippling longing for the past is portrayed as an outgrowth of their grandmother's romantic stories. In an alcohol-fueled conversation the three sisters reveal to one another that they all used to dream of princes that would come and take them away:

> THE MAI. My God, we were some eejits.
> BECK. Too much listenin' to Grandma Fraochlán and her wild stories.
> THE MAI. She didn't prepare us at all.
> CONNIE. She did her best.
> THE MAI. She filled us with hope—too much hope maybe—in things to come. And her stories made us long for something extraordinary to happen in our lives. I wanted my life to be huge and heroic and pure as in the days of yore. I wanted to march through the world up and up, my prince at my side, and together we'd leave our mark on it.[55]

Here the stories of the past become tied up with hope for the future. Romantic nostalgia, applied to the future, becomes an impossible life plan. This idea of the stories, traits, and tendencies that are inescapably passed down in families and even in entire ethnic groups or nations is one of the main ideas informing Carr's plays. In an interview with Adrienne Leavy, Carr discusses the idea of "racial memory":

> It's a fabulous idea really, racial memory, and I think we all have it. You don't realise what you know and what's in there, what's in

> the hard wiring in all of us. We all speak English here, so the idea of the vanished language of Ireland would be one aspect of racial memory. It's part of what we are carrying down in our blood, absolutely. If you look at physically, genetically, what's passed down in families and then there are all the things you can't see. There are all the behavioural patterns, the familial and the racial behaviours . . . Think of the old Irish laments and how they affect you; often you don't understand why something affects you the way it does, but it is like the past calling you.[56]

For Carr and her characters, the past is simultaneously alluring and threatening, inaccessible and inescapable.

In describing the dreams that her grandmother inspired, the Mai uses language suggestive of Irish precolonial mythology. She longs for a life "huge and heroic and pure as in the days of yore," a description that rings of adventure and freedom. And yet even her hazy fantasies are tinged with patriarchal reality. In order to "march through the world" she must have a "prince at [her] side," and the "mark" she makes on the world will not be hers alone but the mark they make "together." For the Mai and her sisters the dream of a prince is a beautiful and romantic one, but it is likely to make an adult audience uneasy, particularly when these three women approaching forty are unable to imagine an alternative. After the Mai's speech about how Grandma Fraochlán's stories have failed them, Connie's response is not to challenge the childish dream of princes but to tell her sister to find a better prince than Robert: "I suggest you look around for another prince."[57] Carr's women long for a more romantic, more beautiful past. But in dreaming of it they are unable to escape the reality of their gender and its constraints. Going back in time would just present them with more domestic drudgery, unless they could somehow find a prince to take them "away to a beautiful land never seen or heard of before."[58]

Even as they long for the past, the Mai and her sisters are imprisoned in it. The myth of the modern world is that women can do as they please: succeed academically, find meaningful and well-compensated work, express their sexuality freely. Yet despite doing many of these things, Carr's women find themselves trapped in the same roles and routines that have imprisoned women for centuries. The Mai moans: "I started off so well, gained entry everywhere I wanted, did exceedingly well academically, and I was good on the cello—I know I was—The more I think about it, the more I began to realize that, one by one, I have let go of all the beautiful things in my life, though I didn't mean to."[59] Though the Mai has a good job as a headmistress of a school, she finds herself married to a man who bristles at any mention of her educational accomplishments and a mother to children whose demands force her to work an exhausting "second shift." When Robert returns from a weekend at the seashore with his mistress, the Mai confronts him with a description of her weekend: "I collected the children from their schools, I did twelve loads of laundry, I prepared eight meals, I dropped the children back to their schools, and I read Plato and Aristotle on education."[60] The Mai's sister Beck initially seems to have chosen a freer, more modern life; she has slept with so many men she says she's "lost count," and has traveled extensively. Yet at thirty-seven she finds herself uneducated, wishing for children but unsure if she'll ever have any, and married to a much older man who only loved her when he thought she was thirty. Both women live in a world that presents the illusion of freedom for women but in reality enshrines many of the same oppressive structures that imprisoned their mother and grandmother. Grandma Fraochlán sums up the play's message when she observes to Robert that "we can't help repeatin', Robert, we repeat and we repeat, the orchestration may be different but the tune is always the same."[61]

In a world where both the past and the future offer only imprisonment, the Mai and Grandma Fraochlán turn to water—and, by extension, drowning—as an image of freedom. Shonagh Hill writes: "In Carr's plays watery landscapes evoke freedom from culturally constructed roles and offer a place of possibility for the central women."[62] While the more prosaic Agnes and Julie love graves and graveyards and visiting family there, both the Mai and her grandmother find fluidity and dissolution more compelling:

BECK. I suppose ye went to the graveyard for Christmas.

AGNES. Of course we did, looked in on the whole family, God rest them all. I love graveyards, so does Julie.

JULIE. The graves were in an awful state after the winter. Michael has sunk another foot and his tombstone's cracked. I'll have to order another one.

AGNES. It's the bog, keeps sinkin'.

JULIE. Such a stupid place to have a graveyard. Maybe my Christmas present wasn't such a good idea after all, Agnes.

AGNES. Julie bought me a plot beside her own for Christmas . . .

THE MAI. It's beautiful there though, the way the tide comes in around it.

GRANDMA FRAOCHLÁN. When my time comes I'm to be thrun into the wide Atlantic! D'ye all hear that? Twenty mile sou'west of Fraochlán where the nine-fingered fisherman's currach went down! D'ye hear me now!

JULIE. Ara, would ya stop such morbid talk on Christmas Day.[63]

This graveyard, sinking into the bog and surrounded by the tide, is a place of memory threatened by water. Agnes and Julie find this fact disturbing and intend to replace the cracked tombstone. But for the Mai the beauty of the graveyard is in its proximity to the ocean, and implicitly in the way that the ocean is encroaching on the bodies buried there. Grandma Fraochlán takes this one step further with her desire to have her body "thrun into the wide Atlantic." While she intends this as a way to be reunited to her beloved husband, lost at sea, there is an element of freedom in her describing the ocean as "wide."

Grandma Fraochlán's request to be buried at sea also recalls the legend of Owl Lake that Millie tells as Robert holds the Mai's drowned body at the end of act 1. The seasonal myth describes the love of Coillte and Bláth, two Irish gods invented by Carr. As autumn approaches, Bláth must return to "live with the dark witch of the bog,": "Coillte lay down outside the dark witch's lair and cried a lake of tears that stretched for miles around. One night, seizing a long-awaited opportunity, the dark witch pushed Coillte into her lake of tears. When spring came round again Bláth was released from the dark witch's spell and he went in search of Coillte, only to be told that she had dissolved."[64] Millie indicates that she should have paid more attention to the myth, that it held the key to her mother's demise. This tale of a lovesick woman not just drowning in her own tears but dissolving completely must have seemed like an image of escape and freedom to the despairing Mai, who could not imagine a reason for living without Robert.

We do not witness Grandma Fraochlán's death or discover whether her desire for a sea burial is observed. In this age of funerary regulations, it seems unlikely, though perhaps achievable via cremation if her family sprinkles her ashes in the ocean. The Mai, though she is able in some sense to escape her miserable situation by drowning, is unable to dissolve in the water like Coillte. Instead her body is carried back home by her errant husband, returned to the house where she sat like a prisoner at the window, waiting for him to return. She cannot escape Robert and her troubled domestic life even in death. Ominously, when Robert first returns early in the play, he does so because he has had a dream that the Mai is dead and his cello case is her coffin. Upon being told this dream, the Mai asks, "So you've come back to bury me?"[65] Unable to disappear into the freedom of the lake, the Mai is given a conventional burial except for her shroud, one small symbolic nod to her choice of death: "No shroud for The Mai. It was her wish. In one of those throwaway conversations which only become significant with time, The Mai had said she wanted to be buried in blue. So here we were in a daze fingering sky blues, indigo blues, navy blues, lilac blues, night blues, finally settling on a watery blue silk affair."[66] Buried in "watery blue silk," the Mai's corpse gestures toward her desire for freedom even as her body is boxed up and entombed in the ground to serve as a place of memory for her family.

Perhaps the most innovative technical feature of *The Mai* and *Portia Coughlan* is the distortion of time that allows Carr to flash forward and depict the heroine's death at the end of act 1 and then return her to life for act 2. Though the Mai's dead body appears in Robert's arms halfway through the play, she returns to the stage very much alive and wearing a cheerful "summer dress" just a page later.[67] A number of goals are accomplished by this clever manipulation of the traditional play's timeline. By seeing into the future and glimpsing the heroine's demise, the audience become detectives in act 2, piecing together the events and emotions that led to the Mai's suicide. As Doyle notes, the structure also resists catharsis, preventing a sense of "wholeness" and emotional closure in the audience.[68] Doyle goes on to note that the theatrical resurrection of Carr's heroines also provides them with a chance to tell their own story: "A greater potential for forceful self-expression: formerly inert bodies become aggressive, vocal, yet that present energy is also juxtaposed in the mind of the audience against the silence—the absence—we have already witnessed."[69] Aware that the living woman onstage is in some sense already dead, the audience attends to her voice more carefully, searching for an explanation for her troubling choice.

Although allowing her heroine a chance to tell her own story posthumously is certainly part of Carr's design in *The Mai*, there is also a darker side to the play's unusual structure. The Mai is not freed by her suicide but forced by the structure of the play to return as a kind of ghost, reliving her humiliation at the hands of her husband, and repeating the monotonous routines and arguments of her daily life. Though we do not know whether the Mai will return as an actual ghost, in a play filled with ghosts who converse and even dance with the characters, it seems likely. Carr herself believes in ghosts; she once claimed, "I had a fist-fight with a ghost one time."[70] Whether or not the Mai will become a literal ghost, she becomes a haunting and destructive presence for her daughter, drawing Millie back into the past and away from "all that is good and hopeful and worth pursuing."[71] Instead Millie sees "The Mai at the window again. The Mai at the window again, and it goes on and on till I succumb and linger among them there in that dead silent world that tore our hearts out for a song."[72] Though *The Mai* follows four generations of women, none of them can escape the past—not through romantic love, education, work, marriage, sexual freedom, or even suicide. Instead they find themselves drawn to the past, both nostalgically and emotionally, and more inadvertently through the structures of oppression that linger and continue to bind them.

In *Portia Coughlan*, written and performed two years after *The Mai*, Carr relies on many of the same theatrical techniques to explore the titular heroine's suicide by drowning. Yet this much darker play makes the demons of the past more explicit: the racism and sexism that continue to resurface in the present day, the domestic imprisonment of women; even the ghosts are more present and more sinister. The past is both more inaccessible and more inescapable than in *The Mai*. In the play's most memorable moment, Portia's drowned body dangles above the stage from a pulley, creating a powerful theatrical spectacle. But this death, which is so shockingly visible, is simultaneously unknowable as Carr overdetermines her heroine's death to the point that it is impossible to say exactly why she dies.

Set "in the Belmont Valley in the Midlands" in "the present," *Portia Coughlan* takes place on Portia's thirtieth birthday and the following day.[73] Unhappily married to the limping, wealthy Raphael Coughlan, with whom she has three young sons, Portia is caught up in mourning her twin, Gabriel, who drowned himself fifteen years ago and who now haunts her and the stage as a singing ghost. Portia refuses to live by the expectations her family and culture demand of a married woman and mother, drinking copiously, ignoring her children and domestic responsibilities, and meeting lovers down by the Belmont River. Act 1 comes to a close as Portia's birthday ends, with her meeting the local barman by the river and missing the romantic dinner Raphael has prepared for her. The couple has a vicious argument in which Portia is terribly cruel to her husband, lying that she has slept with the barman, whom she actually sent away unfulfilled. The lights go down, and act 2 begins with a searchlight shining on Portia's drowned body, being raised from the river by a pulley. Raphael carries Portia's body home, and the next scene unfolds as Portia's family and friends return from her wake and discuss her death (and Gabriel's, which occurred fifteen years ago). Act 3 goes back in time to the morning after Portia's birthday. It follows her through an emotional but otherwise fairly unexceptional day as she meets with various family members, returning frequently in conversation to her grief over Gabriel. In *Portia Coughlan*'s final scene, Portia attempts to reconcile with Raphael by putting the kids to bed, making him dinner, and revealing to him her childhood sexual relationship with her twin, but he is unmoved and goes to bed. Portia's last lines of the play, before her brother's ghostly voice rises "triumphant," are "And though everyone and everythin' tells me I have to forget [Gabriel], I cannot, Raphael, I cannot."[74]

As with *The Mai*, the central story of *Portia Coughlan* remains one that might trouble feminist readers: a woman drowns herself for the love of an absent man. Portia's final assertion that she cannot forget her twin echoes the Mai's admission that she cannot think of a reason to live without Robert. Certainly Portia's love relationship is more complicated than the Mai's. Initially seeming like the powerful attachment of twins, the relationship between Portia and Gabriel develops through *Portia Coughlan* from Damus Halion's claim that he couldn't tell the twins apart to Portia's final admission that "me and Gabriel made love all the time down be the Belmont River among the swale, from the age of five."[75] She tells her mother that she only married Raphael because his name, "an angel's name," made her hope that he would take on the characteristics of her lost brother.[76] When her father tells her to forget Gabriel, she retorts that he is "everywhere": "There's not a corner of any of your forty fields that don't remind me of Gabriel. His name is in the mouths of the starlin's that swoops over Belmont hill, the cows bellow for him from the barn on frosty winter nights. The very river tells me that once he was here and now he's gone. And you ask me to forget him."[77] Like the Mai, Portia is a woman imprisoned in the memory of a love that once was and is no longer. Like the Mai, her suicide speaks to her inability to go on without a beloved man.

More than in *The Mai*, however, where the past seemed essentially knowable if romanticized, in *Portia Coughlan* the past is uncertain and dangerous terrain. This difference is made most apparent in the play's updated and much nastier version of the charming Grandma Fraochlán.[78] Portia's eighty-year-old grandmother, Blaize Scully, serves as the voice of the past in *Portia Coughlan*, but instead of island love stories and old-fashioned Orientalism her voice dredges up explicitly racist and classist vitriol. Blaize hates her daughter-in-law, Portia's mother, Marianne, whose family she calls "tinkers": "Come into this area three generations ago with nothin' goin for yees barrin' flamin' red hair and fat arses. And the County Council buildin' yees houses from our hard-earnt monies. We don't know where ye came from, the histories of yeer blood. I warned ya, Sly! Do ya think you'd listen? There's a devil in that Joyce blood, was in Gabriel, and it's in Portia too. God protect us from that black-eyed gypsy tribe with their black blood and their black souls!"[79] Blaize wants to blame Portia and Gabriel's problems on the distant past, on the unknown "histories" of their ancestors, the handouts provided by the government, and what she calls their "black blood." Later in the play, after Portia's death, Blaize complicates her attribution of blame by drawing on an old Irish legend suggesting that the twins were changelings. She raises her glass "to Portia in the murky clay of the Belmont graveyard where she was headin' from the day she was born, because when you breed animals with humans you can only bring forth poor haunted monsters who've no sense of God or man. Portia and Gabriel, Changelin's. *Sláinte*."[80] It is significant that even Blaize's mythological interpretation of events betrays her racism; instead of blaming the presence of changelings on fairies, she connects it to her ideas of miscegenation, calling Travellers "animals" who should not breed with "humans." If Blaize, as the oldest character in the play, is the voice of the past, than the past is a vile place, spewing forth its hatred into the present day.

Of course, as the audience quickly discovers, both Blaize's racism and her use of Irish mythology are disingenuous attempts to cover up for the truth of Portia and Gabriel's heredity. Blaize's husband had an affair when she was pregnant with Sly, Portia's father. That affair resulted in Marianne, Portia's mother. Though Blaize was aware of her husband's affair and the resulting child, she allowed her son Sly to marry his half-sister because she was too proud—and too afraid of her abusive husband—to reveal the truth. Instead she cloaked her opposition to the marriage in the language of racism, layering an ugly secret past beneath an equally ugly disguise.

As the example of Blaize shows, in *Portia Coughlan* the past is a tangled, confusing place in which nasty lies intermingle with nasty truths. Everyone's story of the past is different and even simple questions, such as whether Portia was a difficult child, receive radically different answers. Portia's best friend, Stacia, says that Portia was "a demon of a child but she grew up alright," and her aunt Maggie immediately replies, "Never knew a gentler child than Portia, like a mouse."[81] Even within a single individual, memory is often shifting and unreliable: In two sentences, Sly moves from calling his dead son a "little outcast from hell" to describing his singing as "beautiful and rare . . . those high notes of God."[82] Local mythology is another victim of this unreliable memory. Fintan the barman recalls the story of how the Belmont River got its name as "some auld river God be the name of Bel and a mad hoor of a witch as was doin' all sorts of evil round here but they fuckin' put her in her place," and Portia retorts, "She wasn't a mad hoor of a witch! And she wasn't evil! Just different, is all, and the people round here impaled her on a stake and left her to die. And Bel heard her cries and came down the Belmont Valley and taken her away from here and the river was born."[83] Whether ancient or recent, in *Portia Coughlan* the past is always suspect, subject to the flawed memories and prejudices of the teller.

The most fiercely contested memory in *Portia Coughlan* is the memory of the day that Gabriel drowned himself. Explanations for his suicide from the play's minor characters include Maggie May's assertion that "young Gabriel Scully was insane from too much inbreedin' and I'd near swear he walked into the Belmont River be accident."[84] Damus and Fintan, Portia's lover and would-be lover, never claim to have an explanation for Gabriel's death, but dance around their suspicions by discussing his gender fluidity and his eerie closeness with his twin. The most important confusion about Gabriel's death, however, comes from Portia, whose story shifts in significant and irreconcilable ways as the play goes on. For the entirety of acts 1 and 2, the audience sees Portia as a grieving sister, left behind by a suicidal twin. It isn't until act 3, after the audience has already witnessed her corpse and her wake, that Portia begins to reveal her own side of the story. First, she confides to her aunt that she and Gabriel had made a suicide pact: "I knew he was goin' to do it, planned to do it together, and at the last minute I got afraid and he just went on in and I called him back but he didn't hear me on account of the swell and just kept on wadin', and I'm standin' on the bank, right here, shoutin' at him to come back and at the last second he turns thinkin' I'm behind him, his face, Maggie May, the look on his face, and he tries to make the bank but the undertow do have him and a wave washes over him."[85] Portia goes on to explain to Maggie the confusion of being a twin, saying, "Times we got so confused we couldn't tell who was who."[86] Although she adds, "We didn't really like each other that much when it came down to it," Portia ends her confession with a moan, "Oh, how can everyone be alive and not him? If I could just see him, just once, I'd be alright, I know I would."[87]

As the last act proceeds, however, the story of Gabriel's death and of Portia's relationship with him becomes increasingly complicated. Portia's mother paints Gabriel as unhealthily "obsessed" with his twin, telling her that he "came out of the womb clutchin' your leg and he's still clutchin' it from wherever he is."[88] To Portia's angry claim that "I was the only one that mattered to him," Marianne responds, "Mattered to him! I seen what he used do to you! How he used start ya chokin' by just lookin' at ya! How he used draw blood from ya when ya tried to defy him!"[89] Finally, Portia accuses her mother of driving Gabriel to suicide by stopping his singing lessons. Marianne's response places the blame for Gabriel's death squarely at Portia's feet: "Gabriel stopped singin', Portia, when you stopped talkin' to him, when ya refused to go anywhere with him, when ya refused to ate at the table with him, when ya ran from every room he walked into, when you started runnin' round with Stacia and Damus Halion. That's when Gabriel stopped singin'. Oh, Portia, you done away with him as if he were no more than an ear of corn at the threshen' and me and your father could do nothin' only look on."[90] This accusation prompts Portia to give a different, more sinister account of Gabriel's suicide: "Mother, the night he died, the night after our fifteenth birthday, I walked down to the river with him and he whispered to me before he went in, 'Portia,' he says, 'I'm goin' now but I'll come back and I'll keep comin' back until I have you' . . . One of us was goin', were killin' each other, and ye just left us to fight it to the death. Well, we fought it to the death and I won."[91] While it seems possible that Portia makes up this story in order to exonerate herself from her mother's assertion that her neglect caused her brother's suicide, it seems equally likely that the version Portia tells Maggie May is a sugarcoated falsehood. Ultimately the audience is not given enough evidence to decide which version of events is most true, or whether they are both fabricated and the truth is something else entirely.

The unknowability of the past sets the stage for the inscrutability of Portia's own suicide in the play's present. While early on in the play the audience has a sense that Portia will drown herself, and certain knowledge of her death by act 2, a satisfying explanation of Portia's motives is frustratingly elusive. As Portia's best friend, Stacia, muses, "Sure, I knew she was unhappy but who isn't these days, must be a terrible state of mind to do what she done and Maggie May told me about Sly and Marianne, but somehow that don't add up to this."[92] Carr presents the audience with no shortage of motives, so many that Portia's death seems overdetermined, but somehow they don't ever completely add up. Depending on how you interpret *Portia Coughlan*, Portia dies because she is struggling with postpartum depression or mental illness, because she is still grief-stricken at the loss of Gabriel, or because Gabriel's malicious ghost haunts her and lures her to her death.[93] Portia may be drawn to the river to escape a loveless marriage and a mundane domestic routine, or to flee an incestuous and diseased family heritage. Ultimately all of these factors combine to create a lethal environment of memory that Portia is unable to escape. Whether in death or life, she cannot escape the past because men keep dragging her back to it, whether in the form of insults and sexual violence or through the endless demands of childbearing and domesticity.

More than her predecessor the Mai, Portia is drawn to water as a space of freedom and release. Her main obsession is with the Belmont River and the place that Gabriel drowned, but an anecdote from her childhood reveals that water has always represented the possibility of escape. On a school trip to the beach at Bettystown, the twins stole a rowboat and headed out to sea. When asked by their distraught teacher where they were going, they responded that they were "just goin' away," and when pressed, added, "Just anywhere that's not here."[94] Thirty-year-old Portia finds in the river both an intimately familiar environment and one that is always moving and changing. She says that she could not imagine enjoying a holiday because her mind would always be returning to the Belmont River: "Wonderin' was it flowin' rough or smooth, was the bank mucky nor dry, was the salmon beginnin' their rowin' for the sea, was the frogs spawnin' the waterlilies, had the heron returned, be wonderin' all of these and a thousand other wonderin's that river washes over me."[95] Interestingly, while the water myth in *The Mai* is about a woman who drowns in a lake of her own tears, the myth Carr creates for the Belmont River seems to hold out more hope for the central woman. When local people impale a female outsider accused of being a witch, the river god has pity on her and takes her away, leaving the river behind them. As Shonagh Hill writes, the river is a place of possibility for Portia: "The river is a free flowing space of movement which evokes Portia's desire for self-invention and renewal."[96] River water manages to be both constantly moving and reassuringly local; Portia can return to the same familiar place every day and never find it fixed or stagnant.

As the site of Portia's suicide, however, the river is an ambivalent place. Depending on how one interprets her death, as an escape or as resignation, the river can ultimately symbolize freedom or entrapment. Hill notes that Portia's obsessive return to the riverbank can be viewed either as a sign of her depression or of her unconventionality: "If we view Portia as a melancholic, trapped in the past, then the river can be interpreted as a place of memory: a shrine to Gabriel. Conversely, the river can be construed as an environment of memory if we link it to an interrogative female mythmaking, the oral tradition of storytelling and female bodily freedom."[97] The river myth, a story that Portia reclaims as feminist, recasting the "mad hoor of a witch" who deserved her punishment as an innocent outsider persecuted by ignorant villagers, suggests Hill's reading of the river as a freeing "environment of memory" that enables female storytelling. A closer reading of the myth, however, reveals its patriarchal side. Reading the Belmont River as a female space is questionable, since it is a male river god who creates it by carrying off a damsel in distress. A final odd touch is that this woman who was supposedly saved still haunts a cave by the river singing arias, which only Gabriel can hear. While the Belmont River may be "an environment of memory" for Portia, Carr's portrayal suggests that environments of memory are not kind to women. Instead, aided by men who profit from the status quo, the past restrains women, carrying them back each time they reach toward freedom.

Although the past takes literal form for Portia in the ghost of Gabriel, it also takes more invisible but equally insidious form in the shape of domestic duties and maternal expectations. Whenever Portia steps outside the bounds of expected behavior for women of her age and class (which is often), someone is there to remind her of the unspoken rules she is breaking. In fact, Portia is not onstage for five minutes before her husband, Raphael, chides her for drinking too early in the morning, not washing the dishes for over a week, and not driving the children to school. Despite the play's setting in the 1990s, this initial exchange and Portia's position as an unemployed housewife to a wealthy man feels regressive, a holdover from the 1950s. Interestingly, unlike the Mai's faithless Robert, Raphael is a sympathetic character who takes on most of the child-rearing as well as his traditional role as breadwinner. Though Raphael reminds Portia in almost every scene of her duties to house, husband, and children, he seems a genuinely unwitting part of Portia's patriarchal prison, blind to the pressures and structures that are slowly stifling her.

Carr literalizes Raphael's well-meaning restriction of Portia in one of the most powerfully visual scenes of *Portia Coughlan*, when he carries her drowned body home. Covered in "water, moss, algae, frogspawn, waterlilies, from the river" and wearing only a slip, Portia's body is raised from the river by a pulley and hangs suspended over the stage.[98] The image recalls the iconic drowned woman, Ophelia, in its interweaving of the drowned body with its natural botanical surroundings. The positioning is also familiar, with Portia's body dangling over the river as Ophelia is pictured climbing over the brook on a hanging willow branch. Ophelia's death is followed by her brother and her lover grappling in her grave, arguing about who loved her more. Similarly, after Portia's death, her body remains an object to be disputed by men. As her husband moves forward to take her from the pulley, Fintan the barman steps in to help, earning Raphael's "measured growl": "Keep your paws off of my wife."[99] The sexual freedom Portia sought in life is revealed as just another facet of male ownership as her husband and would-be lover face off aggressively over her inert body. Though she may have imagined her body floating free in the waters of her beloved Belmont River, Portia's corpse is dredged up and reclaimed by her husband, who immediately carries her "up to the house,"[100] the same house she had earlier compared to a "coffin" where she couldn't "breathe any more."[101]

The image of Raphael carrying Portia's dead body back to the house that imprisoned her in life provides a visual metaphor for the way that men treat her throughout the play each time she asserts herself or does something that belies traditional models of femininity. With the exceptions of Raphael, who reminds Portia of her domestic duties when she steps out of line but does not belittle her in other ways, and Senchil, whose wife says he "wasn't born, he was knitted on a wet Sunday afternoon," the men in Portia's life respond with violent misogyny when she refuses or otherwise threatens them.[102] Fintan, with whom Portia arranges a liaison before changing her mind, describes what he'd do to her "if [he] owned [her]" and upon her decision to "wade home be the river" instead of having sex with him, calls her a "fuckin' mickey-dodger."[103] Damus, Portia's longtime lover, also becomes violently jealous when Portia reveals she prefers the river's company to his:

PORTIA. I'd liefer sit be the Belmont River for five seconds than have you or any other man beside me in bed.

DAMUS. Strong sentiments from a little cock-teaser who used get her joys and thrills from watchin' men drool as she curved by and who, even as she professes to have found sex to be a great let-down, is leanin' up again' me with a flame creepin' up her throat all the way from the backstairs of her hot little arse. *Portia moves away from him.* Sulkin' now, are we?

PORTIA. I didn't come here to see you, Damus Halion. I came here because this is me father's land. This be our part of the Belmont River. So go on off with yourself and your crude readin' of the world and its inhabitants.[104]

Damus's "crude readin' of the world," like Fintan's, cannot encompass a woman who leaves her house to sit by the river for any reason other than to pursue sexual dalliances. Faced with Portia's rejection, Damus retaliates by reducing Portia to her sexuality, calling her a "cock-teaser" and assuming that even the way she walks is a performance, staged for the male gaze.

In this exchange with Damus, Portia sends him away by invoking her father as the owner of the land on which she sits. She knows, like most women, that in a patriarchal world her own autonomy is not enough to earn her respect and safety from angry men. Instead she must call on the ownership of a husband or father. Yet though she uses his name to deflect Damus's misogyny, Portia's father, Sly, treats her in much the same way as her disappointed lover in one of the play's most disturbing scenes. When Portia reveals to her mother that she was present when Gabriel committed suicide, her father overhears and is understandably furious that she kept this information from her parents: "And ya let us search high and low for him, hopin' against hope we'd find him alive, puttin' off draggin' the river and you knew where he was the whole fuckin' time. Me only son and you let him go like a swallow at the close of summer."[105] Sly's anger seems reasonable and appropriate. Like Maurya, he has suffered both the agonizing loss of a child and a period of anxiety where the body is missing and the child is somehow both dead and alive. Portia kept the certain knowledge of Gabriel's death from Sly and let him dwell in that torment. Yet with his next words, Sly's anger takes an unexpected turn: "Ya cunt! Ya dark fuckin' cunt! I watched how you played with him, how ya teased him, I watched yeer perverted activities, I seen yees, dancin' in yeer pelts, disgustin', and the whole world asleep barrin' ye and the river—I'll sort you out once and for all, ya little hoor, ya, ya rip, ya fuckin' bitch ya!"[106] Instead of berating his daughter for her part in his son's death, Sly turns on the twins' incestuous behavior, portraying Portia as a temptress who lured Gabriel to sin. Surprisingly, this passage contains more misogyny and violence than any of the furious accusations leveled by Portia's thwarted lovers. Her own father calls her, in the space of a few sentences, a "cunt," a "hoor," and a "bitch." Portia's response is telling. Instead of calling Sly out for his misogyny or redirecting his anger to the appropriate topic, she yells, "I'm not your wife nor your mother so don't you come in here takin' your rage out on me, ya fuckin' coward ya!"[107] The implication that men have a right to take their sexual aggression out on their wives or mothers but not their daughters is echoed in her mother's dismayed reaction: "Sly! Go home! Now! Your own daughter!"[108] Portia and her mother—and grandmother, a victim of her husband's domestic violence—live in a world where violent misogyny is an expected part of most male-female relationships. Neither woman can see a way out of this cultural norm, thus both resort to a feeble plea that father-daughter relationships remain exempt from misogynistic slurs.

The twin relationship in *Portia Coughlan* appeals because it initially seems like one that exists outside the patriarchal power struggles and misogynistic violence of the rest of the play. Portia and Gabriel are almost literally equals, indistinguishable to outsiders and even at times to themselves. Portia says she remembers sharing the womb with her brother: "Times I close my eyes and I feel a rush of water around me and above we hear the thumpin' of me mother's heart and we're a-twined, his foot on my head, mine on his foetal arm, and we don't know which of us is the other and we don't want to, and the water swells around our ears."[109] This vision of male and female twins together in a fluid, amniotic space suggests that Portia is remembering a better world, where relationships between the sexes are characterized by harmony and equality instead of violence and hierarchy.

But as *Portia Coughlan* progresses and other characters offer their memories of Portia and Gabriel's relationship, it becomes clear that

Portia's memory is a nostalgic construction. Like her other lovers, Gabriel is sexually possessive and violent toward his sister. Marianne, who admits she loved her son more, still recognizes and recounts his abusive treatment of Portia. Like most of the other men in Portia's life, Gabriel reacts violently to her independence; Marianne says he "used draw blood from ya when ya tried to defy him."[110] When Portia steps outside of their incestuous relationship by sleeping with Damus Halion, Gabriel punishes her by no longer talking to her, stopping singing, and eventually by committing suicide and trying to persuade her to kill herself with him. Although Portia has nostalgically reconstructed Gabriel as a beautiful memory and the one true love of her life, Gabriel, like the other men in Portia's life, continually drags her into a past that proves not only damaging but deadly for women. The afternoon before her own suicide Portia reaches out for help to her parents, revealing: "He's closin' in on me, I hear his footfall crossin' the worlds."[111] If Portia's death is, as it has been portrayed in the criticism, a suicide, it is a suicide heavily assisted by a vengeful male ghost, a ghost whose voice rises "triumphant" as the play's final sound, after Portia expresses despair at her inability to move beyond her past: "And you say you want me to talk about ya the way I talk about Gabriel—I cannot, Raphael, I cannot. And though everyone and everythin' tells me I have to forget him, I cannot, Raphael, I cannot."[112] Doyle writes of the paradox of female suicide: "If suicide represents an attempt, as Higonnet terms it, to force 'others to read one's death' by willfully turning a living body into an object, this interpretive act becomes particularly difficult when the doer is, by definition, a 'feminine' mystery; a woman's willful eradication of her own voice risks the appearance of appropriateness."[113] Given this context it seems significant how thoroughly critics and audiences have ignored Portia's attempts to explain her own death. In Portia's final moments onstage she portrays suicide not as a choice but as inevitable, a violent battle with her brother's ghost, a battle she knows that she will lose.[114]

Like the Mai, Portia never haunts the stage as a literal ghost, but as in *The Mai*, the chronological structure makes Portia into a kind of ghost for the entirety of *Portia Coughlan*'s final act. As Carr says in an interview with Mike Murphy, "You're watching her living, knowing she's dead. Everything you see is with that knowledge."[115] As Hill notes, Carr's framing of Portia as a kind of ghost shifts the focus from her love for her dead twin to her domestic imprisonment: "Presenting Portia as a ghostly body or surrogate that evokes cultural memory, rather than focusing solely on Gabriel's ghost as a surrogate that fills a gap in Portia's unfulfilled life, begs the question, is her life unfulfilled due to his absence or unfulfilled due to the stifling restrictions of the familial and domestic roles she is expected to perform."[116] As with the Mai, the "resurrection" of Portia in the final act allows Portia to have a little more agency to reveal the motives behind her suicide, but it also returns her to her stifling domestic routines, preventing her from escaping into the (possible) freedom and silence of death. The play's final scene explicitly dramatizes this return as Portia tries on the role of housewife by putting her children to bed and cooking dinner for Raphael.

More than in *The Mai*, it also seems certain that Portia will return as an actual ghost after the play's end. The river is already haunted, both by Portia's twin and by the woman whose story provides the Belmont River with its name. Portia herself also suggests, early in the play, her plans to haunt the banks of the Belmont after her death: "I come here because I've always come here and I reckon I'll be comin' here long after I'm gone. I'll lie here when I'm a ghost and smoke ghost cigarettes and watch ye earthlin's goin' about yeer pointless days."[117] Perhaps there is some minor freedom in this vision of Portia's ghostly afterlife; she will at least be outside the cycle of "earthlin's pointless days." It is difficult, however, to find any true victory for Portia in an afterlife that has her returning to the place she obsessively and unhappily haunted in life.

Marina Carr's women, as postcolonial women, dwell obsessively in the past. As Wallace writes, "It is notable that these mature characters are essentially conservative, wishing to evade new, perhaps unpredictable or uncontrollable experiences and favouring a return to a previous, often illusory state of affairs . . . Each is bound by the legacy of the past."[118] Yet in a past that offers romantic nostalgia and a vision of prelapsarian wholeness, women find the seeds of their current oppression. Even in nostalgia they cannot escape the misogyny, violence, and domestic drudgery that characterize their present-day lives. Melissa Sihra expresses this well when she writes: "Many critics have expressed discomfort and often derision that there are no 'positive' resolutions in Carr's plays from this period. However, in a society where historical processes of female oppression have only begun to be seriously acknowledged in the social, political and academic arenas in the last decade or so, painful narratives need to be addressed before transformations can occur."[119] Women, Carr suggests, cannot escape a past that continues to structure their modern-day lives, making its insidious and often invisible way into romantic relationships, educational opportunities, the workplace, and mother-child relationships. Carr portrays women who are drawn to the water, seeing in its fluidity and movement the possibility of escape. Yet even after drowning they are unable to free themselves, as their bodies are carried back home by their husbands and their "ghosts" are forced to relive the circumstances leading up to their deaths. For women, Carr suggests, neither places nor environments of memory are enabling. Rather, memory serves as a prison for both the Mai and Portia.

It is worth noting that Carr has not yet finished with the drowned woman. In an interview with Murphy, she muses, "I would like to write a play where I don't have to kill off the heroine."[120] While Carr's 2002 play *Ariel* has a male protagonist, Fermoy Fitzgerald, the play is full of drowned women, including Fermoy's daughter Ariel, whom he kills in a "blood sacrifice" to his own political ambition, and his mother, murdered by his father. When the authorities drag Cuura Lake in search of Ariel's body, they find "the remains a seven people."[121] In a seemingly insignificant laugh line, Boniface says to his elderly aunt Sarah, given to rambling tales of the distant past, "You'd reminisce the future, missus, if ya though ya'd geh away wud ud."[122] The temporal confusion in this statement is deliberate. Women, Carr suggests, are not free to imagine a future unburdened by the baggage of the past. Instead, the bones of our mothers and grandmothers lie submerged in lakes and rivers, waiting to resurface with their stories of violence, misogyny, and loss.

As a postcolonial literary trope, the drowned body nearly always indicates a concern with memory. Yet the additional layers of significance that accrue around drownings allow authors to subtly inflect their discussions of the possibilities, problems, and dangers of remembering postcolonially. For Carr, gender is a necessary facet of the project of memory. Women, she indicates, may long for an idealized precolonial past, but that past proves not only unattainable but destructive.

Afterword

"Remembering Rightly"

Several photographs of drowned bodies have made headlines in recent years. In September 2015 the body of two-year-old Alan Kurdi washed up on a beach in Turkey and was photographed by the Turkish photojournalist Nilüfer Demir.[1] Alan and his family were Syrian refugees attempting to flee Turkey for the Greek island of Kos, hoping to eventually make their way to join family in Canada. When their boat capsized, Alan's mother and five-year-old brother also drowned, leaving their father, Abdullah, as the family's sole surviving member. Demir's photograph of Alan shows the toddler dressed in a red shirt, blue shorts, and tiny sneakers, lying on his stomach with his bottom in the air in the familiar pose of a sleeping child. His face, largely obscured by his shoulder, lies in the shallow Mediterranean waves.

Four years later, a similar picture caught the world's attention. On June 23, 2019, Óscar Alberto Martínez Ramírez and his twenty-three-month-old daughter, Angie Valeria, drowned while attempting to cross the Rio Grande from Mexico to Brownville, Texas.[2] The young El Salvadorian family had traveled to the border of the United States, fleeing poverty and gang violence in their neighborhood. Yet having been forced to wait for two months to cross the bridge and claim asylum, the family grew desperate and attempted to wade across the river. The heartbreaking photograph, taken by Julia Le Duc, shows father and daughter facedown in the water, the little girl tucked inside her father's shirt, her arm draped around his neck.

In a world of social media and easily accessible online news sites, both photographs went viral. According to the *Guardian* (UK), the photograph of Alan Kurdi reached twenty million screens in the first twelve hours after it appeared.[3] While similar statistics on Le Duc's photograph are not available, it was published in newspapers across the world and shared extensively on social media by both average citizens and high-ranking politicians. The photographs became injunctions to look, to see, and to remember.

Part of the visual power of these images may derive from the fact that they depict drowning victims. In both photographs, the subjects appear to be peacefully asleep. They look profoundly human, unlike the ubiquitous photographs of emaciated children dying of famine or more gruesome pictures depicting maimed and bloodied victims of war. The images are deeply disturbing, but not gory; there is no blood or any visceral reason to immediately look away. The viewer, while helpless in the face of the massive refugee crises facing our world, may feel when looking at the pictures as though they arrived on the scene just a moment too late; if they were there they could have waded into the water to rescue Óscar and his daughter, or could have picked up the sleeping body of Alan and gently woken him.

These photographs provide iconic individual faces to a massive and often faceless crisis. At least in the case of the Kurdi photograph, they captured interest and galvanized public support in a way that the much larger statistics about migrant deaths or the crisis in Syria could not. At least 2,638 migrants drowned in the Mediterranean in 2015, the year of Alan Kurdi's death, according to the Missing Migrants Project.[4] Only a few months before Alan drowned, over seven hundred refugees and migrants drowned in a single incident off the coast of the Italian island of Lampedusa. Yet the story passed from the international news cycle in a single day. It was Alan's picture, story, and name that captured public attention, and had real-world effects, at least in the short-term. According to the WNYC podcast *Snap Judgment*, in the twenty-four hours following the picture's release, donations to refugee and migrant charities tripled. UK politicians cited Alan in their decision to settle twenty thousand Syrian refugees.

A German NGO bought a rescue ship to aid migrants and named it the *Alan Kurdi*.[5]

Responses to Le Duc's photograph of Martínez Ramírez and his daughter are harder to quantify, in part because of the event's recency, and in part because of the intractable nature of the partisan immigration debate in the United States. While public figures and politicians on both sides of the political aisle expressed sorrow over the tragic image, each party used it as evidence for their own entrenched position, with Republicans blaming Democrats for blocking stricter immigration policies or even criticizing the young father for risking his daughter's life, and Democrats lambasting President Trump's zero-tolerance and metering policies. As Jens Kjeldsen argues in a piece for *Reading the Pictures*, "In the end, the visual power of the photograph of Óscar and Valeria Ramírez will depend on who wins the verbal war over the meaning of the picture."[6] Their bodies, frozen in time in an iconic photograph, have become blank canvases onto which powerful voices will write the stories that they want others to hear.

Photographs like Le Duc's and Demir's undoubtedly help us to experience, process, and remember tragedies and humanitarian crises. They will retain their power to shock and provoke grief long after the actual crisis has passed. In our modern world they promise to serve as virtual "places of memory" where mourners can gather to remember the individuals depicted or the tragedies they represent. But even with powerful photographic reminders, memory is fickle, and its relationship to action uncertain. A study led by Paul Slovic showed that while the charitable response to Alan Kurdi's photograph was significant, it was also short-lived. The study tracked donations to the Swedish Red Cross campaign for the crisis in Syria. The number of daily donations increased one hundred times in the week following the photograph's publication. But by five weeks after the photo's appearance, the number of donations had declined to pre-photograph levels.[7] This data, while indicating the power of photographs to promote empathy and provoke action, raises important questions about memory. How should we remember? For how long? To be authentic, must our memory be accompanied by action, or is individual feeling and reflection enough?

In his book *The End of Memory: Remembering Rightly in a Violent World*, the theologian Miroslav Volf describes his experience of being interrogated in the 1980s by the Communist government of Yugoslavia. While his treatment was mild compared to many who suffered under the often-brutal Communist regimes of Eastern Europe, Volf writes of being haunted by the memory of his interrogators. In the face of post-Holocaust injunctions to remember, Volf asks how it is possible to use the memory of abuse in the service of good: "From the start the central question for me was not *whether* to remember. I most assuredly would remember and most incontestably should remember. Instead, the central question was *how to remember rightly*."[8] A simple injunction to remember, Volf argues, is not enough; there are many ways to remember that are dangerous or unhealthy:

> To remember a wrongdoing is to struggle against it. The great advocates of "memory" have rightly reminded us of that. But it seemed to me that there were so many ways in which I could remember wrongly that the injunction verged on being dangerous. I could remember masochistically, to use the phrase coined by Milan Kundera in his novel *Ignorance*, by remembering only those things from the incident that made me displeased with myself. Or I could remember sadistically, guided by a vindictive desire to repay evil for evil. Then I would be committing a wrongdoing of my own as I was struggling, with the help of memory, against the wrongdoing committed against me. I would be granting evil its second victory, its full triumph.[9]

Volf goes on to advocate an approach to memory that allows for both justice and forgiveness, one that gestures toward the possibility of renewed community between victims and abusers once the truth of painful memory has been spoken and faced.

Volf's situation, however traumatic, is in many ways more straightforward than that of Irish or Caribbean artists. The memories he deals with are personal—even if distorted or weakened by the passage of time, they happened to him. He can repress them; he can choose to ignore them, but they remain his to access or deny as he chooses. Volf writes of the connection between memory and identity: "Memory, as the argument goes, is central to identity. To the extent that we sever ourselves from memories of what we have done and what has happened to us, we lose our true identity . . . So salvation lies in memory insofar as that memory prevents us from distorting our essential selves and living a lie."[10] Where memory exists, Volf cautions against severing ourselves from it. We ought to preserve and to face the photographs of Alan Kurdi and Óscar and Valeria Ramírez in order to understand "what we have done and what has happened to us." Yet the authors discussed in *Literary Drowning* face the reality of cultures and individuals who have been forcibly severed from memory, who have unwillingly had their "essential selves" distorted. There are no photographs that capture the reality of life in precolonial Africa, no audio recordings of ancient Irish storytellers. The injunction to remember can seem like a mockery to those Africans in the Caribbean who have no way of knowing which part of Africa their ancestors were abducted from, who have no memory of the Middle Passage aside from a few slave narratives, heavily edited by whites. Remembering may also seem elusive to the modern Irish citizen who cannot truly communicate with her Irish-speaking grandparents, who is unable to read the prolific poetry of her cultural past except in translation.

Given the gaps in memory left by colonialism, it would be understandable if postcolonial artists simply rejected memory as a source of cultural identity and artistic inspiration. Derek Walcott comes close in his call for creative amnesia, but ultimately embraces literary and cultural memory as long as it does not become entrenched in past wrongs. Remembering rightly is a central obsession for each of the authors studied here. What, these authors ask, does it mean to *remember rightly*, when remembering at all is difficult or impossible? How is it possible to construct a communal identity out of broken and fractured scraps of memory?

The modern Western response to the waning of memory has often been the construction of monuments or tombs or the preservation of archives and photographs, places that fix and attempt to immortalize certain sanctioned versions of the past. Avishai Margalit describes these places as the modern storehouses of shared or communal memory:

> In traditional society there is a direct line from the people to their priest or storyteller or shaman. But shared memory in a modern society travels from person to person through institutions, such as archives, and through communal mnemonic devices, such as monuments and the names of streets. Some of these monuments are notoriously bad reminders. Monuments, even those located in salient places, become "invisible" or illegible with the passage of time. Whether good or bad as mnemonic devices, these complicated communal institutions are responsible, to a large extent, for our shared memories.[11]

While recognizing the allure of such constructions, the authors examined in this study resist the urge to use the fragments of memory left behind by colonialism to erect fixed places of memory. Instead, they turn to the drowned body, an image that captures the pain of the past while recognizing that all memory is uncertain, multivalent, and shifting.

The psychologist Frederic Bartlett describes memory as an imaginative project: "Remembering . . . is not the re-excitation of innumerable fixed, lifeless, and fragmentary traces. It is an imaginative reconstruction, or construction."[12] Similarly, Volf emphasizes the agency of the individual and the community in deciding how to use memory, how to piece it together to shape personal and communal identities: "The memory that helps make us up is a veritable patchwork quilt stitched together from the ever-growing mountain of discrete, multicolored memories. What will be stitched into the quilt and what will be discarded, or what will feature prominently on the quilt and what will form a background, will depend greatly on how we sew our memories together and how others—from those who are closest to us all the way to our culture as a whole—sew them together for us. We are not just shaped *by* memories; we ourselves *shape* the memories that shape us."[13] The authors studied in *Literary Drowning* examine how fragments of memory can be pieced together to shape cultural and artistic identities. In their novels, poems, plays, and travelogues, these authors shape those memories that have been left to them, fabricating stories to fill the gaps where memory is gone. By emphasizing some memories and allowing others to recede, each author offers a different vision of postcolonial art. Synge's depictions of the drowned body allow the author to step into a role as cultural mourner, but a mourner who lacks complete access to the memories he is grieving. Meanwhile Walcott finds in the drowned body a suggestive blend of forgetting and memory, one that provides a fertile new ground for an artist who desires access to all literary and cultural traditions while not denying the particular pain of the Caribbean past. By fragmenting the drowned body and his narratives, Dabydeen highlights the instability of memory and the unreliability of any artistic vision of the past. Finally, Carr considers the particular problems facing the female postcolonial artist, for whom memory itself may be an alluring but dangerous trap, inviting women to idealize a past that contains the seeds of their own oppression. Their visions of the past and the future differ, with some more pessimistic than others. Yet as Margalit movingly writes, "Even the project of remembering the gloomiest of memories is a hopeful project. It ultimately rejects the pessimist thought that all will be forgotten, as expressed by Ecclesiastes: 'There is no remembrance of former things, nor will there be any remembrance of things that are to come amongst those who shall come after.' The project of memory is not vanity of vanities."[14] By wrestling with the unique challenges of postcolonial memory and by embodying their examinations in the image of the drowned body, these authors provide a glimpse into what *remembering rightly* might look like for postcolonial individuals and communities. In their resistance to official places of memory and sanctioned versions of history, they hold out hope for the return of environments of memory, cultures, or communities in which memory might once again become a living and thriving part of everyday life.

Notes

Bibliography

Index

Notes

Introduction

1. Hamza Hendawi, "Islamic Scholars Question bin Laden's Sea Burial," *Atlanta Journal Constitution*, May 2, 2011; Peter Baker, Helene Cooper, and Mark Mazzetti, "Bin Laden Is Dead, Obama Says," *New York Times*, May 1, 2011.

2. Hendawi, "Islamic Scholars Question Sea Burial."

3. Baker, Cooper, and Mazzetti, "Bin Laden Is Dead."

4. Among the world's major religions, only Hinduism embraces a variation of "burial at sea"; the cremated ashes of Hindus are traditionally sent to the sacred Ganges River for "burial." In reality they are more often sprinkled over the body of water nearest to the home of the deceased. For both Islamic and Judeo-Christian traditions, burial at sea, while permitted in extreme circumstances, raises anxieties about memory and bodily dissolution. Buddhists, who do not share this anxiety about bodily dissolution, most often promote cremation, though practices vary.

5. See Jahan Ramazani, *Poetry of Mourning: The Modern Elegy from Hardy to Heaney* (Chicago: Univ. of Chicago Press, 1994), 16–17.

6. Leela Gandhi, *Postcolonial Theory: A Critical Introduction*, (New York: Columbia Univ. Press, 1998), 8.

7. Neil Lazarus, *The Postcolonial Unconscious* (Cambridge: Cambridge Univ. Press, 2011), 33.

8. Of course, given the reality of neocolonialism, even the historical implications of the term *post* colonialism are problematic, as Lazarus writes: "For, conjoining violence and military conquest with expropriation, pillage, and undisguised grabbing for resources, these developments have demonstrably rejoined the twenty-first century to a long and as yet unbroken history, wrongly supposed by postcolonial theory to have come to a close circa 1975. This is the history of capitalist imperialism." See Lazarus, *Postcolonial Unconscious*, 15.

9. Jahan Ramazani, "Introduction," in *The Cambridge Companion to Postcolonial Poetry*, ed. Jahan Ramazani (Cambridge: Cambridge Univ. Press, 2017), 1–2.

10. According to T. O. Lloyd, "Without the naval strength established during Elizabeth's reign, imperial development would not have been possible." See T. O. Lloyd, *The British Empire 1558–1995* (Oxford: Oxford Univ. Press, 1996), 9.

11. Jonathan Raban, "Introduction," in *The Oxford Book of the Sea*, ed. Jonathan Raban (Oxford: Oxford Univ. Press, 1992), 20.

12. Robert Louis Stevenson, "The English Admirals," in Raban, *Oxford Book of the Sea*, 284. This kind of rhetoric is particularly interesting coming from Stevenson who, as a Scot, may not have been considered by some of his contemporaries as a possessor of the truest form of Englishness.

13. Rupert Brooke, "The Soldier," in *The Collected Poems of Rupert Brooke* (New York: Dodd, Mead and Co., 1915), 115.

14. While emphasizing that popular accounts of the Middle Passage tend to overestimate mortality rates, the historian Herbert Klein estimates that the mean slave mortality rate for all European slave-trading nations between 1590 and 1867 was 12.4 percent. The English mortality rates averaged 21.3 percent in the seventeenth century and fell to 11.1 percent by the second half of the eighteenth century. Assuming that between eleven and twelve million Africans embarked on the Middle Passage and taking into account the much higher mortality estimates of other scholars, it seems reasonable to estimate that between one and two million Africans died as a result of the Middle Passage.

15. Paul Gilroy, *The Black Atlantic: Modernity and Double-Consciousness* (Cambridge, MA: Harvard Univ. Press, 1993), 15.

16. Gilroy, *Black Atlantic*, 4.

17. For a recent example, see Tuire Valkeakari, *Precarious Passages: The Diasporic Imagination in Contemporary Black Anglophone Fiction* (Gainesville: Univ. Press of Florida, 2017).

18. See, for example, Ian Baucom, *Specters of the Atlantic: Finance Capital, Slavery, and the Philosophy of History* (Durham, NC: Duke Univ. Press, 2005), a text that was influential in inspiring and shaping this book.

19. Maria McGarrity, *Washed by the Gulf Stream: The Historic and Geographic Relation of Irish and Caribbean Literature* (Newark: Univ. of Delaware Press, 2008), 25.

20. McGarrity, *Washed by the Gulf Stream*, 24.

21. Alison Donnell, Maria McGarrity, and Evelyn O'Callaghan, "Introduction," in *Caribbean Irish Connections: Interdisciplinary Perspectives*, ed. Alison Donnell, Maria McGarrity, and Evelyn O'Callaghan (Kingston: Univ. of the West Indies Press, 2015), 3.

22. Donnell, McGarrity, and O'Callaghan, *Caribbean Irish Connections*, 10.

23. Liam Kennedy, "Modern Ireland: Post-Colonial Society or Post-Colonial Pretensions?" *Irish Review* 13 (Winter 1992–93): 115.

24. Hilary Beckles, "Foreword: Irish Routes," in Donnell, McGarrity, and O'Callaghan, *Caribbean Irish Connections*, x.

25. In Mootoo's novel, despite the title, the main characters do not actually drown. But the faked drowning at the center of the story has a similar effect to an actual literary drowning, erasing names, identities, and memories, albeit with more hopeful and freeing results.

26. I will be using the English translation, *Realms of Memory*, published in 1996 (see note 27).

27. Pierre Nora, *Realms of Memory*, trans. Arthur Goldhammer (New York: Columbia Univ. Press, 1996), 1.

28. Nora, *Realms of Memory*, 8.

29. According to Nora, there is no adequate equivalent in English for the phrase *lieux de mémoire*: "In French, the association of the words *lieu* and *mémoire* proved to have profound connotations—historical, intellectual emotional [*sic*], and largely unconscious (the effect was something like that of the English word 'roots')." See Nora, *Realms of Memory*, xv–xvi.

30. Nora, 6.

31. Nora, 7.

32. Nora, xv.

33. Nora, 18.

34. Nora, xvii.

35. Nora, 15.

36. Homi K. Bhabha, "Interrogating Identity: Frantz Fanon and the Postcolonial Prerogative," in *Modern Critical Thought: An Anthology of Theorists Writing on Theorists*, ed. Drew Milne (Oxford: Blackwell, 2003), 307.

37. Ian Baucom, *Out of Place: Englishness, Empire, and the Locations of Identity* (Princeton, NJ: Princeton Univ. Press, 1999), 18.

38. Baucom's argument focuses mainly on physical places of memory, memorials to Englishness built on land. Intriguingly, however, the book ends with a gesture toward the sea, citing Ariel's song from *The Tempest* and describing the changes worked on English places of memory by the colonized as a "sea change." See Baucom, *Out of Place*, 222.

39. David Dabydeen, "'A Continual Sense of Isness': An Interview with Derek Walcott," *Agenda* 39, no. 1–3, (2002): 155.

40. Eavan Boland, "That the Science of Cartography Is Limited," in *Collected Poems* (Manchester: Carcanet, 1995), 175.

41. Oona Frawley, "Introduction," in *Memory Ireland: History and Modernity*, ed. Oona Frawley (Syracuse, NY: Syracuse Univ. Press, 2011), xix.

42. Barbara Misztal, "Memory and History," in Frawley, *Memory Ireland*, 3.

43. Misztal, "Memory and History," 3.

44. Frawley, "Introduction," xviii.

45. Avishai Margalit, *The Ethics of Memory* (Cambridge, MA: Harvard Univ. Press, 2002), 17.

46. Margalit, *Ethics of Memory*, 197.

47. Margalit, 13. Margalit primarily considers cases of authoritarian regimes in Eastern Europe and the Soviet Union, but he also mentions South Africa's Truth and Reconciliation Committee, and it is clear that his insights apply equally to countries emerging from colonial regimes.

48. Frawley, "Toward a Theory of Memory in an Irish Postcolonial Context," in *Memory Ireland*, 33.

49. Gandhi, *Postcolonial Theory*, 9.

1. "Full Fathom Five"

1. T. S. Eliot, *The Waste Land*, ed. Michael North (New York: W. W. Norton, 2001), 55. References are to line numbers.

2. Ankhi Mukherjee, *What is a Classic?: Postcolonial Rewriting and Invention of the Canon* (Stanford, CA: Stanford Univ. Press, 2013), 3.

3. Jahan Ramazani, *The Hybrid Muse: Postcolonial Poetry in English* (Chicago: Univ. of Chicago Press, 2001), 6.

4. Gilroy, *Black Atlantic*, 49.

5. Salman Rushdie, qtd. in Mukherjee, *What is a Classic*, 7.

6. William Shakespeare, *Richard III*, in *The Complete Pelican Shakespeare*, ed. Alfred Harbage (London: Penguin, 1969), 1.4.21–33. References are to act, scene, and line.

7. Shakespeare, *Richard III*, 1.4.45–47.

8. William Shakespeare, *Hamlet*, in *The Complete Pelican Shakespeare*, 5.1.24.

9. William Shakespeare, *Pericles, Prince of Tyre*, in *The Complete Pelican Shakespeare*, 3.1.57–64.

10. Shakespeare, *Pericles*, 3.2.71.

11. Shakespeare, 3.1.71.

12. Shakespeare, *Hamlet*, 4.7.180.

13. Shakespeare, 5.1.39–40, 55–66.

14. Shakespeare, 5.1.156–57.

15. Shakespeare, 5.1.160–161.

16. Shakespeare, 5.1.200.

17. Shakespeare, 5.1.1–2.

18. Shakespeare, 5.1.206.

19. Shakespeare, 5.1.214, 218.

20. Michael MacDonald, "Ophelia's Maimed Rites," *Shakespeare Quarterly* 37, no. 3 (1986): 311.

21. Magda Romanska, "Ontology and Eroticism: Two Bodies of Ophelia," *Women's Studies* 34 (2005): 485.

22. Shakespeare, *Hamlet*, 5.1.176–77.

23. Shakespeare, *The Tempest*, 1.2.397–405.

24. Shakespeare, 1.1.14–15.

25. Shakespeare, *Richard III*, 1.4.29–30.

26. Shannon Kelley, "The King's Coral Body: A Natural History of Coral and the Post-Tragic Ecology of *The Tempest*," *Journal for Early Modern Cultural Studies* 4, no. 1 (2014): 115.

27. Kelley, "King's Coral Body," 115.

28. Kelley, 134–35.

29. Dan Brayton, "Shakespeare and the Global Ocean," in *Ecocritical Shakespeare*, ed. Lynne Bruckner and Dan Brayton (Farnham: Ashgate, 2011), 178.

30. Brayton, "Shakespeare and the Global Ocean," 183.

31. Brayton, 184.

32. Lengthy discussions of the poem occur in Elizabeth Bowen's *The Land of Spices* and David Dabydeen's *The Intended*, for example.

33. Edward LeComte, "Introduction," in "*Paradise Lost*" *and Other Poems*, ed. Edward LeComte (New York: New American Library, 1961), xiv.

34. Richard P. Adams, "The Archetypal Pattern of Death and Rebirth in Milton's 'Lycidas,'" *PMLA* 64, no. 1 (1949): 185.

35. John Milton, "Lycidas," in "*Paradise Lost*" *and Other Poems*, 8–9, 12–13. References are to line numbers.

36. *Oxford English Dictionary*, "parching," https://www.lexico.com/en/definition/parching.

37. The moment foreshadows Coleridge's "Water, water everywhere, / Nor any drop to drink." See Samuel Taylor Coleridge, *The Rime of the Ancient Mariner*, in *Selected Poetry and Prose of Coleridge*, ed. Donald A. Stauffer (New York: Random House, 1951), 121–22.

38. Milton, "Lycidas," 154–62.

39. Rosemond Tuve, "Theme, Pattern, and Imagery in 'Lycidas,'" in *Milton's "Lycidas": The Tradition and the Poem*, ed. C. A. Patrides (Columbia: Univ. of Missouri Press, 1983), 190.

40. Milton, "Lycidas," 12–14.

41. Milton, 19–22.

42. Eric Brown, "Underworld Sailors in Milton's 'Lycidas' and Virgil's *Aeneid*," *Milton Quarterly* 36, no. 1 (March 2002): 36.

43. Milton, "Lycidas," 140, 151.

44. Tuve, "Theme, Pattern, and Imagery," 198.

45. Milton, "Lycidas," 158.

46. Milton, 165–77.

47. Romans 6:3–6, New Revised Standard Version (NRSV). For clarity, and because my point is more general and theological than philological, I am using a modern translation of the Bible. Though the language of Milton's Geneva Bible differs, the general concepts are the same.

48. I Peter 3: 18–22, NRSV.

49. Milton, "Lycidas," 173.

50. Milton, 182–86.

51. Lawrence Lipking, "The Genius of the Shore: Lycidas, Adamastor, and the Poetics of Nationalism," *PMLA* 111, no. 2 (1996): 205.

52. Lipking, "Genius of the Shore," 210.

53. LeComte, "Introduction," 401.

54. Lipking, "Genius of the Shore," 213.

55. Eliot, *The Waste Land*, 430.

56. See, among others, Marjorie Donker, "*The Waste Land* and the *Aeneid*," *PMLA* 89, no. 1 (1974): 164–73.

57. Eliot, *The Waste Land*, 335–36.

58. Eliot, 1–7.

59. Eliot, 62.

60. Eliot, 71–75.

61. This quote is found in Michael North's footnotes to the "sources" in his edited edition of *The Waste Land*, 45.

62. Shakespeare, *Hamlet*, 5.1.225–29.

63. Eliot, *The Waste Land*, 46–48.

64. Eliot, 54–55.

65. Eliot, 312–21.

66. Martin Scofield, "Poetry's Sea-Changes: T. S. Eliot and *The Tempest*," in *Shakespeare Survey* 43, ed. Stanley Wells (Cambridge: Cambridge Univ. Press, 1990), 126.

67. Scofield, "Poetry's Sea-Changes," 127.

68. Paul Lewis, "Life by Water: Characterization and Salvation in *The Waste Land*," *Mosaic* 11, no. 4 (Summer 1978): 85.

69. Scofield, "Poetry's Sea-Changes," 127.

70. Eliot, *The Waste Land*, 387, 390, 384.

71. Eliot, 402–9.

72. My reading agrees with that of Aaron Bibb, who writes: "While on its own, this section might appear ambiguous towards Phlebas's condition, his fate seems vastly preferable when contrasted with the agony and sordidness of the characters in the previous sections." See Aaron Bibb, "Death by Water: A Reevaluation of Bradleian

Philosophy in *The Waste Land*," in "*The Waste Land" at 90: A Retrospective*, ed. Joe Moffett (Amsterdam: Rodopi, 2011), 84.

73. Eliot, *The Waste Land*, 430.

74. T. S. Eliot, "Tradition and the Individual Talent," in *Poetry in Theory: An Anthology 1900–2000*, ed. Jon Cook (Oxford: Blackwell, 2004), 99.

75. Eliot, "Tradition and the Individual Talent," 102.

2. The Lost Body

1. Milton, "Lycidas," 411.

2. Lipking, "Genius of the Shore," 205, 207.

3. I am aware of the problems involved in considering Synge, who died before Ireland gained its independence, a postcolonial artist. However, as critics like Declan Kiberd have demonstrated, Synge's works are deeply involved in the project of exposing and dismantling colonialism, making them postcolonial in the less chronologically focused sense of the term.

4. Synge's corpse-crowded sea is oddly similar to that described by Clair Wills in her cultural history of World War II–era Ireland, *That Neutral Island*. She devotes an entire chapter to the recovery of drowned bodies along Ireland's coasts, a gruesome fact of war that, despite its neutrality, Ireland was unable to escape. Wills cites a newspaper report from the time, which estimated that "about 100 dead bodies are floating in the sea off Inniskea [I]sland, on the Western Mayo Coast." See Clair Wills, *That Neutral Island* (Cambridge, MA: Harvard Univ. Press, 2007), 137. While it may seem gauche to compare these real bodies with Synge's often exaggerated or imagined ones, Wills writes movingly about the horror of encountering headless and decaying corpses from a war that the Irish media was attempting to downplay or ignore, a kind of shock Synge could be seen to be creating in his writing. An encounter, even a literary one, with the drowned corpses of young Aran Islands men could potentially awaken a reader to the tragedies of poverty and cultural loss in the west of Ireland, often glossed over by the myths of cultural nationalism.

5. It is almost impossible to accurately enumerate the drowning cases in *The Aran Islands*, since Synge's present experiences are blended together with stories of the recent and ancient past with little clear distinction, a fact that I discuss later in this chapter.

6. In *Gender and Modern Irish Drama*, Susan Cannon Harris provides a thorough reading of the body in Synge's work. Yet while she mentions in passing the role of the corpse on Synge's stage, noting that his "impolite insistence on bringing dead and dying bodies onto his stage gave grievous offense to his audiences," she is much less concerned with the dead or drowned body than with the diseased or degenerate body, whose infection stands in for the corruption, both biological and political, of the Irish

nation. See Susan Cannon Harris, *Gender and Modern Irish Drama* (Bloomington: Indiana Univ. Press, 2002), 8.

7. John C. Messenger, *Inis Beag: Isle of Ireland* (Long Grove, IL: Waveland Press, 1969), 41.

8. J. M. Synge, *The Aran Islands* (London: Penguin, 1992), 3.

9. Declan Kiberd, *Inventing Ireland: The Literature of the Modern Nation* (Cambridge, MA: Harvard Univ. Press, 1995), 174.

10. J. M. Synge, *Travels in Wicklow, West Kerry and Connemara*, (London: Serif, 2005), 62. In another Wicklow travel essay, "The Oppression of the Hills," Synge links the cultural decline of the Gaelic peasantry to their lack of young girls, writing that "there are so few girls left in these neighborhoods that one does not often meet with women that have grown up unmarried." See Synge, *Travels in Wicklow, West Kerry and Connemara*, 30.

11. Kiberd, *Inventing Ireland*, 173; emphasis in original.

12. Ann Saddlemyer, "Art, Nature, and 'the Prepared Personality': A Reading of *The Aran Islands* and Related Writings," in *Sunshine and the Moon's Delight: A Centenary Tribute to John Millington Synge, 1871–1909*, ed. Suheil Badi Bushrui (Gerrards Cross, UK: Smythe, 1979), 107.

13. W. B. Yeats, "J. M. Synge and the Ireland of His Time," in *Essays and Introductions* (London: Macmillan, 1961), 321.

14. Jack B. Yeats, "A Letter about J. M. Synge," in W. B. Yeats, *Collected Works: Prose*, ed. Richard Finneran (New York: Scribner, 1997), 401.

15. Jack B. Yeats, "A Letter about J. M. Synge," 403.

16. J. M. Synge, "Autobiography" in *Collected Works: Prose*, ed. Alan Price (Oxford: Oxford Univ. Press, 1966), 9.

17. Synge, *Aran Islands*, 63.

18. Quoted in Tim Robinson, "Introduction," in Synge, *Aran Islands*, xlviii.

19. For a unique reversal of this reading of the influence of Synge's illness on his work, see Susan Cannon Harris, who makes the intriguing point that it may in fact have been contemporary awareness of Synge's medical state that caused critics to perceive his work as particularly morbid: "Given that many of Synge's later critics explain his 'morbidity' in terms of his illness, it is hard not to read the ad hominem attacks made on Synge by his contemporaries—the accusations of degeneracy, morbidity, unhealthiness—as having some reference to his physical condition, which was deteriorating during the production of *Playboy*." See Harris, *Gender and Modern Irish Drama*, 122. In a later essay, however, she agrees with these critics that Synge's depiction of the male body "replicates his fears about his own body," though not in as straightforward or simplistic a way as has generally been proposed. See Susan Cannon Harris, "Synge and Gender," in *The Cambridge Companion to J. M. Synge*, ed. P. J. Mathews (Cambridge: Cambridge Univ. Press, 2009), 112.

20. Synge, *Travels in Wicklow, West Kerry and Connemara*, 31.

21. Synge, 31. For simplicity's sake, I will refer to the narrator of the travel writings as Synge. Even though there may be cases in which one could benefit from differentiating the author and the narrator, it seems, given Synge's own claim to be striving for documentary realism, quite difficult to do so.

22. Synge, *Travels in Wicklow, West Kerry and Connemara*, 32.

23. Synge, 32.

24. Synge, 32.

25. Synge, 32.

26. Synge, 32.

27. Synge, 61.

28. Synge, 62.

29. Synge, 61–62.

30. Synge, 61.

31. P. J. Mathews, "'In a Landlord's Garden': Synge and Parnell," in Frawley, *Memory Ireland*, 125.

32. Synge, *Travels in Wicklow, West Kerry and Connemara*, 32.

33. Synge, 33.

34. Synge, 33.

35. Synge, qtd. in Kiberd, *Inventing Ireland*, 175.

36. Synge, *Aran Islands*, 89.

37. Synge, 88.

38. Quoted in Mary M. Colum, "Memories of Yeats," *Saturday Review of Literature*, February 25, 1939, 4.

39. Quoted in Nicholas Grene, "Synge in Performance," in *The Cambridge Companion to J. M. Synge*, 149.

40. Messenger, *Inis Beag*, 41.

41. Synge, "When the Moon Has Set," in *Collected Works: Plays*, ed. Ann Saddlemyer (Gerrards Cross, UK: Colin Smythe, 1982), 159.

42. Synge, *The Playboy of the Western World* in *The Complete Plays*. (New York: Vintage, 1960), 67.

43. Nora, *Realms of Memory*, 2.

44. Nora, 3.

45. Misztal, "Memory and History," in Frawley, *Memory Ireland*, 5.

46. Leslie D. Foster's article provides a helpful survey of early to mid-twentieth-century critical readings of Maurya's character. Some of these readings saw Maurya as a Christian hero, her relative peace and calm at Bartley's death a sign of "Christian resignation." Others saw Maurya as ultimately uninteresting because her suffering was too passive, denying her the role of tragic heroine. See Leslie D. Foster, "Maurya: Tragic Error and Limited Transcendence in *Riders to the Sea*," *Éire-Ireland* 16, no. 3 (1981): 101.

47. T. R. Henn, "*Riders to the Sea*: A Note," in Bushrui, *Sunshine and the Moon's Delight*, 35.

48. Synge, *Riders to the Sea*, in *Collected Works: Plays*, 86.

49. Synge, *Riders to the Sea*, 86.

50. Synge, 87.

51. Synge, 95.

52. Daniel Davy, "Tragic Self-Referral in *Riders to the Sea*," *Éire-Ireland* 29, no. 2 (1994): 85.

53. Synge, *Riders to the Sea*, 86, 93.

54. Synge, 95, 96.

55. Synge, 97.

56. Nina Witoszek and Patrick Sheeran, *The Irish Funerary Tradition* (Galway: Social Sciences Research Center, 1990), 7.

57. Qtd in Anne Ridge, *Death Customs in Rural Ireland: Traditional Funerary Rites in the Irish Midlands* (Dublin: Arlen House, 2009), 91.

58. Ridge, *Death Customs in Rural Ireland*, 151.

59. Anthony Roche, "J. M. Synge: Christianity versus Paganism," in *A J. M. Synge Literary Companion*, ed. Edward A. Kopper Jr. (Westport, CT: Greenwood, 1988), 119.

60. Edward. A. Kopper Jr., "*Riders to the Sea*," in Kopper, *A J. M. Synge Literary Companion*, 44.

61. Declan Kiberd, *Synge and the Irish Language* (Lanham, MD: Rowman & Littlefield, 1979), 166.

62. Synge, *Riders to the Sea*, 93.

63. Kiberd, *Synge and the Irish Language*, 172. Maurice Bourgeois calls Maurya "a lonely, stately figure as majestic as the sea itself," and claims that "their conflict with the Ocean makes [the characters] great because nothing stands between them and the fierce onset of ineluctable circumstance; it actually raises them to heroic proportions." Maurice Bourgeois, *John M. Synge and the Irish Theatre* (London: Constable & Co., 1913), 162, 63.

64. Bert Cardullo, "*Riders to the Sea*: A New View," *Canadian Journal of Irish Studies* 10, no. 1 (1984): 95, 96; emphasis in original.

65. Cardullo, "*Riders to the Sea*," 98, 106.

66. David Clark makes a similar assertion, noting that "one of the disconcerting peculiarities of the life pictured in the play is that many of the objects that relate to the dead are brand new, whereas the living must be content with old things." See David R. Clark, "Synge's 'Perpetual "Last Day"': Remarks on *Riders to the Sea*," in Bushrui, *Sunshine and the Moon's Delight*, 43. The importance of good burial to Maurya reveals itself in the things she purchases and the way she treats them.

67. Synge, *Riders to the Sea*, 97.

68. Synge, 97.

69. Henn, for example, asks, "Is Michael the beloved son, and is it for that reason that Bartley's death is received with a terrible resignation? . . . Are 'sorrow's springs' exhausted; did the death of Michael numb Maurya's capacity to lament?" See Henn, "*Riders to the Sea*," 38.

70. Synge, *Riders to the Sea*, 97.

71. Synge, 84.

72. Judith Remy Leder, "Synge's *Riders to the Sea*: Island as Cultural Battleground," *Twentieth Century Literature* 36, no. 2 (Summer 1990): 208.

73. Leder, "Synge's *Riders to the Sea*," 218.

74. Synge, *Riders to the Sea*, 96.

75. Synge, 86.

76. Synge, 90. The focus on cloth is not accidental and would have had great meaning to Synge's nationalist colleagues. In Douglas Hyde's "The Necessity for De-Anglicising Ireland," delivered in 1892, he called for nationalists to embrace homespun Irish clothing: "Why have we discarded our own comfortable frieze? Why does every man in Connemara wear home-made and home-spun tweed, while in the midland counties we have become too proud for it, though we are not too proud to buy at every fair and market the most incongruous castoff clothes imported from English cities, and to wear them? Let us, as far as we have any influence, set our faces against this aping of English dress, and encourage our women to spin and our men to wear comfortable frieze suits of their own wool, free from shoddy and humbug." See Douglas Hyde, "The Necessity for De-Anglicising Ireland," in *The Revival of Irish Literature* (London: T. Fisher Unwin, 1904), 158.

77. Leder, "Synge's *Riders to the Sea*," 216. Nora's witlessness also serves the simple dramaturgical function of introducing the props to the audience. These props themselves, as critics such as Eugene Benson have noted, have both a practical purpose in the cottage and a symbolic purpose within the play: "These are everyday Aran household items which persuade us that the action is naturalistic, but as the play unfolds they become charged with enormous symbolic voltage." See Eugene Benson, *J. M. Synge* (London: MacMillan, 1983), 54. The deep meanings attributed to such simple items are another mark of the folk culture that is dying out in characters like Nora, who recognizes none of this multilayered significance.

78. Synge, *Riders to the Sea*, 92.

79. Synge, 92.

80. Synge, 93.

81. It is worth noting that Maurya names only her sons and not her husband and father-in-law. She does not even call her husband by the title *husband*, but instead refers to him as Sheamus's father. Given the relative sexual freedom displayed in Synge's other plays, it seems significant that *Riders to the Sea* depicts a world from which sex is strangely absent. Both Federico García Lorca and D. H. Lawrence reinsert sex into

their versions of *Riders to the Sea*, to the extent that in both plays the central crisis is an erotic one. Although sex is not completely absent from Derek Walcott's *The Sea at Dauphin*, it plays a relatively unimportant role in the lives of the fisherman, and the play as a whole lacks the erotic charge of Lorca's or Lawrence's.

82. Synge, *Riders to the Sea*, 95.

83. Synge, 94.

84. Synge, 94.

85. Margalit, *Ethics of Memory*, 21.

86. Synge, *Riders to the Sea*, 94.

87. Synge, 94.

88. Synge, 94.

89. Synge, 94.

90. Nora, *Realms of Memory*, 1.

91. Synge, *Riders to the Sea*, 94.

92. Frawley, "Introduction," in *Memory Ireland*, xxiv; emphasis in original.

93. Synge, *Aran Islands*, 44.

94. Kiberd, *Inventing Ireland*, 172.

95. Synge, *Aran Islands*, 30.

96. Synge, 31.

97. Synge, 31.

98. Synge, 31.

99. Weldon Thornton, *J. M. Synge and the Western Mind* (Gerrards Cross, UK: Colin Smythe, 1979), 69.

100. Although not linking his observation to a difference between the two funerals, Daniel Davy does notice that the account of the first funeral is delivered in the style of a "'reporter' giving an objective account," and observes that "such a 'normative' and objective perspective on the relationship of the psyche of the islanders to their environment is in fact very atypical of *The Aran Islands*." See Davy, "Tragic Self-Referral in *Riders to the Sea*," 80. Synge, in other words, tends to be aware of his own subjectivity in reporting his experiences on Aran.

101. Synge, *Aran Islands*, 112.

102. Synge, 112.

103. Synge, 113.

104. Synge, 110.

105. Synge, 110.

106. Synge, 110.

107. Synge, 110.

108. Synge, 31.

109. Synge, 31.

110. Synge, 114; emphasis mine.

111. Quoted in Robinson, "Introduction," in *Aran Islands*, xxxix.
112. Kiberd, *Inventing Ireland*, 173; emphasis in original.
113. Kiberd, 173.
114. Synge, *Travels in Wicklow, West Kerry, and Connemara*, 91
115. Synge, 92.
116. Synge, 98.
117. Synge, *Aran Islands*, 133.
118. Synge, *Travels in Wicklow, West Kerry, and Connemara*, 85.
119. Synge, *Aran Islands*, 52.
120. Synge, 31.
121. Synge, 32.

3. The Regenerative Body

1. Frawley, "Toward a Theory of Memory in an Irish Postcolonial Context," in Frawley, *Memory Ireland*, 33.

2. In the now plentiful critical monographs on Walcott it is not uncommon for *The Sea at Dauphin* to completely escape mention or to earn only a few glancing references. The three pages of analysis that Edward Baugh devotes to the play seem extravagant by comparison to most. This paucity of critical interest is partially understandable given that Walcott was incredibly prolific, and that most studies focus on his poetry rather than his dramatic output. The play, however, deserves more attention, both as an early indication of the themes and concerns that would shape Walcott's work, and as a fascinating piece in its own right.

3. Edward Hirsch, "An Interview with Derek Walcott," *Contemporary Literature* 20, no. 3 (1978): 288.

4. Hirsch, "Interview with Derek Walcott," 288.

5. Hirsch, 289.

6. Derek Walcott, *The Sea at Dauphin*, in "*Dream on Monkey Mountain*" *and Other Plays* (New York: Farrar, Straus and Giroux, 1970), 45.

7. Walcott, *Sea at Dauphin*, 47.

8. Walcott, 49.

9. Walcott, 69.

10. Walcott, 73.

11. Walcott, 76.

12. Michael Malouf agrees that this is the play's major departure from Synge, flagging "Walcott's foregrounding of masculine concerns that are not only lacking in Synge but often critically undermined . . . In its use of a female perspective, *Riders to the Sea* might be seen as embodying a critique of the self-sacrificing, isolationist masculinity that is memorialized . . . in *The Sea at Dauphin*." See Michael Malouf, "Dissimilation

and Federation: Irish and Caribbean Modernisms in Derek Walcott's *The Sea at Dauphin*," *Comparative American Studies* 8, no. 2 (June 2010): 147.

13. Lawrence Breiner, "Walcott's Early Drama," in *The Art of Derek Walcott*, ed. Stewart Brown (Bridgend, Wales: Seren Books, 1991), 73.

14. Walcott, *Sea at Dauphin*, 46.

15. Leif Schenstead-Harris, "The Haunted Ocean: Mourning Language with J. M. Synge and Derek Walcott" in Donnell et al., *Caribbean-Irish Connections*, 211.

16. Walcott, *Sea at Dauphin*, 62.

17. Walcott, 76.

18. Walcott, 76.

19. Walcott, 76.

20. Robert Hamner, *Derek Walcott* (Woodbridge, CT: Twayne, 1981), 56.

21. Walcott, *Sea at Dauphin*, 77.

22. Walcott, 60–61.

23. Walcott, 52.

24. The same could be said of the culture of the Aran Islanders in *Riders to the Sea*; the difference is in the playwright's focus.

25. Walcott, *Sea at Dauphin*, 66.

26. Walcott, 77.

27. Edward Baugh, *Derek Walcott* (Cambridge: Cambridge Univ. Press, 2006), 70.

28. Baugh points out that in positioning Hounakin as such a sympathetic character, Walcott makes an important statement about race in the Caribbean: "In the portrait of Hounakin, Walcott also shows his own characteristic racial compassion, all the more remarkable here because the (East) Indian presence in St. Lucia was, then as now, very much a minority . . . Walcott's portrait of Hounakin signifies his early, deeply sympathetic recognition of the Indian diaspora." See Baugh, *Derek Walcott*, 70.

29. Walcott, *Sea at Dauphin*, 54.

30. Walcott, 66.

31. Walcott, 67.

32. Walcott, 47.

33. Walcott, 53.

34. Walcott, 61.

35. Walcott, 69.

36. Walcott, 64.

37. Walcott, 67–68. Note the possible echo of Shakespeare's *Pericles*; Pericles envisions his wife's corpse "lying with simple shells." See William Shakespeare, *Pericles, Prince of Tyre*, in *The Complete Pelican Shakespeare*, 3.1.57–64.

38. Walcott, *Sea at Dauphin*, 73.

39. Walcott, 73.

40. Though all of the islanders seem certain that his death is a suicide, while in the presence of the priest they are careful to say he "fell." Thus it seems unlikely that he will be denied a church burial.

41. Though the priest's role in *Riders to the Sea* is minimal, the religious angle of the play is one that has been popular among adaptors. In *Die Gewehre der Frau Carrar*, Brecht brings the priest onstage, solely for the purpose of excoriating him and verbally dismantling his world view.

42. Walcott, *Sea at Dauphin*, 73.

43. Walcott, 73.

44. Walcott, 80.

45. The difference between memory and forgetfulness is an important and deliberate way that Walcott distances his play from Synge's. Malouf argues that while it has been typical to read *The Sea at Dauphin* "in terms of a 'comparison' to Synge's *Riders*," it would be more accurate to read it as a project of "dissimilation." The differences between the two plays are more telling than their similarities, Malouf claims, locating the most significant changes in Walcott's disagreement with Synge's nationalism, and his search for "a federationist aesthetics." See Malouf, "Dissimilation and Federation," 142, 143.

46. Derek Walcott, "The Muse of History," in *Poetry in Theory*, ed. Jon Cook (Oxford: Blackwell, 2004), 421.

47. Walcott, "Muse of History," 422. For Walcott, the New World includes not just the Caribbean but North and South America as well, a fact he indicates in *Omeros* by including the character of Catherine Weldon, a nineteenth-century white settler on the American Plains.

48. Walcott, "Muse of History," 421.

49. George Handley, *New World Poetics: Nature and the Adamic Imagination of Whitman, Neruda, and Walcott* (Athens: Univ. of Georgia Press, 2007), 292.

50. Walcott, "Muse of History," 428.

51. Maria McGarrity, *Allusions in "Omeros"* (Gainesville: Univ. Press of Florida, 2015), 3.

52. Edouard Glissant, *Caribbean Discourse: Selected Essays*, trans. J. Michael Dash (Charlottesville: Univ. of Virginia Press, 1989), 66–67.

53. For a fuller exploration of Walcott's symbolic use of seascapes, see Tobias Döring and Bernhard Klein's article, "Of Bogs and Oceans." The authors compare Walcott's relationship to history with Seamus Heaney's through an exploration of their central metaphors: the ocean and the bog. Their reading agrees with mine on the significance of the ocean as a space of forgetfulness: "The sea, for him, operates as central agent in the passionate rejection of the poetics of memory and his championing, instead, of what we may call a poetics of passages and spatial reconnection." See

Tobias Döring and Bernhard Klein, "Of Bogs and Oceans: Alternative Histories in the Poetry of Seamus Heaney and Derek Walcott," in *Common Ground? Crossovers between Cultural Studies and Postcolonial Studies*, ed. Bernhard Klein (Trier: Wissenschaftlicher, 2001), 122.

54. Derek Walcott, "The Sea Is History," in *Selected Poems*, ed. Edward Baugh (New York: Farrar, Straus, and Giroux, 2007), 137.

55. Walcott, "Sea Is History," 138.

56. Walcott, "Sea Is History," 139.

57. This more ambivalent version of the sea is almost certainly an important influence on Dabydeen's "Turner."

58. There are several monographs focusing on *Omeros* that follow the various threads of the poem in greater detail than I can do here, including Robert Hamner's *Epic of the Dispossessed: Derek Walcott's "Omeros"* and Lance Callahan's *In the Shadows of Divine Perfection: Derek Walcott's "Omeros."*

59. Michael Malouf, *Transatlantic Solidarities*, 124.

60. The influence of Joyce on *Omeros* has been carefully examined both by Malouf and by McGarrity in *Washed by the Gulf Stream*.

61. Walcott, *Omeros*, 94.

62. Walcott, 311.

63. Walcott, 44.

64. Walcott, 44.

65. Walcott, 46.

66. Walcott, 128.

67. Walcott, 128.

68. William Butler Yeats, "Easter, 1916," in *The Collected Works of W. B. Yeats: Volume I: The Poems*, ed. Richard Finneran (New York: Scribner, 1997), 184.

69. Walcott, *Omeros*, 129.

70. Walcott, 129.

71. Walcott, 130.

72. Walcott, 130.

73. Given the time period in which the poem is set and the youth of Achille, it is of course impossible that he had a father who came to St. Lucia on a slave ship. Walcott uses the words *father* and *ancestor* interchangeably for Afolabe, and the poem often breaks the rules of linear time. Nonetheless, Achille retains the sense that he has a true, given African name, if only he could remember it.

74. Martin McKinsey, "Missing Sounds and Mutable Meanings: Names in Derek Walcott's *Omeros*," *Callaloo* 31, no. 3 (2008): 892.

75. Walcott, *Omeros*, 139.

76. Walcott, 136.

77. Walcott, 140.

78. Walcott, 137.

79. Walcott, 141.

80. Walcott, 143.

81. McKinsey, "Missing Sounds and Mutable Meanings," 895.

82. Walcott, *Omeros*, 145.

83. Walcott, 149.

84. Walcott, 149.

85. Walcott, 149.

86. Walcott, 320.

87. Walcott, 148.

88. Walcott, 296.

89. Walcott, 296.

90. Walcott, 297.

91. Walcott, 297.

92. Walcott, 297.

93. My reading of this passage agrees with Sarah Senk's: "If the Middle Passage represents the most forceful cultural trauma for the poem's black West Indian characters, what might we make of the fact that it takes place on an expanse of water where roots could not possibly take hold? The figure of the ocean as the primary site of wounding, which repeatedly conjures and re-submerges the memories of the dead, complicates the linear model of rupture and return because there is no rupture immediately distinguishable from regeneration. Taking this into account, I suggest that the ocean is not a model for 'memory-as-forgetting,' as much as it is a model for memory in which complete forgetting (and complete healing) is never completely possible." See Sarah Senk, "Mourning's Spiral: Trauma, Time, and Memory in Derek Walcott's *Omeros*," *Symbolism: An International Annual of Critical Aesthetics* 16 (October 2016): 44.

94. Walcott, "Muse of History," 421. I use the male pronoun deliberately. Walcott's artist is almost always gendered male, a fact I discuss later.

95. David Dabydeen, "'A Continual Sense of Isness': An Interview with Derek Walcott," *Agenda* 39 (2002): 155.

96. Dabydeen, "Interview with Derek Walcott," 156.

97. Walcott, "Muse of History," 431.

98. Malouf, "Dissimilation and Federation," 146.

99. For Handley, there is an important distinction between a neocolonial Adamic vision, one which dismisses history in its urge to name and possess the land "for the first time," and an adamic vision, which does not dismiss history but stands in awe of nature's continuing ability to makes things new and gives them new names accordingly. See Handley, *New World Poetics*, 2. This is a useful distinction; however, given Walcott's tendency to dismiss the actual art and history of the West Indies, to claim that nothing came before him and his work was "total originality," it seems that his

work is constantly slipping between the Adamic and the adamic. See Hirsch, "Interview with Derek Walcott," 289.

100. Jana Gohrisch, "Gender and Hybridity in Contemporary Caribbean Poetry," in *Anglistentag 1997 Giessen*, ed. Raimund Borgmeier et al. (Trier: Wissenschaftlicher Verlag Trier, 1998), 139.

101. Gohrisch, "Gender and Hybridity," 139.

102. Handley, *New World Poetics*, 4.

103. Patricia Ismond highlights racial and cultural hybridity in *Omeros* specifically, noting that "in the narratives of *Omeros*, Homer the arch myth maker/griot of European literary tradition, African griot, Amerindian shaman, and Seven-Seas, the Caribbean island-diasporic-wanderer and encompasser of all myths, meet and cross each other." See Patricia Ismond, *Abandoning Dead Metaphors: The Caribbean Phase of Derek Walcott's Poetry* (Kingston: Univ. of the West Indies Press, 2001), 14.

104. Jahan Ramazani, *The Hybrid Muse: Postcolonial Poetry in English* (Chicago: Univ. of Chicago Press, 2001), 63.

105. Carole Boyce Davies, *Black Women, Writing and Identity* (Abingdon, UK: Routledge, 1994), 50.

106. For the article often credited with initiating the feminist critique of Walcott, see Elaine Savory Fido, "Value Judgements in Art and the Question of Macho Attitudes: The Case of Derek Walcott," *Journal of Commonwealth Literature* 21, no. 1 (1986): 109–19.

107. This point is significant, but I do not wish to overstate it. Just as Walcott's sea is complicated and multivalent, his artist figure is a complex one. He seems most comfortable when the authorial voice is a stable, fixed point, yet he does not blindly or simplistically construct it as a source of power and authority. Rather, by including his authors as characters in his narrative, he reveals them as vulnerable, wounded men who struggle within and against dominant discourses.

108. Paula Burnett, *Derek Walcott: Poetics and Politics* (Gainesville: Univ. Press of Florida, 2000), 73.

109. Derek Walcott, "What the Twilight Says," in "*Dream on Monkey Mountain*" *and Other Plays*, 39. This moment seems deliberately reminiscent of Stephen Dedalus's moment of artistic inspiration in *A Portrait of the Artist as a Young Man:* "He was alone . . . A girl stood before him in midstream, alone and still, gazing out to sea . . . She was alone and still, gazing out to sea; and when she felt his presence and the worship of his eyes her eyes turned to him in quiet sufferance of his gaze, without shame or wantonness . . . —Heavenly God! cried Stephen's soul, in an outburst of profane joy . . . Her image had passed into his soul for ever." See James Joyce, *A Portrait of the Artist as a Young Man*, in *The Portable James Joyce*, ed. Harry Levin (London: Penguin, 1976), 433–34. Both Stephen and Walcott consistently imagine artistic inspiration as arriving in the form of female muse characters.

110. Victor Figueroa, "Encomium of Helen: Derek Walcott's Ethical Twist in *Omeros*," *Twentieth-Century Literature* 53, no. 1 (2007): 30.

111. Figueroa, "Encomium of Helen," 29.

112. Figueroa, 30.

113. Figueroa, 36.

114. Quoted in Figueroa, "Encomium of Helen," 26.

115. Walcott, *Omeros*, 211.

116. Walcott, 211.

117. Walcott, 212.

118. Walcott, 212.

119. Handley, *New World Poetics*, 46.

120. Figueroa, "Encomium of Helen," 34.

121. Walcott, *Omeros*, 34.

122. Walcott, 153.

123. Walcott, 14.

124. Walcott, 14–15.

125. Baugh, *Derek Walcott*, 186.

126. Renée Ater, "Slavery and Its Memory in Public Monuments," *American Art* 24, no. 1 (2010): 21.

127. Ater, "Slavery and Its Memory," 21.

128. Ater, 20.

129. Ater, 21.

130. Walcott, *Omeros*, 297.

4. The Disintegrating Body

1. William Devlin, "Cremation," in *The Catholic Encyclopedia*, vol. 4 (New York: Robert Appleton Company, 1908), http://catholicencyclopedia.newadvent.com/cathen/04481c.htm.

2. A distaste for sea burials is generally shared by Islamic and Orthodox Jewish traditions. Hinduism embraces a variation of "burial at sea"; the cremated ashes of Hindus are traditionally sent to the sacred Ganges River for "burial." It seems significant that, while neither Walcott nor Dabydeen would claim to be particularly religious, Walcott was raised as a Methodist, while Dabydeen's background is Hindu.

3. George Herbert, "Doomsday," in *George Herbert and the Seventeenth-Century Religious Poets*, ed. Mario A. Di Cesare (New York: W. W. Norton, 1978), 68.

4. I am indebted to Sarah Dawson Ellison, whose unpublished paper "Metaphysical Bodies: George Herbert Palmer's 'Costly Monument' and the New Critical Judgement" drew my attention to this aspect of Herbert's work.

5. David Dabydeen, *A Harlot's Progress* (London: Jonathan Cape, 1999), 49.

6. Dabydeen, *Harlot's Progress*, 49.

7. David Dabydeen, "*Turner*"*: New and Selected Poems* (London: Cape Poetry, 1994), ix. Lines from "Turner" reprinted courtesy of David Dabydeen.

8. Dabydeen, *Harlot's Progress*, 49.

9. Herbert, "Doomsday," 68.

10. Kevin Davey, "Mongrelisation Is Our Original State: An Interview with David Dabydeen," in *Altered States: Postmodernism, Politics, Culture*, ed. Mark Perryman (London: Lawrence and Wishart, 1994), 189.

11. I am aware of the difficulties involved in considering Dabydeen, who was educated in the United Kingdom and lives there as a poet, as a Caribbean writer. This chapter occasionally mentions European resonances in his work, but given his usual subject matter as well as his frequently stated sense of connection with writers in or from the Caribbean, its main focus considers his work within that tradition.

12. David Dabydeen, "David Dabydeen with Mark Stein," in *Writing across Worlds: Contemporary Writers Talk*, ed. Susheila Nasta (Abingdon, UK: Routledge, 2004), 233–34.

13. Dabydeen, "With Mark Stein," 234.

14. See Tobias Döring's examination of Dabydeen's intertextual interaction with Naipaul, "The Passage of the Eye / I: David Dabydeen, V. S. Naipaul and the Tombstones of Parabiography," in *Postcolonialism and Autobiography*, ed. Alfred Hornung and Ernstpeter Ruhe (Amsterdam: Rodopi, 1998), 149–66.

15. Although the publication dates are close, *Omeros* is arguably the crowning achievement of a sixty-year old soon-to-be Nobel Laureate, while "Turner" is the third volume of poetry by Dabydeen, who was thirty-nine years old at its publication.

16. Walcott, *Omeros*, 61.

17. Walcott, "Muse of History," 428.

18. Stuart Hall, "New Ethnicities," in *Black British Cultural Studies: A Reader*, ed. Houston Baker et al. (Chicago: Univ. of Chicago Press, 1996), 166.

19. Davies, *Black Women, Writing and Identity*, 56.

20. Hall, "New Ethnicities," 166.

21. Bhabha, "Interrogating Identity," 309; emphasis in original.

22. Elizabeth DeLoughrey, *Routes and Roots: Navigating Caribbean and Pacific Island Literatures* (Honolulu: Univ. of Hawai'i Press, 2007), 21.

23. Kwame Dawes, "David Dabydeen (b. 1955)," *Talk Yuh Talk: Interviews with Anglophone Caribbean Poets*, ed. Kwame Dawes (Charlottesville: Univ. of Virginia Press, 2001), 202.

24. Dabydeen, "Mongrelisation Is Our Original State," 186.

25. David Dabydeen, *The Intended* (London: Secker & Warburg, 1991), 141.

26. Dabydeen, *Intended*, 143.

27. Dabydeen, 144.

28. Dabydeen, 144.

29. Dabydeen, 146.

30. Dabydeen, 146.

31. Dabydeen, 146.

32. Joseph's character is in some ways a familiar one, kin to Yeats's "wise and simple man" "in grey Connemara clothes," the idealized peasant reader who by an untutored sympathy with literary expression legitimates the artistic productions of the cultural elite. See W. B. Yeats, "The Fisherman," in *The Collected Works of W. B. Yeats: The Poems*, 148. Joseph, however, is more complex and tortured than Yeats's peasant, more scarred by the oppressions and erasures of colonialism.

33. Dabydeen, *Intended*, 147.

34. Dabydeen, 148–49.

35. This title is itself an ironic (and self-aware) indication of Dabydeen's indebtedness to Western models, as it is borrowed from a poem by Tony Harrison.

36. Lars Eckstein, *Re-Membering the Black Atlantic: On the Poetics and Politics of Literary Memory* (Amsterdam: Rodopi, 2006), 164; emphasis in original.

37. Erik Falk, "How to Really Forget: David Dabydeen's 'Creative Amnesia,'" in *Readings of the Particular: The Postcolonial in the Postnational*, ed. Anne Holden Ronning and Lene Johannessen (Amsterdam: Rodopi, 2007), 194.

38. Dawes, "David Dabydeen," 202.

39. For the purposes of this chapter, I refer to the narrator as Mungo, since that is the name most frequently used in the novel. Like the other names given to the narrator it is an imposed one; like Sambo it was a general name applied to slaves, usually mockingly. See Sofia Muñoz-Valdivieso, "Africa in Europe: Narrating Black British History in Contemporary Fiction," *Journal of European Studies* 40, no. 2 (2010): 171.

40. Dabydeen, *Harlot's Progress*, 2.

41. Dabydeen, 139.

42. Dabydeen, 3.

43. Dabydeen, 34–35.

44. Dabydeen, 243.

45. Dabydeen, 244.

46. Dabydeen, 67.

47. Dabydeen, 3.

48. Muñoz-Valdivieso, "Africa in Europe," 164.

49. Walcott, "Muse of History," 422.

50. Since he himself is descended from both slaves and slave owners, this move on Walcott's part can be read less cynically as an attempt to confront his own hybrid past and to reach out to those who, like him, have ties to both traditions.

51. Dabydeen, *Harlot's Progress*, 65.

52. Dabydeen, 65.

53. In an interview with Kevin Davey, Dabydeen explains the danger of an idyllic retelling of the African past: "Although one can play with idylls, at the end of the day there is nothing to go back to. One has to make actual returns to actual places, and the actualities are far more painful in Africa, or India, or wherever you originate, than the literary imagination will allow for, or confess." See Dabydeen, "Mongrelisation," 178.

54. Dabydeen, *Harlot's Progress*, 64.

55. Bhabha, "Interrogating Identity," 309.

56. Dabydeen, "With Mark Stein," 237.

57. Heike Härting and Tobias Döring, "Amphibian Hermaphrodites: Marina Warner and David Dabydeen in Dialogue," *Third Text* 30 (1995): 41.

58. Dabydeen, "Turner," 39.

59. Dabydeen, 1.

60. Walcott, *Omeros*, 275.

61. Dabydeen, "Day's End," in *Coolie Odyssey* (Hertford, UK: Hansib Publishing, 1988), 19.

62. Benita Parry, "Between Creole and Cambridge English: The Poetry of David Dabydeen," *Kunapipi* 10, no. 3 (1988): 6.

63. David Dabydeen, *Molly and the Muslim Stick* (New York: Macmillan, 2008), 38.

64. David Dabydeen, "*On Not Being Milton*: Nigger Talk in England Today," in *The State of the Language*, ed. Christopher Ricks and Leonard Michaels (Berkeley: Univ. of California Press, 1990), 3.

65. Dabydeen, "*On Not Being Milton*," 3.

66. Kuti juxtaposes the stories of a nineteenth-century Dublin Quaker couple, a sexually unsatisfied woman and her socially respected but secretly prostitute-frequenting husband, with the tale of a syphilitic prostitute dying in poverty. Into their midst she inserts a freed slave, Sarah, whose powerful speeches on the abolition circuit include the tale of the Zong massacre, during which her pregnant great-grandmother is raped and kills her attacker. Sarah's purchaser is also her lover; he is a photographer and an artist who is attracted to pain. Erotics and economics are further imbricated as the Quaker man, Samuel, the owner of a large tea and sugar import business, tries to decide whether to compromise his Quaker principles by importing sugar from the West Indies, where slavery is still legal. Like Kuti, Dabydeen is interested in exposing the way in which colonialism was driven by an erotic fascination with the Other.

67. Dabydeen, "Turner," 38.

68. Obviously this is not the case with the pedophilic rape of young boys described in these lines. While the rape of women may result in "new life," Dabydeen most often portrays sexual violence against boys or prepubescent girls as a kind of teaching or mentoring relationship that results in their learning language or new ideas.

69. Dabydeen, *Harlot's Progress*, 72.

70. David Dabydeen, *Hogarth's Blacks: Images of Blacks in Eighteenth Century English Art* (Manchester: Manchester Univ. Press, 1987), 108.

71. Härting and Döring, "Amphibian Hermaphrodites," 40.

72. Lazarus, *Postcolonial Unconscious*, 162.

73. Lazarus, 33.

74. Abigail Ward, "'Word People': A Conversation with David Dabydeen," *Atlantic Studies* 11 (2014): 41.

75. Ward, "'Word People,'" 41.

76. Bhabha, "Interrogating Identity," 290.

77. Bhabha, 294.

78. John McCoubrey contests the almost ubiquitous identification of the ship as the slave ship *Zong*, arguing that the atrocity of the *Zong* case rested partly on the fact that the slaves were thrown overboard during a calm spell. He argues that the ship, beleaguered by the oncoming storm, is more likely meant to remind viewers of illicit post-abolition slavers, who would jettison slaves in an attempt to avoid Royal Navy ships that would liberate the slaves and prosecute the slavers.

79. For a fuller description of this debate, see Abigail Ward, "'Words Are All I Have Left of My Eyes': Blinded by the Past in J. M. W. Turner's *Slavers Throwing Overboard the Dead and the Dying* and David Dabydeen's 'Turner,'" *Journal of Commonwealth Literature* 42, no. 1 (2007): 47–58. Note that Ward's argument rests on the identification of the ship as the *Zong*, a problematic one given McCoubrey's evidence to the contrary.

80. John Ruskin, *Modern Painters*, vol. 1 (Hoboken, NJ: Wiley, 1853), 376.

81. Ruskin, *Modern Painters*, 377.

82. Paul Gilroy, "Art of Darkness: Black Art and the Problem of Belonging to England," *Third Text* 10 (1990): 49.

83. Dabydeen, "Turner," x.

84. Dabydeen, 1.

85. Turner, the captain of the slave ship in "Turner," is essentially the same character as the slave captain Thomas Thistlewood in *A Harlot's Progress*. Both are pedophiles; both teach their victims to love the English language.

86. Dabydeen, "Turner," 16, 28, 39.

87. Dabydeen, 16.

88. Dabydeen, 28.

89. Dabydeen, 28.

90. Shakespeare, *The Tempest*, 1.2.397–99.

91. Dawes, "David Dabydeen," 213. At moments like these it is worth recalling that Dabydeen is of Indian, not African, descent. His scholarship and the shared experience of racism have led him to identify closely with the African experience. His

ancestors were brought from India to Guyana as indentured servants, little better than slaves but still a difference worth noting.

92. Dabydeen, "Turner," 28.

93. Walcott, *Omeros*, 15.

94. Gohrisch, "Gender and Hybridity," 147.

95. Dabydeen, "Turner," 31.

96. Dabydeen, "Turner," 39.

97. Dabydeen, "Coolie Odyssey," in *Coolie Odyssey*, 9. For more on Dabydeen's relationship to the Barbarian poetry movement, see Lee Jenkins, *The Language of Caribbean Poetry: Boundaries of Expression* (Gainesville: Univ. Press of Florida, 2004).

98. Dabydeen, "Coolie Odyssey," 13.

99. Dabydeen, "Turner," 9. This last line alludes to one of the earliest Biblical mentions of slavery, which links it directly to shame, and implicitly to race. In the story, Noah has become drunk and is lying naked in his tent, where his son Ham sees him and tells his brothers Shem and Japheth. Unlike their brother, Shem and Japheth refuse to "see their father's nakedness," and cover him with their faces turned away (Gen. 9:23). When Noah awakes, he curses Ham's son Canaan, saying: "Cursed be Canaan; / lowest of slaves shall he be to his brothers" (Gen 9:25). The next chapter seems to link the story and the institution of slavery directly to race by providing a genealogy of the people groups that descend from each of the three brothers. While this allusion may or may not be intended by Dabydeen, it connects questions of the gendered body, parentage, origins, race, and slavery, much like "Turner."

100. Dabydeen, "Turner," 14.

101. Dabydeen, 17.

102. Dabydeen, 35–37.

103. Dabydeen, 5.

104. Bhabha, "Interrogating Identity," 299.

105. Dabydeen, "Turner," 39–40.

106. Dawes, "David Dabydeen," 197–98.

107. Tobias Döring, *Caribbean-English Passages: Intertextuality in a Postcolonial Tradition* (Abingdon, UK: Routledge, 2002), 167.

108. Douglas Kearney, "Swimchant for Nigger Mer-Folk (An Aquaboogie Set in Lapis)," in *The Black Automaton* (New York: Fence Books, 2009).

109. M. NourbSe Philip, *Zong!* (Middletown, CT: Wesleyan Univ. Press, 2008), 193.

110. Philip, *Zong!*, 195.

111. Eckstein, *Re-Membering the Black Atlantic*, 156.

112. Eckstein, 155.

113. Eckstein, 158.

114. Dabydeen, "Turner," 39.

115. Stef Craps, "Learning to Live with Ghosts: Postcolonial Haunting and Mid-Mourning in David Dabydeen's 'Turner' and Fred D'Aguiar's *Feeding the Ghosts*," *Callaloo* 33, no. 4 (2010): 469.

116. Craps, "Learning to Live with Ghosts," 473.

5. The Ghostly Body

1. Helen Emmitt, "'Drowned in a Willing Sea': Freedom and Drowning in Eliot, Chopin, and Drabble," *Tulsa Studies in Women's Literature* 12, no. 2 (1993): 317.

2. Mary Jane Lupton, "Women Writers and Death by Drowning," in *Amid Visions and Revisions: Poetry and Criticism on Literature and the Arts*, ed. Burney Hollis (Baltimore, MD: Morgan State Univ. Press, 1985), 98.

3. Kevin Haworth, "Famous Drownings in Literary History," *Fourth Genre: Explorations in Nonfiction* 14, no. 1 (2012): 55.

4. "Irish Water Safety Data Report on Drowning in the Republic of Ireland 1988–2012," Irish Water Safety, http://www.iws.ie/_fileupload/Statistics/Irish%20Water%20Safety%20Report%20on%20Drowning%20in%20the%20Republic%20of%20Ireland_For%20Web.pdf.

5. George Eliot, *The Mill on the Floss* (New York: Bantam, 1987), 471.

6. Emmitt, "'Drowned in a Willing Sea,'" 319.

7. Hélène Cixous, "The Laugh of the Medusa," trans. Keith Cohen and Paula Cohen *Signs* 1, no. 4 (1976): 881.

8. Quoted in Juliet Yates, "Feminine Fluidity: Mind Versus Body in *Pilgrimage*," *Pilgrimages: A Journal of Dorothy Richardson Studies* 2 (2009): 63.

9. George Eliot, *Daniel Deronda* (New York: Penguin, 1967), 264.

10. Maria Doyle, "Dead Center: Tragedy and the Reanimated Body in Marina Carr's *The Mai* and *Portia Coughlan*," *Modern Drama* 49, no. 1 (2006): 44.

11. Doyle, "Dead Center," 44.

12. Marina Carr, *Portia Coughlan*, in *Marina Carr: Plays One* (London: Faber and Faber, 1999), 224.

13. Carr, *Portia Coughlan*, 225.

14. Margaret Higonnet, "Suicide: Representations of the Feminine in the Nineteenth Century," *Poetics Today* 6, no. 1 (1985): 108. Note the name. Carr has discussed *The Merchant of Venice* as her inspiration for Portia Coughlan's name, but this earlier Portia who committed suicide for love also seems like a ghostly presence in this multilayered play.

15. Owl Lake, though named after Lough Owel near Mullingar, may be inspired by Pallas Lake, where Carr lived for much of her childhood. In an interview with Mike Murphy, she observes: "We moved to Pallas Lake. My first seven or eight summers were spent running around the fields, eating grass, chasing tractors, picking

mushrooms, blueberries, all that stuff. It was quite idyllic for a child. It's a beautiful part of the country and still not very well known. Now people go fishing there, so it's beginning to have a bit of a tourist season. But when I was growing up it was quite remote. There was little traffic and there were very few outsiders in the area. It was a close-knit community and we knew everyone." See Mike Murphy, "Interview by Mike Murphy," in *Reading the Future: Irish Writers in Conversation with Mike Murphy*, ed. Clíodhna Ní Anluain (Dublin: Lilliput Press, 2000), 45. Carr also shares with many of her protagonists the experience of having lost her mother young; she was seventeen when her mother died. In another interview, Carr describes *The Mai* as "part autobiography, part creation." See Marina Carr, "Interview," in *Rage and Reason: Women Playwrights on Playwriting*, ed. Heidi Stephenson and Natasha Langridge (York: Methuen, 1997), 147.

16. Marina Carr, *The Mai*, in *Marina Carr: Plays One* (London: Faber and Faber, 1999), 147, 148.

17. Carr, *The Mai*, 149.

18. Carr, 185.

19. Carr, 186.

20. Clare Wallace, "Tragic Destiny and Abjection in Marina Carr's *The Mai*, *Portia Coughlan*, and *By the Bog of Cats*," *Irish University Review* 31, no. 2 (2001): 435.

21. The Bechdel test, used to evaluate films for their treatment of women, asks whether a film has at least two women who talk to each other about something other than a man. *The Mai* would pass the test. Grandma Fraochlán's opium-fueled discussion with Beck about escaping to Zanzibar is, ironically, a breath of fresh air. Connie and the Mai discuss aging, and there are several minor conversations about the house. But for a play in which a family of women sit onstage talking for hours, there are surprisingly few conversations that don't revolve around men or their effects on the women.

22. Carr, *The Mai*, 177.

23. Carr, 115.

24. Carr, 182.

25. Carr, 145.

26. Kelly Marsh, "'This Posthumous Life of Mine': Tragic Overliving in the Plays of Marina Carr," *Tulsa Studies in Women's Literature* 30, no. 1 (2011): 118.

27. Carr, *The Mai*, 185.

28. Eileen Battersby, "A Double Take of Savage Realism," *Irish Times*, February 7, 2009, https://www.irishtimes.com/news/a-double-take-of-savage-realism-1.695286.

29. Carr, *The Mai*, 111.

30. The play names three of Grandma Fraochlán's daughters: Julie, Agnes, and Ellen. Only one son, Donal, is named, and only as a footnote in the love story of how the nine-fingered fisherman lost his finger.

31. If we assume that *Riders to the Sea* is set during the late 1890s, when Synge visited the Aran Islands, Maurya, who describes herself as an old woman, would be a few decades older than Grandma Fraochlán, possibly the age of her mother.

32. Carr, *The Mai*, 119.

33. Carr, 133.

34. Anthony Roche, "Women on the Threshold: J. M. Synge's *The Shadow of the Glen*, Teresa Deevy's *Katie Roche* and Marina Carr's *The Mai*," in *The Theatre of Marina Carr: "Before Rules Was Made*," ed. Cathy Leeney and Anna McMullan (Dublin: Carysfort, 2003), 41.

35. Carr, *The Mai*, 182.

36. Carr, 116.

37. Carr, 169.

38. Carr, 169.

39. Carr, 117.

40. Carr, 121.

41. Carr, 142.

42. Carr, 121.

43. Carr, 167.

44. Carr, 168.

45. Carr, 153.

46. Carr, 160, 165.

47. Carr, 141. Ironically, the insult that prompts this accusation is one of the few in the play that contains an Irish word; Grandma Fraochlán tells her daughter to wipe that "self-righteous *straois* [grin] off your puss." The implication by Carr is that the old woman's vulgarity is part of her Irish heritage, and that Julie fails to recognize her own mother's use of the Irish language.

48. Carr, 140.

49. Carr, 147.

50. Along this line, it seems significant that the most racist character in this play is not, as one might expect, the oldest. Though Grandma Fraochlán is ignorant of the outside world and makes laughably uninformed comments about it, she is generally portrayed as open-minded. When Julie expresses her opposition to divorce, Grandma Fraochlán retorts, "I didn't bring you up to think like that!" See Carr, 141.

51. Victor Merriman, "'Poetry Shite': Towards a Postcolonial Reading of Portia Coughlan and Hester Swane," in *The Theatre of Marina Carr*, 149.

52. Victor Merriman, "Besides the Obvious: Postcolonial Criticism, Drama, and Civil Society," *Modern Drama* 47, no. 4 (Winter 2004): 625.

53. Victor Merriman, "Decolonisation Postponed: The Theatre of Tiger Trash," *Irish University Review* 29, no. 2 (1999): 309.

54. Merriman, "Decolonisation Postponed," 313.

55. Carr, *The Mai*, 163.

56. Adrienne Leavy, "Marina Carr Interview: 'There Is an Affinity between the Russian Soul and the Irish Soul,'" *Irish Times*, December 6, 2016, https://www.irishtimes.com/culture/books/marina-carr-interview-there-is-an-affinity-between-the-russian-soul-and-the-irish-soul-1.2893945.

57. Carr, *The Mai*, 163.

58. Carr, 162.

59. Carr, 163.

60. Carr, 155.

61. Carr, 123.

62. Shonagh Hill, "Ghostly Surrogates and Unhomely Memories: Performing the Past in Marina Carr's *Portia Coughlan*," *Etudes Irlandaises* 37, no. 1 (2012): 183.

63. Carr, *The Mai*, 180.

64. Carr, 147.

65. Carr, 125.

66. Carr, 129.

67. Carr, 149.

68. Doyle, "Dead Center," 42.

69. Doyle, 50.

70. Murphy, *Reading the Future*, 49.

71. Carr, *The Mai*, 184.

72. Carr, 184.

73. Carr, *Portia Coughlan*, 191.

74. Carr, 255.

75. Carr, 253.

76. Carr, 210.

77. Carr, 213–14.

78. As Melissa Sihra writes, Carr's short story "Grow a Mermaid" serves as the origin for *The Mai*. In the story, the grandmother is called Grandma Blaize. See Melissa Sihra, "The House of Woman and the Plays of Marina Carr," in *Women in Irish Drama: A Century of Authorship and Representation*, ed. Melissa Sihra (London: Palgrave, 2007), 207.

79. Carr, *Portia Coughlan*, 215.

80. Carr, 229.

81. Carr, 244.

82. Carr, 230.

83. Carr, 219.

84. Carr, 245.

85. Carr, 240.

86. Carr, 241.

87. Carr, 241.
88. Carr, 247.
89. Carr, 249.
90. Carr, 250.
91. Carr, 250–51.
92. Carr, 227.
93. It strikes me as odd that critics and audiences seem to universally accept Portia's death as a suicide. Given Gabriel's active and eerie presence onstage and Portia's claim that the twins were out to kill one another, isn't it worth considering that what we are witnessing may be a kind of ghostly homicide?
94. Carr, *Portia Coughlan*, 225.
95. Carr, 207–8.
96. Hill, "Ghostly Surrogates and Unhomely Memories," 183.
97. Carr, *Portia Coughlan*, 184.
98. Carr, 223.
99. Carr, 223.
100. Carr, 224.
101. Carr, 207.
102. Carr, 240.
103. Carr, 220.
104. Carr, 236.
105. Carr, 251.
106. Carr, 251.
107. Carr, 251.
108. Carr, 251.
109. Carr, 254.
110. Carr, 249.
111. Carr, 251.
112. Carr, 255.
113. Doyle, "Dead Center," 45.
114. Perhaps our reluctance to take Gabriel's ghostly intervention seriously is proof of what Carr says of theater audiences: "People don't believe in things anymore. They go to the theatre and they want two episodes of a soap opera. They don't want to be told about a ghost." See Murphy, *Reading the Future*, 48.
115. Murphy, 53.
116. Hill, "Ghostly Surrogates and Unhomely Memories," 179.
117. Carr, *Portia Coughlan*, 203.
118. Wallace, "Tragic Destiny and Abjection," 438.
119. Sihra, "House of Woman and the Plays of Marina Carr," 214.
120. Murphy, *Reading the Future*, 152.

121. Marina Carr, *Ariel*, in *Marina Carr: Plays 2* (London: Faber and Faber, 2009), 135.

122. Carr, *Ariel*, 120.

Afterword

1. The boy's name was originally misspelled in many news sources as Aylan Kurdi. Other sources have reported that the family's last name is actually Shenu, but in *The Boy on the Beach*, Tima Kurdi, the boy's aunt, refers to her nephew as Alan Kurdi.

2. In 2018 ninety-six migrants drowned attempting to cross the Rio Grande. See Reis Thebault, Luis Velarde, and Abigail Hauslohner, "The Father and Daughter Who Drowned at the Border were Desperate for a Better Life, Family Says," *Washington Post*, June 26, 2019, https://www.washingtonpost.com/ world/2019/06/26/father-daughter-who-drowned-border-dove-into-river-desperation/.

3. "Alan Kurdi Image Appeared on 20m Screens in Just 12 Hours," *Guardian* (UK), December 15, 2015, https://www.theguardian.com/media/2015/dec/15/alan-kurdi-image-appeared-on-20m-screens-in-just-12-hours.

4. "Missing Migrants: Tracking Deaths along Migratory Routes," International Organization for Migration, last update March 9, 2020, https://missingmigrants.iom.int/region/mediterranean.

5. Tima Kurdi and Anna Sussman, "The Boy on the Beach," *Snap Judgment* (podcast), produced by Anna Sussman, May 30, 2019, MP3 audio, 18:41, https://www.wnycstudios.org/podcasts/snapjudgment/podcasts/2.

6. Jens Kjelsden, "Photo of a Drowned Migrant Father and Daughter Is Fading Fast," Reading the Pictures, July 7, 2019, https://www.readingthepictures.org/2019/07/drowned-migrants-photo/.

7. Paul Slovic, Daniel Västfjäll, Arvid Erlandsson, and Robin Gregory, "Iconic Photographs and the Ebb and Flow of Empathic Response to Humanitarian Disasters," *PNAS* 114, no. 4 (January 2017): 640–44.

8. Miroslav Volf, *The End of Memory: Remembering Rightly in a Violent World* (Grand Rapids, MI: William B. Eerdmans Publishing, 2006), 11.

9. Volf, *End of Memory*, 11.

10. Volf, 24.

11. Margalit, *Ethics of Memory*, 54.

12. Qtd in Frawley, *Memory Ireland*, 24.

13. Volf, *End of Memory*, 25.

14. Margalit, *Ethics of Memory*, 82.

Bibliography

Adams, Richard P. "The Archetypal Pattern of Death and Rebirth in Milton's 'Lycidas.'" *PMLA* 64, no. 1 (1949): 183–88.

"Alan Kurdi Image Appeared on 20m Screens in Just 12 Hours." *Guardian* (UK), December 15, 2015, https://www.theguardian.com/media/2015/dec/15/alan-kurdi-image-appeared-on-20m-screens-in-just-12-hours.

Ater, Renée. "Slavery and its Memory in Public Monuments." *American Art* 24, no. 1 (2010): 20–23.

Baker, Peter, Helene Cooper, and Mark Mazzetti. "Bin Laden Is Dead, Obama Says." *New York Times*, May 1, 2011.

Battersby, Eileen. "A Double Take of Savage Realism." *Irish Times*, February 7, 2009. https://www.irishtimes.com/news/a-double-take-of-savage-realism-1.695286.

Baucom, Ian. *Out of Place: Englishness, Empire, and the Locations of Identity.* Princeton, NJ: Princeton Univ. Press, 1999.

———. *Specters of the Atlantic: Finance Capital, Slavery, and the Philosophy of History*. Durham, NC: Duke Univ. Press, 2005.

Baugh, Edward. *Derek Walcott*. Cambridge: Cambridge Univ. Press, 2006.

Beckles, Hilary. "Foreword: Irish Routes." In *Caribbean Irish Connections: Interdisciplinary Perspectives*, edited by Alison Donnell, Maria McGarrity, and Evelyn O'Callaghan. Kingston: Univ. of the West Indies Press, 2015.

Benson, Eugene. *J. M. Synge*. New York: MacMillan, 1983.

Bhabha, Homi K. "Interrogating Identity: Frantz Fanon and the Postcolonial Prerogative." In *Modern Critical Thought: An Anthology of Theorists Writing on Theorists*, edited by Drew Milne, 286–310. Oxford: Blackwell, 2003.

Bibb, Aaron. "Death by Water: A Reevaluation of Bradleian Philosophy in *The Waste Land*." In *The Waste Land at 90: A Retrospective*, edited by Joe Moffett, 73–92. Amsterdam: Rodopi, 2011.

Boland, Eavan. "That the Science of Cartography Is Limited." In *Collected Poems*, 174–75. Manchester: Carcanet, 1995.

Bourgeois, Maurice. *John M. Synge and the Irish Theatre*. London: Constable & Co., 1913.

Brayton, Dan. "Shakespeare and the Global Ocean." In *Ecocritical Shakespeare*, edited by Lynne Bruckner and Dan Brayton, 173–90. Farnham, UK: Ashgate, 2011.

Breiner, Lawrence. "Walcott's Early Drama." In *The Art of Derek Walcott*, edited by Stewart Brown. 69–84. Bridgend, UK: Seren Books, 1991.

Brooke, Rupert. "The Soldier." In *The Collected Poems of Rupert Brooke*, 115. New York: Dodd, Mead and Co., 1915.

Broom, Sarah. *Contemporary British and Irish Poetry*. London: Palgrave, 2006.

Brown, Eric. "Underworld Sailors in Milton's 'Lycidas' and Virgil's *Aeneid*," *Milton Quarterly* 36, no. 1, (March 2002): 34–45.

Burnett, Paula. *Derek Walcott: Poetics and Politics*. Gainesville: Univ. Press of Florida, 2000.

Bushrui, Suheil Badi, ed. *Sunshine and the Moon's Delight: A Centenary Tribute to John Millington Synge, 1871–1909*. Gerrards Cross, UK: Smythe, 1972.

Byron, George Gordon. *Childe Harold's Pilgrimage*. New York: Mershon Company, n.d.

Callahan, Lance. *In the Shadows of Divine Perfection: Derek Walcott's "Omeros."* Abingdon, UK: Routledge, 2003.

Cardullo, Bert. "'Riders to the Sea': A New View." *Canadian Journal of Irish Studies* 10, no. 1 (1984): 95–112.

Carr, Marina. *Ariel*. In *Marina Carr: Plays 2*. London: Faber and Faber, 2009.

———. "Interview." In *Rage and Reason: Women Playwrights on Playwriting*, edited by Heidi Stephenson and Natasha Langridge, 146–55. London: Methuen, 1997.

———. "Interview by Mike Murphy." In *Reading the Future: Irish Writers in Conversation with Mike Murphy*, edited by Clíodhna Ní Anluain. 43–58. Dublin: Lilliput Press, 2000.

———. *The Mai*. In *Marina Carr: Plays One*. London: Faber and Faber, 1999.

———. *Portia Coughlan*. In *Marina Carr: Plays One*. London: Faber and Faber, 1999.

Cixous, Helene. "The Laugh of the Medusa." Translated by Keith Cohen and Paula Cohen. *Signs* 1, no. 4 (1976): 875–93.

Coleridge, Samuel Taylor. *The Rime of the Ancient Mariner.* In *Selected Poetry and Prose of Coleridge*, edited by Donald A. Stauffer, 6–23. New York: Random House, 1951.

Colum, Mary M. "Memories of Yeats." *Saturday Review of Literature*, February 25, 1939, 3–4, 14.

Clark, David R. "Synge's 'Perpetual "Last Day': Remarks on *Riders to the Sea.*" In *Sunshine and the Moon's Delight: A Centenary Tribute to John Millington Synge, 1871–1909*, edited by Suheil Badi Bushrui, 41–51. Gerrards Cross, UK: Smythe, 1972.

Craps, Stef. "Learning to Live with Ghosts: Postcolonial Haunting and Mid-Mourning in David Dabydeen's 'Turner' and Fred D'Aguiar's *Feeding the Ghosts.*" *Callaloo* 33, no. 4 (2010): 467–75.

Cregan-Reid, Vybarr. "Bodies, Boundaries, and Queer Waters: Drowning and Prosopopoeia in Later Dickens." *Critical Survey* 17, no. 2 (2005): 20–33.

Dabydeen, David. "'A Continual Sense of Isness': An Interview with Derek Walcott." *Agenda* 39 no. 1–3 (2002): 154–65.

———. *Coolie Odyssey*. Hertford, UK: Hansib Publishing, 1988.

———. "David Dabydeen with Mark Stein." In *Writing across Worlds: Contemporary Writers Talk*, edited by Susheila Nasta, 229–36. Abingdon, UK: Routledge, 2004.

———. *A Harlot's Progress*. London: Jonathan Cape, 1999.

———. *Hogarth's Blacks: Images of Blacks in Eighteenth-Century English Art.* Manchester: Manchester Univ. Press, 1987.

———. *The Intended*. London: Secker & Warburg, 1991.

———. *Molly and the Muslim Stick*. London: Macmillan, 2008.

———. "On Not Being Milton: Nigger Talk in England Today." In *The State of the Language*, edited by Christopher Ricks and Leonard Michaels, 3–14. Berkeley: Univ. of California Press, 1990.

———. *Slave Song*. London: Dangaroo Press, 1984.

———. *"Turner": New and Selected Poems*. London: Cape Poetry, 1994.

Davies, Carole Boyce. *Black Women, Writing and Identity*. Abingdon, UK: Routledge, 1994.

Davey, Kevin. "Mongrelisation Is Our Original State: An Interview with David Dabydeen." In *Altered States: Postmodernism, Politics, Culture*, edited by Mark Perryman, 174–94. London: Lawrence and Wishart, 1994.

Davy, Daniel. "Tragic Self-Referral in *Riders to the Sea.*" *Éire-Ireland* 29, no. 2 (1994): 77–91.

Dawes, Kwame. "David Dabydeen (b. 1955)." In *Talk Yuh Talk: Interviews with Anglophone Caribbean Poets*, edited by Kwame Dawes, 196–214. Charlottesville: Univ. of Virginia Press, 2001.

DeLoughrey, Elizabeth. *Routes and Roots: Navigating Caribbean and Pacific Island Literatures.* Honolulu: Univ. of Hawai'i Press, 2007.

Devlin, William. "Cremation." In *The Catholic Encyclopedia.* New York: Robert Appleton Company, 1908. http://catholicencyclopedia.newadvent.com/cathen/04481c.htm.

Donker, Marjorie. "*The Waste Land* and the *Aeneid.*" *PMLA* 89, no. 1 (1974): 164–73.

Donnell, Alison, Maria McGarrity, and Evelyn O'Callaghan, eds. *Caribbean Irish Connections: Interdisciplinary Perspectives.* Kingston: Univ. of the West Indies Press, 2015.

Döring, Tobias. *Caribbean-English Passages: Intertextuality in a Postcolonial Tradition.* Abingdon, UK: Routledge, 2002.

———. "The Passage of the Eye/I: David Dabydeen, V. S. Naipaul and the Tombstones of Parabiography." In *Postcolonialism and Autobiography*, edited by Alfred Hornung and Ernstpeter Ruhe, 149–66. Amsterdam: Rodopi, 1998.

Döring, Tobias, and Bernhard Klein. "Of Bogs and Oceans: Alternative Histories in the Poetry of Seamus Heaney and Derek Walcott." In *Common Ground? Crossovers between Cultural Studies and Postcolonial Studies*, edited by Bernhard Klein, 113–36. Trier, Germany: Wissenschaftlicher, 2001.

Doyle, Maria. "Dead Center: Tragedy and the Reanimated Body in Marina Carr's *The Mai* and *Portia Coughlan.*" *Modern Drama* 49, no. 1 (2006): 41–59.

Eckstein, Lars. *Re-Membering the Black Atlantic: On the Poetics and Politics of Literary Memory.* Amsterdam: Rodopi, 2006.

Eliot, George. *Daniel Deronda.* London: Penguin, 1967.

———. *The Mill on the Floss.* London: Bantam, 1987.

Eliot, T. S. "Tradition and the Individual Talent." In *Poetry in Theory: An Anthology 1900–2000*, edited by Jon Cook, 97–105. Oxford: Blackwell, 2004.

———. *The Waste Land.* Edited by Michael North. New York: W. W. Norton, 2001.

Emmitt, Helen. "'Drowned in a Willing Sea': Freedom and Drowning in Eliot, Chopin, and Drabble." *Tulsa Studies in Women's Literature* 12, no. 2 (1993): 315–32.

Falk, Erik. "How to Really Forget: David Dabydeen's 'Creative Amnesia.'" In *Readings of the Particular: The Postcolonial in the Postnational*, edited by Anne Holden Ronning and Lene Johannessen, 187–204. Amsterdam: Rodopi, 2007.

Fido, Elaine Savory. "Value Judgements in Art and the Question of Macho Attitudes: The Case of Derek Walcott." *Journal of Commonwealth Literature* 21, no. 1 (1986): 109–19.

Figueroa, Victor. "Encomium of Helen: Derek Walcott's Ethical Twist in *Omeros*." *Twentieth-Century Literature* 53, no. 1 (2007): 23–39.

Foster, Leslie D. "Maurya: Tragic Error and Limited Transcendence in *Riders to the Sea*." *Éire-Ireland* 16, no. 3 (1981): 98–117.

Frawley, Oona, ed. *Memory Ireland: History and Modernity*. Syracuse, NY: Syracuse Univ. Press, 2011.

Gandhi, Leela. *Postcolonial Theory: A Critical Introduction*. New York: Columbia Univ. Press, 1998.

Gilroy, Paul. "Art of Darkness: Black Art and the Problem of Belonging to England." *Third Text* 10 (1990): 45–52.

———. *The Black Atlantic: Modernity and Double-Consciousness*. Cambridge, MA: Harvard Univ. Press, 1993.

Glissant, Edouard. *Caribbean Discourse: Selected Essays*. Translated by J. Michael Dash. Charlottesville: Univ. of Virginia Press, 1989.

Gohrisch, Jana. "Gender and Hybridity in Contemporary Caribbean Poetry." In *Anglistentag 1997 Giessen*, edited by Raimund Borgmeier et al., 139–56. Trier, Germany: Wissenschaftlicher Verlag Trier, 1998.

Grene, Nicholas. "Synge in Performance." In *The Cambridge Companion to J. M. Synge*, edited by P. J. Mathews, 149–61. Cambridge: Cambridge Univ. Press, 2009.

Hall, Stuart. "New Ethnicities." In *Black British Cultural Studies: A Reader*, edited by Houston Baker et al., 163–72. Chicago: Univ. of Chicago Press, 1996.

Hamner, Robert. *Derek Walcott*. Woodbridge, CT: Twayne, 1981.

———. *Epic of the Dispossessed: Derek Walcott's "Omeros."* Columbia: Univ. of Missouri Press, 1997.

Handley, George. *New World Poetics: Nature and the Adamic Imagination of Whitman, Neruda, and Walcott*. Athens: Univ. of Georgia Press, 2007.

Harris, Susan Cannon. *Gender and Modern Irish Drama*. Bloomington: Indiana Univ. Press, 2002.

———. "Synge and Gender." In *The Cambridge Companion to J. M. Synge*, edited by P. J. Mathews, 104–17. Cambridge: Cambridge Univ. Press, 2009.

Haw, Camilla, and Keith Hawton. "Suicide and Self-Harm by Drowning: A Review of the Literature." *Archives of Suicide Research* 20, no. 2 (2016): 95–112.

Haworth, Kevin. "Famous Drownings in Literary History." *Fourth Genre: Explorations in Nonfiction* 14, no. 1 (2012): 53–59.

Härting, Heike, and Tobias Döring. "Amphibian Hermaphrodites: Marina Warner and David Dabydeen in Dialogue." *Third Text* 30 (1995): 39–46.

Hendawi, Hamza. "Islamic Scholars Question bin Laden's Sea Burial." *Atlanta Journal Constitution*, May 2, 2011.

Henn, T. R. "*Riders to the Sea*: A Note." In *Sunshine and the Moon's Delight: A Centenary Tribute to John Millington Synge, 1871–1909*, edited by Suheil Badi Bushrui, 33–39. Gerrards Cross, UK: Smythe, 1972.

Herbert, George. "Doomsday." In *George Herbert and the Seventeenth-Century Religious Poets*, edited by Mario A. Di Cesare, 67. New York: W. W. Norton, 1978.

Higonnet, Margaret. "Suicide: Representations of the Feminine in the Nineteenth Century." *Poetics Today* 6, no. 1 (1985): 103–18.

Hill, Shonagh. "Ghostly Surrogates and Unhomely Memories: Performing the Past in Marina Carr's *Portia Coughlan*." *Etudes Irlandaises* 37, no. 1 (2012): 173–87.

Hirsch, Edward. "An Interview with Derek Walcott." *Contemporary Literature* 20, no. 3 (1978): 279–92.

Hyde, Douglas. "The Necessity for De-Anglicising Ireland." In *The Revival of Irish Literature*, by Charles Gavan Duffy, George Sigerson, and Douglas Hyde, 117–61. London: T. Fisher Unwin, 1904.

Ismond, Patricia. *Abandoning Dead Metaphors: The Caribbean Phase of Derek Walcott's Poetry*. Kingston: Univ. of the West Indies Press, 2001.

Jenkins, Lee M. *The Language of Caribbean Poetry: Boundaries of Expression*. Gainesville: Univ. Press of Florida, 2004.

Joyce, James. *A Portrait of the Artist as a Young Man*. In *The Portable James Joyce*, edited by Harry Levin. London: Penguin, 1976.

Kearney, Douglas. "Swimchant for Nigger Mer-Folk (An Aquaboogie Set in Lapis)." In *The Black Automaton*. New York: Fence Books, 2009.

Kelley, Shannon. "The King's Coral Body: A Natural History of Coral and the Post-Tragic Ecology of *The Tempest*." *Journal for Early Modern Cultural Studies* 14, no. 1 (2014): 115–42.

Kennedy, Liam. "Modern Ireland: Post-Colonial Society or Post-Colonial Pretensions?" *Irish Review* 13 (1992–93): 107–21.

Kiberd, Declan. *Inventing Ireland: The Literature of the Modern Nation*. Cambridge, MA: Harvard Univ. Press, 1995.

———. *Synge and the Irish Language*. Lanham, MD: Rowman and Littlefield, 1979.

Kjelsden, Jens. "Photo of a Drowned Migrant Father and Daughter Is Fading Fast." Reading the Pictures, July 7, 2019, https://www.readingthepictures.org/2019/07/drowned-migrants-photo/.

Klein, Herbert S. *The Atlantic Slave Trade*. Cambridge: Cambridge Univ. Press, 2010.

Kopper, Edward A., Jr. "Riders to the Sea." In *A J. M. Synge Literary Companion*, edited by Edward A. Kopper Jr., 39–47. Santa Barbara, CA: Greenwood, 1988.

Kurdi, Tima, and Anna Sussman. "The Boy on the Beach." *Snap Judgment* (podcast), produced by Anna Sussman, May 30, 2019, MP3 audio, 18:41, https://www.wnycstudios.org/podcasts/snapjudgment/podcasts/2.

Lawrence, D. H. *"The Widowing of Mrs. Holroyd" and Other Plays*. Oxford: Oxford Univ. Press, 2001.

Lazarus, Neil. *The Postcolonial Unconscious*. Cambridge: Cambridge Univ. Press, 2011.

Leavy, Adrienne. "Marina Carr Interview: 'There Is an Affinity between the Russian Soul and the Irish Soul.'" *Irish Times*, December 6, 2016. https://www.irishtimes.com/culture/books/marina-carr-interview-there-is-an-affinity-between-the-russian-soul-and-the-irish-soul-1.2893945.

LeComte, Edward. "Introduction." In *"Paradise Lost" and Other Poems*, edited by Edward LeComte, vii–xxxii. New York: New American Library, 1961, xiv

Leder, Judith Remy. "Synge's *Riders to the Sea*: Island as Cultural Battleground." *Twentieth-Century Literature* 36, no. 2 (Summer 1990): 207–25.

Leeney, Cathy, and Anna McMullan, eds. *The Theatre of Marina Carr: "Before Rules Was Made."* Dublin: Carysfort, 2003.

Lewis, Paul. "Life by Water: Characterization and Salvation in *The Waste Land*." *Mosaic* 11, no. 4 (Summer 1978): 81–90.

Lipking, Lawrence. "The Genius of the Shore: Lycidas, Adamastor, and the Poetics of Nationalism." *PMLA* 111, no. 2 (1996): 205–21.

Lloyd, David, and Peter D. O'Neill, eds. *The Black and Green Atlantic: Cross-Currents of the African and Irish Diasporas*. London: Palgrave Macmillan, 2009.

Lloyd, T. O. *The British Empire 1558–1995*. Oxford: Oxford Univ. Press, 1996.

Lupton, Mary Jane. "Women Writers and Death by Drowning." In *Amid Visions and Revisions: Poetry and Criticism on Literature and the Arts*, edited by Burney Hollis, 95–101. Baltimore, MD: Morgan State Univ. Press, 1985.

MacDonald, Michael. "The Inner Side of Wisdom: Suicide in Early Modern England." *Psychological Medicine* 7, no. 4 (1977): 565–82.

———. "Ophelia's Maimed Rites." *Shakespeare Quarterly* 37, no. 3 (1986): 309–17.

Madsen, Deborah. *Feminist Theory and Literary Practice*. London: Pluto Press, 2000.

Malouf, Michael. "Dissimilation and Federation: Irish and Caribbean Modernisms in Derek Walcott's *The Sea at Dauphin*." *Comparative American Studies* 8, no. 2 (June 2010): 140–54.

———. *Transatlantic Solidarities: Irish Nationalism and Caribbean Poetics*. Charlottesville: Univ. of Virginia Press, 2009.

Margalit, Avishai. *The Ethics of Memory*. Cambridge, MA: Harvard Univ. Press, 2002.

Marsh, Kelly. "'This Posthumous Life of Mine': Tragic Overliving in the Plays of Marina Carr." *Tulsa Studies in Women's Literature* 30, no. 1 (2011): 117–39.

Mathews, P. J. "'In a Landlord's Garden': Synge and Parnell." In *Memory Ireland: History and Modernity*, edited by Oona Frawley, 115–28. Syracuse, NY: Syracuse Univ. Press, 2011.

McCoubrey, John. "Turner's *Slave Ship*: Abolition, Ruskin, and Reception." *Word & Image* 14, no. 4 (1998): 319–53.

McGarrity, Maria. *Allusions in "Omeros."* Gainesville: Univ. Press of Florida, 2015.

———. *Washed by the Gulf Stream: The Historic and Geographic Relation of Irish and Caribbean Literature*. Newark: Univ. of Delaware Press, 2008.

McKinsey, Martin. "Missing Sounds and Mutable Meanings: Names in Derek Walcott's *Omeros*." *Callaloo* 31, no. 3 (2008): 891–902.

Merriman, Victor. "Besides the Obvious: Postcolonial Criticism, Drama, and Civil Society." *Modern Drama* 47, no. 4 (Winter 2004): 624–35.

———. "Decolonisation Postponed: The Theatre of Tiger Trash." *Irish University Review* 29, no. 2 (1999): 305–17.

———. "'Poetry Shite': Towards a Postcolonial Reading of Portia Coughlan and Hester Swane." In *The Theatre of Marina Carr: "Before Rules Was Made,"* edited by Cathy Leeney and Anna McMullan, 145–59. Dublin: Carysfort, 2003.

Messenger, John C. *Inis Beag: Isle of Ireland*. Long Grove, IL: Waveland Press, 1969.

Milton, John. "Lycidas." In *"Paradise Lost" and Other Poems*, edited by Edward LeComte, 401–12. New York: New American Library, 1961.

"Missing Migrants: Tracking Deaths along Migratory Routes." International Organization for Migration, last update March 9, 2020, https://missingmigrants.iom.int/region/mediterranean.

Misztal, Barbara. "Memory and History." In *Memory Ireland: History and Modernity*, edited by Oona Frawley, 3–17. Syracuse, NY: Syracuse Univ. Press, 2011.

Mukherjee, Ankhi. *What is a Classic?: Postcolonial Rewriting and Invention of the Canon*. Stanford, CA: Stanford Univ. Press, 2013.

Muñoz-Valdivieso, Sofia. "Africa in Europe: Narrating Black British History in Contemporary Fiction." *Journal of European Studies* 40, no. 2 (2010): 159–74.

Nora, Pierre. *Realms of Memory*. Translated by Arthur Goldhammer. New York: Columbia Univ. Press, 1996.

Parry, Benita. "Between Creole and Cambridge English: The Poetry of David Dabydeen." *Kunapipi* 10, no. 3 (1988): 1–14.

Philip, M. NourbeSe. *Zong!* Middletown, CT: Wesleyan Univ. Press, 2008.

Raban, Jonathan. "Introduction." In *The Oxford Book of the Sea*, edited by Jonathan Raban, 1–34. Oxford: Oxford Univ. Press, 1992.

Ramazani, Jahan, ed. *The Cambridge Companion to Postcolonial Poetry*. Cambridge: Cambridge Univ. Press, 2017.

———. *The Hybrid Muse: Postcolonial Poetry in English*. Chicago: Univ. of Chicago Press, 2001.

———. *Poetry of Mourning: The Modern Elegy from Hardy to Heaney*. Chicago: Univ. of Chicago Press, 1994.

Ridge, Anne. *Death Customs in Rural Ireland: Traditional Funerary Rites in the Irish Midlands*. Galway, Ireland: Arlen House, 2009.

Robinson, Tim. "Place/Person/Book: Synge's *The Aran Islands*." In *The Aran Islands*, edited by Tim Robinson, vii–liii. London: Penguin, 1992.

Roach, Joseph. *Cities of the Dead: Circum-Atlantic Performance*. New York: Columbia Univ. Press, 1996.

Roche, Anthony. "J. M. Synge: Christianity versus Paganism." In *A J. M. Synge Literary Companion*, edited by Edward A. Kopper Jr., 107–34. Santa Barbara, CA: Greenwood, 1988.

———. "Women on the Threshold: J. M. Synge's *The Shadow of the Glen*, Teresa Deevy's *Katie Roche* and Marina Carr's *The Mai*." In *The Theatre of Marina Carr: "Before Rules Was Made,"* edited by Cathy Leeney and Anna McMullan, 17–42. Dublin: Carysfort, 2003.

Romanska, Magda. "Ontology and Eroticism: Two Bodies of Ophelia." *Women's Studies* 34, no. 6 (2005): 485–513.

Ruskin, John. *Modern Painters*. Vol. 1. Hoboken, NJ: Wiley, 1853.

Saddlemyer, Ann. "Art, Nature, and 'The Prepared Personality': A Reading of *The Aran Islands* and Related Writings." In *Sunshine and the Moon's Delight: A Centenary Tribute to John Millington Synge, 1871–1909*, edited by Suheil Badi Bushrui, 107–20. Gerrards Cross, UK: Smythe, 1972.

Schenstead-Harris, Leif. "The Haunted Ocean: Mourning Language with J. M. Synge and Derek Walcott." In *Caribbean Irish Connections: Interdisciplinary Perspectives*, edited by Alison Donnell, Maria McGarrity, and Evelyn O'Callaghan, 203–20. Kingston: Univ. of the West Indies Press, 2015.

Schneider, Ryan. "Drowning the Irish: Natural Borders and Class Boundaries in Henry David Thoreau's *Cape Cod*." *American Transcendental Quarterly* 22, no. 3 (2008): 463–76.

Scofield, Martin. "Poetry's Sea-Changes: T. S. Eliot and *The Tempest*." In *Shakespeare Survey* 43, edited by Stanley Wells. Cambridge: Cambridge Univ. Press, 1990.

Senk, Sarah. "Mourning's Spiral: Trauma, Time, and Memory in Derek Walcott's *Omeros*." *Symbolism: An International Annual of Critical Aesthetics* 16 (2016): 35–52.

Shakespeare, William. *The Complete Pelican Shakespeare*. Edited by Alfred Harbage. London: Penguin, 1969.

———. *Hamlet*. In *The Complete Pelican Shakespeare*, edited by Alfred Harbage, 930–77. London: Penguin, 1969.

———. *Pericles, Prince of Tyre*. In *The Complete Pelican Shakespeare*, edited by Alfred Harbage, 1259–89. London: Penguin, 1969.

———. *Richard III*. In *The Complete Pelican Shakespeare*, edited by Alfred Harbage, 551–99. London: Penguin, 1969.

———. *The Tempest*. In *The Complete Pelican Shakespeare*, edited by Alfred Harbage, 1373–95. London: Penguin, 1969.

Sihra, Melissa. "The House of Woman and the Plays of Marina Carr." In *Women in Irish Drama: A Century of Authorship and Representation*, edited by Melissa Sihra, 201–18. London: Palgrave, 2007.

Slovic, Paul, Daniel Västfjäll, Arvid Erlandsson, and Robin Gregory. "Iconic Photographs and the Ebb and Flow of Empathic Response to Humanitarian Disasters." *PNAS* 114, no. 4 (January 2017): 640–44.

Stevenson, Robert Louis. "The English Admirals." In *The Oxford Book of the Sea*, edited by Jonathan Raban, 284–85. Oxford: Oxford Univ. Press, 1992.

Synge, J. M. *The Aran Islands*. London: Penguin Books, 1992.

———. *Collected Works: Prose*. Edited by Alan Price. Oxford: Oxford Univ. Press, 1966.

———. *The Complete Plays*. New York: Vintage Books, 1960.

———. *Travels in Wicklow, West Kerry, and Connemara*. London: Serif, 2005.

———. *When the Moon Has Set*. In *Collected Works: Plays*, vol. 3, edited by Ann Saddlemyer. 153–78. Gerrards Cross, UK: Colin Smythe, 1982.

Thebault, Reis, Luis Velarde, and Abigail Hauslohner. "The Father and Daughter Who Drowned at the Border were Desperate for a Better Life, Family Says." *Washington Post*, June 26, 2019, https://www.washington post.com/world/2019/06/26/father-daughter-who-drowned-border-dove -into-river-desperation/.

Thornton, Weldon. *J. M. Synge and the Western Mind*. Gerrards Cross, UK: Colin Smythe, 1979.

Tuve, Rosemond. "Theme, Pattern, and Imagery in *Lycidas*." In *Milton's "Lycidas": The Tradition and the Poem*, edited by C. A. Patrides, 171–204. Columbia: Univ. of Missouri Press, 1983.

Valkeakari, Tuire. *Precarious Passages: The Diasporic Imagination in Contemporary Black Anglophone Fiction*. Gainesville: Univ. Press of Florida, 2017.

Volf, Miroslav. *The End of Memory: Remembering Rightly in a Violent World*. Grand Rapids, MI: William B. Eerdmans Publishing, 2006.

Walcott, Derek. *"Dream on Monkey Mountain" and Other Plays*. London: Farrar, Straus and Giroux, 1970.

———. "The Muse of History." In *Poetry in Theory: An Anthology 1900–2000*, edited by Jon Cook, 420–36. Oxford: Blackwell, 2004.

———. *Omeros*. London: Farrar, Straus and Giroux, 1990.

———. *The Sea at Dauphin*. In *"Dream on Monkey Mountain" and Other Plays*, 41–80. London: Farrar, Straus and Giroux, 1970.

———. "The Sea Is History." In *Selected Poems*, edited by Edward Baugh, 137–39. London: Farrar, Straus and Giroux, 2007.

———. "What the Twilight Says: An Overture." In *"Dream on Monkey Mountain" and Other Plays*, 3–41. London: Farrar, Straus and Giroux, 1970.

Wallace, Clare. "Tragic Destiny and Abjection in Marina Carr's *The Mai*, *Portia Coughlan*, and *By the Bog of Cats*." *Irish University Review* 31, no. 2 (2001): 431–49.

Ward, Abigail. "'Word People': A Conversation with David Dabydeen." *Atlantic Studies* 11 (2014): 30–46.

———. "'Words Are All I Have Left of My Eyes': Blinded by the Past in J. M. W. Turner's *Slavers Throwing Overboard the Dead and the Dying* and David Dabydeen's 'Turner.'" *Journal of Commonwealth Literature* 42, no. 1 (2007): 47–58.

Wills, Clair. *That Neutral Island: A Cultural History of Ireland During the Second World War*. Cambridge, MA: Harvard Univ. Press, 2007.

Witoszek, Nina, and Patrick Sheeran. *The Irish Funerary Tradition*. Galway, Ireland: Social Sciences Research Center, Univ. College Galway, 1990.

Yates, Juliet. "Feminine Fluidity: Mind versus Body in *Pilgrimage*." *Pilgrimages: A Journal of Dorothy Richardson Studies* 61, no. 2 (2009): 61–75.

Yeats, Jack B. "A Letter about J. M. Synge." In *Collected Works: Prose*, by J. M. Synge, edited by Alan Price, 401–3. Oxford: Oxford Univ. Press, 1966.

Yeats, William Butler. "Easter, 1916." *The Collected Works of W. B. Yeats: Volume I: The Poems*, edited by Richard Finneran, 182–84. New York: Scribner, 1997.

———. "The Fisherman." In *The Collected Works of W. B. Yeats: The Poems*, edited by Richard Finneran, 148–49. New York: Scribner, 1997.

———. "J. M. Synge and the Ireland of His Time." In *Essays and Introductions*, 311–42. New York: Macmillan, 1961.

Index

Stephanie Pocock Boeninger is an associate professor of English at Providence College, specializing in modern drama. She has authored numerous articles on Irish and Caribbean literature in journals such as *Modern Drama*, *Contemporary Literature*, and *Theatre Journal.*